PIAZZA

Catcher * Slugger * Icon * Star

Greg W. Prince

SPORTS
PUBLISHING

Copyright © 2017 by Greg W. Prince

Sports Publishing books may be purchased in bulk at special discounts for sales promotion, corporate gifts, fund-raising, or educational purposes. Special editions can also be created to specifications. For details, contact the Special Sales Department, Sports Publishing, 307 West 36th Street, 11th Floor, New York, NY 10018 or sportspubbooks@ skyhorsepublishing.com.

Sports Publishing® is a registered trademark of Skyhorse Publishing, Inc.®, a Delaware corporation.

Visit our website at www.sportspubbooks.com.

10 9 8 7 6 5 4 3 2 1

Library of Congress Cataloging-in-Publication Data is available on file.

Cover design by Tom Lau
Cover photo courtesy of AP Images
All photos in insert courtesy of AP Images

ISBN: 978-1-68358-007-2
Ebook ISBN: 978-1-68358-008-9

Printed in the United States of America

FOR STEPHANIE
With whom every season is a cause for celebration.

CONTENTS

PART I
FROM SEAVER TO PIAZZA

ISN'T IT ROMANTIC?
Preface to a Baseball Love Story

It is tempting to frame the book you are about to read as a quintessential romantic comedy.

Scene 1, one side of the country: TEAM is hurting. Hurting bad.

Scene 2, other side of the country: PLAYER is excelling. Excelling lots.

TEAM and PLAYER are barely aware of each other.

Ensuing scenes, back and forth between the coasts: TEAM and PLAYER go on with their lives, never knowing something is pulling them inexorably closer until they find themselves thrown together.

Next scene: TEAM brings PLAYER home to meet THE FANS. PLAYER and THE FANS feel each other out. They arouse something in one another. Is it excitement? Is it mistrust?

Is it love?

What becomes of TEAM, PLAYER, and THE FANS constitutes the rest of the story, laid out in the pages ahead. It's as emblematic a romantic comedy with dramatic overtones as any movie of its time. Seriously, Los Angeles superstar Mike Piazza coming to the previously downtrodden Mets and becoming one of New York's enduring baseball icons was *Pretty Woman* meets *Jerry Maguire* in spikes.

They Met cute.

He rescued them.

They rescued him right back.

They completed him.

He had them at hello.

There were misunderstandings. There were reconciliations. There were laughs. There were tears. There was an undeniable attraction that, in the end, you knew would win out.

In the final scene, there is PLAYER and there is TEAM strolling arm in arm into a loving stadium filled with THE FANS and—together—all three entities ascend to a state of grace and eternal embrace.

Roll credits?

* * *

Actually, that is pretty much the story, save for the necessary baseball details which imbue the tale of Mike Piazza, New York Met, with its layers of depth, encompassing prevailing circumstances, business considerations, overlapping eras, ingrained processes, historical forces, recurring rituals, and supporting casts, a.k.a. the other players the team's fans also loved/liked/tolerated/sometimes couldn't stand. Those fellas are the constants of a fan's existence, members of a person's extended emotional family until, suddenly, they are not. Trades, waivers, unconditional releases, free agent eligibility, and cash considerations continually tear the family apart, redefine it, and, if a fan is lucky, make a standout collection or two indelible. Some editions of the Mets wind up enshrined in the heart and are repeatedly invited home to relive the great old days. Others linger in the soul where nobody else can see them, or rattle around in the subconscious like a vague dream.

They're all part of the tapestry, though. Mike Piazza may have been the most Amazin' Met of his time, but his time was shared with others. His story, particularly at its New York peak, was their story, too. To tell of Mike is also to tell of those who preceded him, joined him, complemented him, left him, and outlasted him.

Ultimately, this book traces the journey Mike Piazza took toward going into the Hall of Fame as a New York Met, and why it meant so much to Mets fans that he'd go in that way. Our first step, then, must be a chronologically slight pre-Piazza step backward to touch precedent. Only one other Met reached the same destination as Mike cloaked in the same identity as Mike.

A Met in the Hall of Fame? Nearly a quarter-century before Piazza made it two, there was only one.

PLAQUE IN THE DAY
August 2, 1992

Literally, it's just a plaque in a room full of plaques. Within a museum brimming with treasures and mementoes from a century-and-a-half of the sport's organized history, the room is arguably the least interesting portion of the building, whether gauged by aesthetics or content. Nearly everything else in the National Baseball Hall of Fame and Museum in Cooperstown, New York, came from somewhere. The lockers. The gloves. The caps. The rings. The turnstiles. The documents. The bats. The balls. They tell the story of the game with only an implied sheen of judgment lacquered to them. Those items were out there—in America, around the world, on the scene of baseball being played, negotiated, celebrated, and embraced. They'd been preserved and curated for exhibition in one place: this place. It's the best reason to come to Cooperstown, a village that couldn't be less easily accessed from major population centers if that was the goal. It's what elevates the Hall of Fame from terrain for debate to a baseball pilgrim's Valhalla.

You can sit home and argue about who's a Hall of Famer. To be immersed in its truly compelling elements, you've got to make, at least once in your life, the pilgrimage to Cooperstown and breathe in all the stuff they've gone to the trouble of collecting and displaying. It's all the stuff and what it represents that makes the Hall of Fame the Hall of Fame.

The plaques, though, are of the institution itself. They weren't excavated from Ebbets Field or handled by Honus Wagner in service to a 6–4–3 double play. They were the logical conclusion of a bookkeeping exercise. Ballots were printed, distributed, returned, and counted. An announcement was made. This person and that person and maybe another person surpassed an arbitrary fraction of total votes. Congratulations, people, you are Baseball Hall of Famers.

Months later, on those walls in that least interesting room, the evidence hangs. Plaques, plaques, and more plaques. The information is written down somewhere as well, not at all hard to look up. A generation ago, any respectable almanac would keep track. These days, just enter "baseball hall of fame members" or "baseball hall of fame inductees" into your search engine of choice, and the list loads for your leisurely perusing pleasure.

Really, you don't need to visit the Plaque Gallery, as it's officially dubbed, to know who's in the Hall of Fame, and you don't need to see the plaques while you're there to have a sense of what makes your surroundings so special.

The plaque's most noble purpose is as prop. You do need something tangible to present to a Hall of Famer to let him know he's been inducted. The phone call from the secretary-treasurer of the Baseball Writers' Association of America is hard to frame. For the ceremonial moment on the high summer Sunday when induction is conducted and a player shifts from "going into the Hall" to "in the Hall," the eye needs an object on which to focus.

Ergo, the plaque. It says to visitors who show up after the ceremonies have concluded that, in essence, "TY WAS HERE." Or Babe, Christy, Walter, or Honus. The original 1936 class of Hall of Fame inductees—Cobb, Ruth, Mathewson, Johnson, and Wagner—made Cooperstown a destination when the shrine itself opened in 1939. Once a reliable selection process was hammered out and normalized (give or take the inevitable tweaks), baseball fans began to count on certain truisms in order to count down to certain Hall of Famers. Great players would make the Hall of Fame. The greatest of players would make the Hall of Fame as soon as possible, meaning once five full seasons of retirement had passed. When that fifth season was over, a player could be considered for election. If election occurred, induction followed the very next summer. That precise waiting period was implemented in 1954 and remained in place for decades thereafter. If you took notice that Bob Feller threw his last pitch in 1956, you could reasonably look forward to his Hall of Fame induction in 1962 (unless the voters were comically incapable of recognizing greatness). Rapid Robert was the first pitcher since Mathewson and Johnson to gain election with first-ballot rapidity. Vagaries, values, and customs explained some of the lag between 1936 and 1962, but after a fashion, with a precedent established, the first ballot began to serve as a ticket stamped "ADMIT WITHOUT FURTHER ADO" when unquestionably warranted.

Sandy Koufax was the next pitcher for whom the velvet rope was lifted on the spot. Koufax's lightning-bolt of a career ended abruptly in 1966; he was inducted just as abruptly in 1972. Warren Spahn drifted about the minors for two years after winning 363 major-league games between 1942 and 1965. The BBWAA in those days defined 1967 as his retirement date, thus making a pitcher who didn't want to quit pitching somewhere/anywhere just because he'd passed his forty-sixth birthday wait until 1973 for eligibility. Nevertheless, Spahn went in as soon as he was deemed eligible.

A first-ballot rhythm emerged on behalf of superstar position players— Ted Williams, Stan Musial, and Mickey Mantle setting the pace among those who hung 'em up in the 1960s. But the voters were slower to bestow their blessing on pitchers. Still, some arms could not be denied. Bob Gibson retired in 1975 and was subsequently inducted in 1981. Jim Palmer last pitched in 1984. He became a Hall of Famer in 1990. Gibson collected two Cy Young Awards, Palmer three (Cy Young himself wasn't elected to the Hall until his second ballot, 1937). Every serious observer of baseball believed they were both among the best pitchers of their overlapping eras. And if you were going to contemplate the primes of Gibson and Palmer, you couldn't think about those times without thinking of their absolute peer and not imagine the same immediate induction on tap for him.

Which was why everything in the hearts of Mets fans had been leading to one Sunday, one moment, one honor, one juxtaposition for so long. Tom Seaver was being inducted into the National Baseball Hall of Fame. As were, by implication, Mets fans.

* * *

For any player good enough and lucky enough to gain induction into the Hall, Cooperstown is the last stop on the longest road trip imaginable. Seaver, who couldn't have been any better as a pitcher and didn't lack for luck when his name arrived on the ballot in the winter of 1991–92, could have booked his nonrefundable passage to Upstate New York the moment he knew his active pitching career was over. He'd been playing organized baseball since he was nine, when he was at last old enough to qualify for Little League (he was turned away at eight, which drove him to tears). He kept at it from that point in 1954 until he made the majors on April 13, 1967. His perpetually beleaguered team won his first start. He was the pitcher of record in his second, another win, which was no small feat in those post-toddler Met years. He excelled from practically the moment he debuted until the moment he reluctantly called it a career. Tom didn't judge himself too far gone to compete at the sport's highest level until he was forty-two. He had pitched his final official game, for Boston, on September 19, 1986, and aborted a final tryout to rejoin the Mets—the franchise with whom The Franchise made his indelible mark—nine months later, when he decided, after a few rounds of glorified batting practice, that "no more competitive pitches" could possibly arise from his right arm.

If he wasn't going to pitch for real in 1987, that meant the clock could be set back to 1986 and the countdown would be on for January 1992. Sure enough, shortly after the New Year, the news Mets fans anticipated dropped. Via an overwhelming vote of the Baseball Writers' Association of America, Seaver's performance and persona were deemed immortal.

That's the word that's reflexively applied to Hall of Famers, no matter that it's technically inaccurate. Hall of Fame status won't really save a retired baseball player from designation for assignment to that great clubhouse in the sky. It won't even guarantee that every last Hall of Famer will be uniformly remembered widely and deeply. Check Cooperstown's all-time roster and try to come up with something substantive to say for each member listed. Time bulldozes on and obscurity eventually enshrouds a portion of those who were extraordinarily famous in their day. Still, *immortal* fits the Hall of Fame ideal, particularly if you pitched on the plane where Tom Seaver pitched.

More than 300 wins, back when wins were treated as the gospel truth of pitching (it was a threshold Feller, Koufax, Gibson, and Palmer did not approach). An earned run average comfortably under three across 20 years in the majors. More strikeouts than all but two pitchers ever at the time of his retirement. Three seasons—1969, 1973, 1975—deemed the best in his league inside a seven-season span. A couple more that were probably just as Cy-worthy, but the vote didn't break his way. More often than not an

All-Star. Almost always his team's opening day starter. The main man on the most unlikely of World Champions.

Immortal enough of an aura for ya?

* * *

No argument from 98.84 percent of the voting members of the BBWAA, comprised of the 425 print media professionals who entered a check mark next to Seaver's name in late 1991. When those results were made public on January 7, 1992, Seaver's proportion came accompanied by a news flash: he'd attracted the highest percentage of support of any Hall of Famer ever elected by the writers. Every year, nobody was installed unanimously; most years, heads were shaken at the thought that Williams or Musial or Willie Mays or Henry Aaron couldn't entice every sentient voter to say yes.

Not that Seaver did, either, but he came closest, breaking the mark of 98.23 percent held by Ty Cobb since 1936, the first year of voting. Tom would have come closer had three writers not sent back blank ballots as their way of protesting the omission of Pete Rose from the ranks of the eligible. Like Seaver, Rose had played his final game in 1986, automatically making him a candidate for consideration in 1991 and, given the breadth of his accomplishments, a presumed lock to join Seaver in the Class of '92. However, Rose was permanently expelled from baseball in 1989, when the owner of the all-time record for base hits was found to have gambled on baseball games while manager of the Cincinnati Reds. You couldn't break a more inviolable rule. Though the ban Bart Giamatti handed down from the commissioner's office didn't extend to the Hall, the Hall took its cue from the late Giamatti's successor and dear friend, Fay Vincent, who was not of a forgiving mindset. In 1991, its board said if someone can't be in baseball, then he can't be on the Hall of Fame ballot.

Seaver himself looked forward to Rose, his Reds teammate in 1977 and 1978 and his opponent for 158 separate plate appearances (the most he faced any single batter), someday attaining the honor he was receiving. "This is a country in which we forgive and we forget—and we do forgive," the pitcher said upon his election. The BBWAA would have preferred a say in the matter themselves and, likely, the chance to reject the disgraced Rose on its own. A trio of Pennsylvanians—Bob Hunter and Paul Hagen from

Philadelphia and Bob Hertzel in Pittsburgh—protested by going blank on their ballots. Those votes, officially filed, counted as no's for everybody, Seaver included, even though each third of the trio insisted Seaver was a Hall of Famer in his eyes.

Deane McGowen, who'd been retired from the *New York Times* longer than Tom had been done pitching, resisted Seaver's achievements on the basis of it being his initial appearance on the ballot. "I just ordinarily don't vote for guys in their first year of eligibility," McGowen said, admitting Seaver deserved election and suspecting he wouldn't have the chance to vote for him on a second go-round. The barrier to entry was 75 percent; McGowen's seal of approval was hardly required.

As for the fifth voter to pass on Seaver, Bud Tucker, a Southern California BBWAAer who, like McGowen, was no longer covering baseball, simple human error was involved. Tucker had recently undergone bypass surgery and somehow missed Seaver's name while in the process of voting. Nobody, Tom could have told him on the night he kept every Chicago Cub but Jimmy Qualls off the Shea Stadium bases, was perfect.

Otherwise, that was it. Five out of 430 didn't, by omission or commission, certify Seaver a Hall of Famer. Four-hundred twenty-five voted aye. The ayes had it. And so did Mets fans. They had themselves their very first Hall of Famer they could call their own. Seaver, you see, wasn't just immortal. He was their immortal.

If he was in, they were gonna be there to show their approval. There was no doubting he was in. There was no doubting, judging from the composition of the crowd gathered on the field adjacent to the Clark Sports Gymnasium (where the Hall had moved its induction ceremonies for the first time), who the headline act was on Induction Day, August 2, 1992. Due respect to the other inductees—ace reliever Rollie Fingers, the late American League umpire Bill McGowan, and 1940s pitching star Hal Newhouser—it was a Mets crowd filling the majority of the lawn chairs. A throng estimated at between 15,000 and 20,000 was on hand, and given the relative proximity to New York City and the pull of the afternoon's marquee inductee, it was clearly a Seaver Sunday.

Seaver and Fingers made it in with the BBWAA's blessing; Rollie, the second-ever reliever elected, required two years on the ballot and made it seven years after Hoyt Wilhelm broke the late-inning barrier. McGowan, who officiated from the mid-1920s to the mid-1950s, and Newhouser, the Tigers ace during and after World War II, were products of the Veterans Committee's machinations. Following the presentations of the J. G. Taylor Spink Award to Dayton, Ohio, writer Ritter Collett and the Ford C. Frick Award to broadcaster Milo Hamilton—best known for his *"There's a new home run champion of all time"* call on behalf of Aaron when he announced for the Braves—the warm and sunny festivities turned their focus on the one ump and the three players.

Rollie, despite his talent for closing games in Oakland, San Diego, and Milwaukee, kicked off the affair. "I'm not used to starting things," he joked. Fingers poked fun at his anachronistic handlebar mustache and paid homage to those who preceded him in developing the role of relief pitcher. Bill McGowan Jr. remembered his father as "Old Number One." Prince Hal reflected, "Everything that I have has been because of baseball, and may I say, baseball, I thank you." After the wartime Tiger had his say, Vincent, in his role as the sport's high priest, began to read from the inscription on the plaque dedicated to GEORGE THOMAS SEAVER. In doing so, the commissioner was essentially raising his right arm and signaling to the pen for the most Terrific starting pitcher of his generation.

NEW YORK, N.L., 1967–1977, 1983
CINCINNATI, N.L., 1977–1982
CHICAGO, A.L., 1984–1986
BOSTON, A.L., 1986

Tom Seaver was in the game. He'd pitched in relief six times as a Met and three times with the White Sox, most famously when prevailed upon by Tony La Russa to throw the 24th and 25th innings of a marathon suspended from the night before. Tom won that one for Chicago and then the regularly scheduled contest that followed as starter. So it's not like he didn't know how to make an impression coming on toward the end.

* * *

When the chants of "SEAVER! SEAVER!" died down, the man of the final hour toed the oratorical rubber with a touch of the poet, an ounce of humility, a dose of respect, and a determination to express gratitude to all those who, as one of his managers and now fellow Hall of Famers, Yogi Berra, might have put it, made this day necessary: "The kinds of friends, the kinds of people, the kinds of support, the kinds of education and, most importantly, the kinds of family" who helped "a young kid from Fresno, California," wind up in Cooperstown, New York, after "forty-seven years of living."

"For me," Seaver summed at the outset, "it is the last beautiful flower in the perfect bouquet, because the twenty years that I had as a professional athlete playing for those four wonderful teams, and that twenty-year period before my professional career began, all came together for me in this induction in the Hall of Fame."

He acknowledged his "brothers," those he was humbly joining "in the fraternity" of immortals, contemporaries and idols who he now thought of as "another part of my family."

He singled out childhood chum Russ Scheidt for showing him how to wear a uniform in Little League. "I didn't know how to wear my socks, I didn't know how to wear my shirt," Seaver admitted. "He showed me how to look like a ballplayer."

He counted off several of his "very best friends" from the major leagues who were on hand: Buddy Harrelson, Jerry Koosman, Tom Hume.

He credited three pitching coaches—Rube Walker from the Mets ("I taught him everything he knew," Tom joked), Bill Fischer from the Reds and Red Sox, Dave Duncan from the White Sox.

He hailed the "three people who were my basic catchers during a twenty-year career." Mention of "Jerry Grote of the New York Mets" drew a heartier response than Tom's nods to Carlton Fisk, still active with the White Sox, and Johnny Bench, "the man I worked for for five and a half years," who happened to be sitting on stage with the rest of the fraternity. Fisk, Seaver said, would be initiated into the brotherhood as well when his time came, but as long as the Clark crowd's composition was Mets-oriented, no catcher was going to get as big a hand as Grote.

He testified to the importance of up-the-middle defense, giving props to Buddy again, to Dave Concepcion and to Ozzie Guillen, his three basic shortstops from 1967 until 1986. "For those of us who know the essence of the game, from the defensive standpoint," Tom insisted (noting his new brother Palmer agreed with him), "it's not necessarily the numbers of home runs and RBIs that you put on the board, but the numbers you keep off the board from an opposition standpoint . . . those guys that take away the base hit in the hole." Spoken like a true pitcher who toiled for so long without adequate offensive support.

He slipped in a plug of sorts for another shortstop, "a guy Ted Williams talks about, the Scooter, Phil Rizzuto," perennially discussed—and to this point rejected—as a Veterans Committee candidate for induction. Rizzuto, unlike Harrelson, Concepcion, and Guillen, never played defense behind Seaver, but Tom wasn't shy about going to bat for a teammate. He and the Scooter had been broadcasting Yankees games together on Channel 11 in New York since 1989.

He thanked his dad, Charles Seaver, a name famous in its own right from Walker Cup golf and familiar from Ralph Kiner's tales from the links (Ralph had played with Charles at the Bing Crosby Pro-Am and asked for an autographed picture for his then twelve-year-old son). The elder Seaver was "a man that was always there as a pillar of strength to our entire family," as well as a man who made Tom do all the pitching in backyard games, an exercise that clearly paid off.

He showered affection on his daughters, Sara, twenty-one, and Annie, sixteen: "God love you both. There cannot be a prouder father in all of America."

He introduced Nancy Lynn Seaver, his wife who needed no introduction to anybody who remembered the beautiful blonde wearing the tam o'shanter in the box seats at Shea during the 1969 World Series. Nancy was on TV almost as much as Tom was that October. "When I talk of family," he said, his trademark composure beginning to get away from him like few late-inning leads ever did, "I have been very blessed."

He came down, at last, to "the only two people that are not here today which I would want to be here, and I miss them very much." First, "the one guy who taught me how to be a professional, to really be a pro, Gil Hodges. If all these other people taught me how to get here and what to do when I got here, Gil Hodges told me how to be a pro and stay here—the most important man in my life from the professional standpoint of my career. And God, I know that you're letting Gil look down here today and I know that he is part of this."

Finally, "the other person who is watching now, God love her, my mom."

With that, Seaver finished. Nine minutes of speaking from the man who regularly compiled nine innings of pitching. He didn't need Hodges to come out and tell him it was time to exit the mound. Like that ever-so-slightly Qualls-pocked night in 1969 against the Cubs, Tom was as perfect as he needed to be.

Something was missing, though. Or somebody. Millions of them, if you were scoring at home. Unmentioned among the litany of those Tom thanked or at least acknowledged? Mets fans. Reds, White Sox, and Red Sox fans, too, but they—whatever fondness they developed and appreciation they nurtured for the segments of a career that the business of baseball directed into their laps—were also-rans in this particular posterity pennant race. It was Mets fans who finished first by association here. Cincinnati, Chicago, and Boston may have applauded Seaver warmly. New York held him tight and embraced him forever.

Tom was not a demonstrative enough type to hug the metropolitan area back. He didn't explicitly say "thank you" to his fans during his remarks. He didn't do it implicitly, either. There was nothing said to those who trekked to Cooperstown, nor anything for those who had filled Shea during so many of his starts. Maybe, with so many cherished individuals on his mind, it didn't occur to him to think more broadly. Maybe on some level he concluded he didn't have to. Excellence in a New York Mets uniform for parts of twelve seasons and representation by a New York Mets cap on his Hall of Fame plaque were all New York Mets fans could have wanted out of Tom Seaver. He did what he did best in their name, even if he never bothered to specify the vicarious recipients of his largesse.

Yet tagging alongside him and taking their place on the very same plaque that enshrined him for all time as the FRANCHISE POWER PITCHER WHO TRANSFORMED METS FROM LOVABLE LOSERS INTO FORMIDABLE FOE, even if you couldn't see them, was everybody who had ever rooted for the team with which he was and would always be inextricably linked.

The artistry of the plaque made certain there was no doubt. On Seaver's head, visible in bronze and to be hung forever after in the Plaque Gallery, was proof of how Seaver identified for eternity. It was indeed a Mets cap, distinguished by an NY with the little curls at all its extremities. When visitors to Cooperstown paused to contemplate the pitcher on the plaque, the cue they would be given would be clear. Don't worry about the other lines etched into his résumé. Forget the evil trade that made him a Red in 1977, the veritable bookkeeping error (a.k.a. the compensation pool) that sent him to the White Sox in 1984 and the stint with the American League champion Boston Red Sox in 1986 when he sat opposite the Mets dugout during that fall's World Series. Never mind that it took an aborted comeback defined by unsuccessful "simulated games" before the Mets ensured he'd retire as one of theirs. Considering how rarely any player retired as a Met, it was more of an achievement than face value would indicate. Just look at that cap. Look at those letters. This Seaver fellow was, first and foremost, NEW YORK, N.L.

For Mets fans, that was a hat to hang their own on. Tom Seaver went into the Hall of Fame in 1992 because of what Tom Seaver did as a Met. It was all enshrined so as to be marveled at: 198 of 311 wins; 2,541 of 3,640 strikeouts; all of his Cy Youngs; his only World Series ring; and, if you still weren't sure, the NY on the cap on the plaque. When Tom Seaver went into the Hall of Fame as a New York Met, then so, spiritually, did the population of fans that made the Mets their cause. Tom Terrific was a verifiable baseball immortal. Tom Terrific's Met-loving legions were thrilled simply to have their background presence in his story validated.

In the summer of 1992, a Mets fan had to be thrilled to be thrilled by anything Mets-related, for by the summer of 1992, the thrill in being a Mets fan was becoming harder and harder to find.

LET'S CHECK THE
OUT-OF-TOWN SCOREBOARD
August 2, 1992–September 1, 1992

On the day Tom Seaver was inducted into the Hall of Fame, the sun shone on Shea Stadium. Any opposing atmospheric condition would have been wrong. Nature wasn't always the Mets' ally—their first scheduled game ever, at St. Louis on April 10, 1962—was rained out, but Mets fans always believed deep down that Somebody Somewhere was prone to tipping the scales in their favor. Even Seaver, dispassionate professional who made his own luck, allowed that perhaps God was alive and well and renting an apartment somewhere within the five boroughs during the summer and fall of 1969.

Based on recent evidence, it was hard to surmise the Lord still lived in New York City in 1992, though on Sunday, August 2, you couldn't be blamed for thinking He put in a call to Al Roker, Mr. G, or some other local weather deity. Not only was it a beautiful day at Shea, there was a handsome result on the field, as if a loss on the afternoon when Seaver was sanctified as once and for all immortal would have constituted an ethereal insult.

David Cone, an All-Star Mets right-hander in the tradition if not exactly the mold of Seaver, pitched eight innings, scattered eight hits and struck out eight Cubs. Eddie Murray's 408th career home run, a two-run shot off Mike Morgan, provided Cone the margin he would need. Once John Franco came on to collect his 12th save of the season, Cone had his 13th win against four losses and the Mets could take satisfaction in a 4–2 victory that leapfrogged them over the Cubs and into third place, 5 1/2 games behind the front-running Pirates, 3 1/2 to the rear of the second-place Expos. Two months remained in the season. The standings weren't sensational, but they weren't out of hand. On the same date in 1969, the Mets sat a little further than that behind the Cubs, and evidence of what happened the rest of that year was on full display in Cooperstown. If you looked at nothing more than the games behind column, you'd think maybe Seaver the immortal could chat with God and arrange an Astoria sublet.

A broader view of where the 1992 Mets were on the day Seaver ascended into baseball's highest ranks revealed something closer to a hellscape shrouding Shea, sunshine or not. No, the Mets were not out of contention, but it was hardly through their own doing. Their record on August 2, 1992, was 51–53. Only in the National League East could have that kept them on the fringes of a pennant race. The four-team jumble at the top of the division was mostly attributable to nobody having yet put together a convincing stretch of baseball. Pittsburgh was vying for its third crown in three years, but wasn't a lock, having been depleted of one of its big-name sluggers, Bobby Bonilla.

The Mets signed Bonilla the preceding offseason. It was as much a cause for winter warmth as the word that Seaver had been elected to the Hall. The Mets were making all kinds of moves designed to shake off the blahs of 1991, their first losing season since 1983. The post-1986 period had been highly competitive, yet ultimately disappointing. Every season from 1987 through 1990 ended shy of another world championship, which had become the standard for success in Flushing ever since Frank Cashen built his behemoth. The GM who lost the Franchise to that silly compensation pool did most everything else right from '84 forward.

He promoted, at Davey Johnson's urging, nineteen-year-old Dwight Gooden, the closest thing to a reincarnation of Seaver as existed. He traded for Montreal Expo Gary Carter, the best all-around catcher since the heyday of Johnny Bench. He resisted free agency and kept cultivating from within. Gooden and Carter, alongside Keith Hernandez (another brilliant trade, from 1983) and Darryl Strawberry (chosen wisely with the first draft pick in the nation in 1980) and twenty others—plus maybe just a touch of help from above on a ground ball that rolled up the first base line to and through Seaver's Boston teammate Bill Buckner—led the Mets to the mountaintop in 1986. At the City Hall ceremony that followed the ticker-tape parade that ensued, Mookie Wilson, he who trickled that ball toward Buckner, declared what the immediate future would look like.

"1986: Year of the Mets!
"1987: Year of the Mets!
"1988: Year of the Mets!"

Mookie may have had more Mets years in mind, but the crowd drowned him out with their approval. Who wouldn't have ordered every calendar Wilson described?

Fate failed to print them. The rest of the 1980s had their moments, including a division title in '88, but the Mets kept coming up short. Terry Pendleton hit a home run one year, Mike Scioscia the next. Each became infamous. Meanwhile, the 1986 pedigree began to fade from the picture like the siblings from Marty McFly's snapshot in *Back to the Future*. There went Kevin Mitchell (for Kevin McReynolds) and Ray Knight (mostly out of pique), two of Wilson's co-conspirators from the bottom of the tenth inning in Game Six of the World Series. There went Ed Hearn, though in a good cause, the steal that brought Cone from Kansas City. There went Wally Backman, so superprospect Gregg Jefferies could settle in. There went Roger McDowell and Lenny Dykstra—the spit to Backman's vinegar—in a misguided grab at what used to be Juan Samuel. There went Rick Aguilera, the right place/right time winner from the Buckner Game, with four less-proven arms, for Frank Viola when Gooden was hurt. There even went Mookie, plus Lee Mazzilli, each landing in Toronto to help another budding dynasty, while the one that never quite was receded.

Three seasons passed. The 1986 Mets were done. The shedding of their championship skin continued. Shortly after the 1989 season was complete, the Mets called a press conference. Keith Hernandez and Gary Carter were saying good-bye, the terms of their contracts fulfilled. Hernandez was brought in to provide professionalism and leadership. Carter was imported to power and push the Mets to a World Series. Mission accomplished. Nobody on this October day, however, was retiring as a Met. Gary and Keith were free to keep playing for whoever would have them.

Seven months later, Davey Johnson was told essentially the same thing regarding his managing. The man who led the Mets from the depths to the clouds was fired at the end of May 1990 for not keeping them forever aloft. An average of 96 wins a year from '84 through '89 was trumped by a 20–22 start. Buddy Harrelson, who had served several generations of Mets teams as shortstop, instructor, and goodwill ambassador, put his reputation on the line as a manager. For a while, he was exactly what the Mets needed. Viola couldn't lose. Gooden, previously mired in a slump, began to win. Franco, the Bensonhurst-bred lefty acquired in the offseason closer swap that sent Randy Myers to Cincinnati, filed away save after save. Everybody hit, particularly Strawberry, a slugger who had matured into one of baseball's most potent weapons just as he was approaching free agency. The Mets and Pirates conducted a heartstopping race on the order of the Mets and Cardinals in 1985 and 1987. The ending, sadly, was just as familiar. The Mets finished second.

Then Strawberry left for Los Angeles, his hometown. Cashen wasn't big on dispensing free agent contracts, not even for his own pending free agents. But faced with a 37 HR, 108 RBI-sized void, the Mets needed to replace an irreplaceable part. They traded another 1986 star, Bobby Ojeda, to those very same Dodgers and brought back Hubie Brooks, the third baseman-turned-shortstop they used to help dislodge Carter from Montreal six years before. Brooks was now an outfielder, and he'd be asked to fill Darryl's footprints in right. The lineup would need another boost, and since there weren't any monster bats lying around, the Mets went in another, speedier direction.

They signed Vince Coleman, as fast as anybody in baseball, and as much of a thorn in their side as anybody during the height of the Mets-Cardinals rivalry. He played left in artificially turfed Busch Stadium. He was going to be asked to man center amid the natural grass of Shea, but mostly to catalyze the offense from the top of the order, steal a plethora of bases like no Met before him, and, if all went to plan, make Mets fans forget they had just lost Darryl Strawberry.

Little went to plan in 1991. Backman's platoon partner, Tim Teufel, was dispatched to San Diego. Ron Darling was dealt to Montreal. The Mets, ever less resembling their 1986 selves, hung in with the Pirates until early August despite Coleman clearly being an ill fit physically, functionally, and temperamentally. Injuries limited Vince to 72 games. Pitchers limited him to a .255 average. Third base coach Mike Cubbage tried to tell him prior to a game in July that it wasn't his turn to hit during batting practice. Coleman pushed back, throwing his bat and a tantrum. Harrelson, who was proving an ill fit for the role of manager, did not rush to support his coach. The press took note. Before the season was over—with the Mets en route to fifth place—the Mets let Buddy take the fall, replacing him with Cubbage for the final week of play. Cashen, who was anticipating a smoother succession, stepped aside as GM at the tail end of this 77–84 debacle, handing the keys to the front office to Al Harazin, his longtime lieutenant in charge of business affairs.

* * *

Harazin decided the best business for the Mets to be in was that of major player in the offseason. Nineteen ninety-one needed to be the aberration, not the rule, so for 1992, he stocked up on marquee names. Murray, a longtime RBI machine for the Orioles and Dodgers, was lured to New York as a free agent. Jefferies and McReynolds, each of them having tried the patience of the fan base at large, were bundled and sent to Kansas City for another American League Cy Young owner, Bret Saberhagen, ticketed to replace Viola, who left of his own volition. Bonilla, the cream of the winter crop, was signed for five years and $29 million, as rich as it got in baseball. Bobby Bo and Barry Bonds had just led the Pirates to another division title, but there was no chance Pittsburgh could afford to keep them both. Bonds would be a free agent the following year, and he was a long enough shot to stay, but at least he'd be around for one more run.

Bonilla. Saberhagen. Murray. Willie Randolph, the grand old Yankee with perhaps just enough second base left in him in at age thirty-seven to make one more stand at Shea. Even Coleman, if you were willing to assume his second season in New York had to be better than his first. With all of their credentials and all of their track record, how could the 1992 Mets not return, at last, to their 1986 perch? Five years had gone by, and, on the eve of the sixth, only four '86 World Series alumni—Gooden, Howard Johnson, Sid Fernandez, and Kevin Elster—lingered, but this figured to be a strong team. Even the new skipper, Jeff Torborg, was a get. In 1990, he was AL Manager of the Year, turning the White Sox into surprise contenders. The success anticipated here would be no surprise.

Four months into the season, the only surprise was that the Mets were still alive in the NL East. It was a year of morose chemistry and myriad injuries, and even on the day upwards of 15,000 Mets fans in Cooperstown celebrated Seaver's induction while a paid attendance of 32,086 was enjoying Cone's pitching, clouds that were less puffy and cumulus than dark and foreboding continued to gather over Flushing. HoJo had been diagnosed with a fractured wrist and was out indefinitely. Bonilla fractured a rib in an attempt to catch a foul ball. The DL was his immediate destination, too. It was a familiar stop for Mets all year, as Gooden, Saberhagen, Coleman, Elster, and Franco had each paid it a visit; Elster had never returned from it. The Mets lined up for the disabled list like their fans did for the concession stands.

"Work and scratch, that's all we can do," Torborg said after Cone beat the Cubs. "We have a full club in the trainer's room."

The injuries were real, but at no point when healthy did the Mets emit the impression they were ready to do whatever needed to be done to win. Their high-water mark came in May, six games above .500. They slid from a half-game out in early June to 8 behind within two weeks. And the players, old and new, set the tone for the season ahead in spring training by instituting a media boycott in response to what they considered intrusive coverage of rape allegations against three Mets—Gooden, Coleman, and Daryl Boston. The trio was never formally charged and the team resumed talking, but less and less did many want to hear what they had to say.

Yet despite all that, they were within wishing distance of the Pirates on the second of August, if a person chose to wish these Mets well. Maybe they could take a cue from their freshly certified Hall of Famer and be terrific just long enough to make the stretch drive one that would takes its place alongside 1969 and 1973.

Instead, the clouds thickened and blocked out the sun over the next thirty days. The Mets lost twelve of thirteen directly after Seaver's day of jubilee. The only game they won was on the night they held a brief Hall of Fame celebration of their own for Tom (giving out posters of the pitcher as portrayed by LeRoy Nieman), and on that evening the rain shortened Tom's remarks and kept away half the advance sale. They lost four in their final inning. They lost so often to Pittsburgh that the Pirates padded their first-place lead and never really had to look back to the rest of the division. They lost Dave Magadan, the hero from the '86 NL East clincher, for the year; he never played for the Mets again. They lost Randolph until he was inserted into the lineup on what turned out to be the final day of his career. By August 23, the Mets were 53–67. Their participation in the 1992 pennant race was long over.

* * *

Somebody Up There had no use for them anymore. Then, on August 27, Mets fans learned the management of their team had no use for their best pitcher, trading Cone to the Blue Jays for rookie infielder Jeff Kent and a player to be officially named later who was identified immediately as minor league outfielder Ryan Thompson. Kent was part of a first-place outfit in Toronto, but Thompson was touted as the more glittering gem, packing power, speed . . . more or less what was said about Dan Norman fifteen years earlier when Seaver was sent to Cincinnati.

Dealing Cone away wasn't quite on the level of giving up Tom Terrific—nothing could be—but it was shocking enough to Mets fans. Cone sported a 13–7 record, a 2.88 ERA , and had struck out more than 200 batters in fewer than 200 innings. He hadn't notched a win since August 2, but he'd done plenty to keep the Mets viable to that point. Free agency, however, loomed, and the Mets, who invested so much in so many big names a winter earlier, weren't eager to pay Cone what he'd be worth. They figured they'd get something from a contender for him before he left them, though they apparently hadn't shopped him very vigorously. Four days remained before players had to be obtained by organizations who envisioned them playing in the postseason for them. There was time for the Mets to stir the David Cone market. Harazin chose to cut bait rather than dangle it for very long.

Thus, it would be the Mets of Kent and Thompson, once he was promoted, taking on another postseason-bound team to start September. On this, the thirtieth day since Seaver went into the Hall, the Mets descended fully into hell.

The devil in their midst was Coleman. Injuries had sapped much of his second season in New York. August was the first month in which he lasted from beginning to end, though he lost a few plate appearances after getting himself tossed by Bruce Froemming for arguing a called strike three leading off the home first on August 30. By the end of that Sunday evening, a Turn Back the Clock promotion at Shea won by the recently reactivated Bonilla on a walk-off home run versus the Reds' Rob Dibble, Vince's ejection was forgotten. The Mets had prevailed in their 1962 garb, celebrating the franchise's thirtieth anniversary and getting Dibble's goat in the process. An ESPN audience saw the Reds reliever disgustedly tear his vintage vest off his torso and slam it onto the Shea grass, leaving his mess for somebody else to clean up. The Reds had been chasing the Braves in the West. The Mets completed a four-game sweep, lengthening an unlikely winning streak of their own to seven. They were done contending, but perhaps, even though they were Coneless, they could cotton to the role of spoiler. The Braves were due in next, on August 31. The Mets could take a shot at doing to Atlanta what they had just done to Cincinnati.

Instead, on September 1, Coleman spoiled whatever infinitesimal scintilla of good feeling still connected to the 1992 Mets. In the bottom of the second, he struck out on a checked swing. He didn't think he swung. The third base ump, Dana DeMuth, was asked to adjudicate by Braves catcher Damon Berryhill. DeMuth ruled it was a swing. Another argument and another ejection ensued. Coleman didn't go quietly, taking out his ire on home plate umpire Gary Darling. Contact between player and ump was made. Darling ejected Coleman. Torborg came out less to protest on behalf of his player than direct him away from further trouble. The manager gave his player a literal push toward the dugout. The player pushed the manager back.

That is just not done. There are rules against players touching umpires, but there is unwritten etiquette against players shoving managers. Then again, there was an implicit code that said players don't show up coaches, and Coleman had done that the year before to Cubbage. Torborg wasn't with the Mets then, but he'd been with them all through 1992, shepherding their journey down the tubes until it landed here, on the first of September, he and his leadoff hitter jawing viciously at each other in the clubhouse while the game went on, Thompson, incidentally, making his major-league debut by taking Coleman's vacant place in the lineup.

Thompson went 0-for-2. Coleman was suspended for "insubordination" for two games. The Mets lost, 4–1, to another rookie just breaking in, David Nied. It was their third defeat in a row at the hands of the Braves, who had taken a doubleheader from them the night before and secured their grip on first place in the NL West. By this point, the Mets were buried in fifth place in the East, 14 1/2 games out of first, the notion that they were in the same race as the Pirates a dim memory. Fans conditioned to keep tabs on Shea's out-of-town scoreboard, if they were at Shea at all, had to look elsewhere for distraction from the disaster that was ruining the grass. But on the off chance that they did glance upward on the night of September 1, they could have seen a result from Chicago, already completed, that had it been detailed beyond winner, loser, and pitchers of record, might have told them something was on the verge of happening in Los Angeles.

THE ROSTER EXPANDS
September 1, 1992

September 1 is the day clubhouses and dugouts annually get crowded, the day major-league teams can and generally do expand their rosters beyond the normally authorized twenty-five players. It's the day organizations can begin to gauge how their most prepared prospects might adjust to competition at the highest level of baseball. Ryan Thompson was able to replace Vince Coleman upon Coleman's ejection while the Mets attempted to play Atlanta because the Mets had extra space to allocate to a raw rookie. The September 1 rule also allows managers and general managers to bring back previously injured players from the disabled list and not have to sweat the math of making every healthy player they desire to have around go into twenty-five.

If a team is in contention, as the Braves were in 1992, the opportunity to fortify the ranks is welcome. The rich got more pitching on September 1 when Atlanta augmented a rotation that already boasted Tom Glavine, John Smoltz, Steve Avery, and Charlie Liebrandt with David Nied, its top-ranked starter prospect. Nied was thrown right into the fire and hosed the Mets on the night Coleman and Jeff Torborg had steam coming out of their ears.

Earlier that same day, as they faced the Cubs at Wrigley Field, the Dodgers took advantage of roster expansion. Their situation was closer to that of the Mets than the Braves. They were in Chicago to play out the string and, as will happen when players debut, inadvertently bridge an era or two. As bad a year as New York was having, Los Angeles was having it worse. The Dodgers fell from any pretension of contention by mid-June via a ten-game losing streak, so if they were stretching their roster in September, it was in hope of seeing what their future had in store and maybe getting some work in for those who were hoping to heal.

The latter application of the expanded roster meant the Dodgers could activate, for the first time since July, Darryl Strawberry. This had been the worst season of Straw's career, the first in which he wouldn't, thanks to a bad back, play anywhere close to 120 games. Against the Cubs, Tommy Lasorda had Darryl at his disposal, along with three players set to make their major-league debuts: outfielder Billy Ashley, infielder Rafael Bournigal, and catcher Mike Piazza.

The date and the circumstances dovetailed perfectly, for the Dodgers and Cubs needed plenty of bodies. They had thirteen innings to fill between them and used a combined forty-three players. Bournigal started at short before being pinch-hit for in the sixth. Ashley was announced as a pinch-hitter, but a Cubs pitching change forced Lasorda's hand, so veteran catcher Mike Scioscia pinch-hit for the pinch-hitter, meaning Billy's first official major-league appearance was box score only. Scioscia was available to pinch-hit because Lasorda decided to write Piazza's name into the starting lineup.

The newer Mike, three days shy of his twenty-fourth birthday, wore No. 25 and batted sixth, two slots below Strawberry. Coming into 1992, he was ranked the tenth-best Dodgers prospect by *Baseball America*. That was before he hit .377 for Double-A San Antonio and .341 at Triple-A Albuquerque . . . and before he drew a second-inning walk from the Cubs' Mike Harkey to earn him more than Ashleyesque zeroes in his nascent *Baseball Encyclopedia* entry.

That first plate appearance was followed by three at-bats for Piazza, every one of them a success for the youngster from Norristown, Pennsylvania. In the fourth inning, he produced a double; in the sixth, a single; and to lead off the eighth, another single. Lasorda removed his catcher for pinch-runner Eric Young in hope of generating the two runs L.A. needed to tie Chicago. Sure enough, Young and Mike Sharperson scored on Lenny Harris's single later in the inning (after Scioscia popped out), tying the score and setting the course for extra innings.

* * *

Strawberry, having started in right, played the entire game, but not to much avail. He went 1-for-7 and struck out three times in what became a

5–4, 13-inning L.A. victory. But it was a positive experience for the Straw-man in that, "I didn't have the pain out there that I have felt before. No pain running down my legs." Two other ex-Mets appeared in the box score as well. Roger McDowell, long-relief hero of the legendary sixth game of the 1986 NLCS, earned the win for the Dodgers, while thirty-eight-year-old John Candelaria, who had passed through Flushing as a pennant race pickup in 1987, recorded the fifth save of his 18th season. Candelaria's career stretched back to 1975. His first major-league win, as a Pirate, came at Shea Stadium against the longtime ace of the Mets staff. The Candy Man proved a formidable foe to a star named Seaver when he broke in and was now a venerable teammate to a rookie named Piazza as he hung on. Last long enough in baseball, and you never know the careers you'll touch.

Piazza was now directly connected to Strawberry, McDowell, Cande-laria, and each of the Dodgers and Cubs who played that day through the brotherhood of agate type. He had, by his participation in this September 1 contest, linked in to forty-two other major leaguers who shared the same box score. Given the instinct baseball has for reaching across generations and shaking hands, their connections became his connections.

For now, on 9/1/92, Mike Piazza had exactly one game under his belt as a big leaguer, and like most every big leaguer who had just arrived, swore he was just happy to be there. "A couple of times," he told reporters, "I looked around and said, 'I can't believe this is happening.'" Whereas Strawberry appraised himself running well in the aftermath of his back ailments, Piazza acknowledged he didn't have any idea how he legged out his first major-league double: "I don't think I hit the ground the whole time I was running those bases."

It was an elevated day for the Dodgers, one of only a handful they experienced in 1992. By the time their season was over, they had lost 99 games, the most by the franchise since the Brooklyn Superbas dropped 101 in 1908. Their last-place finish was the Dodgers' first since 1905. Straw-berry, despite the optimism he expressed about his health, played in just four more games in September before deciding to submit to back surgery. Piazza's tryout wasn't spectacular on the surface—one homer, seven RBIs, a .232 average—but it was enough to convince Lasorda he knew who his catcher was going to be in 1993. Scioscia left Los Angeles for free agency, *Baseball America* identified Piazza as the Dodgers' No. 1 prospect, and once

Tommy was sure he was coming back for his 17th season at the helm (99 losses would make any manager's tenure suspect), the rookie's path to a spot where he could squat regularly behind home plate was cleared.

Back in New York, the Mets couldn't help but want to look ahead as well. September was no better than August, and when the 1992 Mets played their last game on October 4, they absorbed their 90th loss and second consecutive fifth-place finish. Their final statement wasn't in the standings, but in an ad they took out in the city's dailies once their '92 campaign was history. "Our season wasn't exactly one to remember," the advertisement acknowledged before it thanked Mets fans for their support and promised, "Spring training is only four months away."

Those fans being thanked could only hope that wasn't a threat.

PART II
EMERGENCE &
EMERGENCY

SPRING AWAKENING
April 5, 1993–June 30, 1993

Hope throbbed up and down the East Coast a little past two o'clock. Lined up in two places were two teams granted the opportunity to erase a blighted recent past and two other teams licensed to lay the cornerstone of both a present and a future. On Opening Day, April 5, 1993, the Colorado Rockies would play their very first game ever at Shea Stadium, visiting the New York Mets. The Florida Marlins would break their seal, too, hosting the Los Angeles Dodgers at Joe Robbie Stadium.

Two brand-new teams. Four brand-new seasons. The same sun shining on everybody. If the 95,461 patrons who filled the ballparks in Flushing and Miami Gardens had been issued a symbolism surcharge, they'd pass over the money without even thinking about it. Fields of dreams were abundant this first Monday in April. Baseball court was in session. All oral arguments on opening day are pro. There is no dissenting opinion.

The Rockies and the Marlins didn't have to be good. They were already better than nothing to fans who had exactly that on the major-league level prior to 1993. The Mets and Dodgers simply couldn't be worse than they'd been in 1992. It was a low bar to clear. Ninety losses in Queens. Ninety-nine in SoCal. Accumulating fewer defeats was just about the least you could ask from the franchises representing the National League's media capitals. Giving them just-happy-to-be-there opponents on opening day was a nice nudge in the right direction.

In New York, the presumed renaissance and its attendant trimmings arrived right on time via a 3–0 victory. Dwight Gooden went the distance, giving up only four singles, including one to ex-Dodger Eric Young, who stole the first Rockies base. But the Mets were not to be outpaced in any facet of the game. They stole three bases. Bobby Bonilla homered off top expansion draft pick and former Brave David Nied and made a sliding catch in right. Doc pitching, Bobby Bo slugging, everybody aggressive . . . this was how it was designed to work a year earlier when New York was assured Hardball was Back. The only headline Mets addition in the offseason was shortstop Tony Fernandez, obtained along with impeccable credentials (four Gold Gloves, four All-Star selections), from San Diego. Other ostensible upgrades were installed around the roster's margins, but the bulk of the projected improvement was centered on good health. So many key Mets had missed so many weeks and months in '92. Get them all on the same field game after game, and how could they fail again?

* * *

Down in Florida, where big-league attention traditionally evaporated once spring training expired, the Dodgers and Marlins were the objects of ESPN's affection. Joe Robbie, unlike Shea, was never a multipurpose stadium. It was built solely for football, yet retrofitting made it passable for the national pastime. An oversized, old-timey scoreboard was in play in left. A local resident by the name of Joe DiMaggio was engaged to throw out the first pitch. The Greatest Living Player, as he liked to be introduced, was the baseball idol of Carl Barger, the Marlins' president in their nascent stages. Barger suffered a fatal aneurysm in December and Florida announced it would retire DiMaggio's No. 5 in Barger's memory. There was enough nostalgia baked in to the setting and ceremonies to make it seem as if the teal-tinged Marlins weren't being born on the spot.

The opening day battery indicated a stalwart of the senior circuit was hosting the Dodgers. The Marlins pitcher was Charlie Hough, forty-five-year-old knuckleballer who graduated from nearby Hialeah High School, class of '66, and was picked in the subsequent amateur draft by Los Angeles when its rotation was still headed by a lefty called Koufax and a righty named Drysdale. Charlie bridged geography and generations. His catcher was of uncommon quality for an expansion outfit, but this was not your father's startup, or like any Hough might have remembered from his youth. When the Mets and Houston Colt .45s came along in 1962, they were limited to the shallowest talent pool the National League establishment could furnish. "There is something wrong with him," Lindsey Nelson would say of the typical player teams made available in that first expansion draft, "or they wouldn't be willing to give him up."

That, however, was fifteen years before free agency. When the Marlins and Rockies coalesced, they not only drafted from a better class of castoffs than the Mets and eventual Astros had, but they could throw money at free agents. One of whom took a deal from Florida was Benito Santiago, recognized as one of the premier all-around catchers in the game since breaking in with San Diego in 1986. He had multiple Silver Sluggers to go with his collection of Gold Gloves. In assessing the Marlins' composition, ESPN analyst Buck Martinez pointed first and foremost to strong-armed Santiago— "a genuine big leaguer and a guy who can lead them behind the plate . . . probably, without a doubt, the best expansion team catcher ever." Martinez caught for the first-year Kansas City Royals of 1969, so he certainly had a feel for the subject.

Buck's partner on the telecast, Chris Berman, introduced America to the Marlins primarily via his nickname fetish. The second baseman was Bret "Put Another Shrimp on the" Barberie; at first base, Orestes "Emotionally" Destrade; the best catcher any expansion team ever had became Benito "Il Duce" Santiago, a fascistic formulation that made Berman (if no one else) chuckle. "Jeff Conine the Barbarian" was in left, while Walt "Three Blind" Weiss manned short. Third baseman Dave Magadan was merely "former Met Dave Magadan."

And the Dodgers' catcher, Santiago's lesser-known opposite number? Berman heralded him as "Tommy Lasorda's godson," which technically Mike Piazza wasn't. Also, Berman pronounced Piazza with a soft "z" sound, "z"as in zero, zero as in the total of silly nicknames ESPN's star announcer bestowed when reciting the Dodgers lineup. Perhaps the Berman flair was judged necessary only for the team no one had ever seen before.

Piazza—the double-z forming a "ts" sound, as in pizza or, for that matter, Mets—wasn't totally unfamiliar. There were those 74 plate appearances in September and October 1992, but those weren't enough to keep him from losing his rookie eligibility. That was intact as he began 1993, catching 1988 Mets tormentor Orel Hershiser in the bottom of the first at Joe Robbie and batting against Hough in the top of the second. Mike's first at-bat of the new season produced a net-negative. With one out, and with Berman and Martinez marveling over the "butterfly net" glove Santiago was using to catch the knuckler, Piazza grounded to Magadan, who threw the ball to Barberie to retire Eric Karros, who had just walked. Barberie relayed to Destrade. Piazza, like Karros, was out by a mile but in the record books. One at-bat, two outs. Mike had just hit into the first double play in Florida Marlins history.

Seven innings later, Piazza would collect his first hit of the season, a single to right off closer Bryan Harvey, but it was the last Los Angeles hit of the day. The Marlins came away from their first game with something neither the '93 Rockies nor the '62 Mets could garner: a win, 6–3 over the Dodgers. The Original Mets didn't triumph until their tenth game, by which time they'd already fallen 9 1/2 out of first. The Original Rockies would be beaten in their second game by the current Mets, 6–1, Bret Saberhagen picking up more or less where Doc left off. The folks back in Denver weren't fazed. More than 80,000 jammed into Mile High Stadium to watch their new team post their first win, 11–4 over the Expos. The Marlins, meanwhile, saw their dream of an unblemished season fall away in their second game, as they fell to the Dodgers, 4–2. Piazza singled, doubled, and drove in a run.

* * *

Once the Mets were done with the Rockies, they, too, tasted defeat. And then some. The Astros came to Shea and swept a weekend series. Between the second and third games, to make it more interesting than it had to be, Bonilla added another incident to his ledger. Earlier in the week, a book was released, titled *The Worst Team Money Could Buy*. It was about the 1992 Mets, with its most expensive player in one of the lead roles. Bonilla was not portrayed kindly, though his highlighted behavior—calling the press box during a game to protest an error, wearing earplugs to drown out the booing—was well known. Perhaps he didn't care to be reminded in detail of his *annus horribilis* so soon. He expressed his displeasure to one of the co-authors, Bob Klapisch of the *Daily News*, in the Mets clubhouse. Specifically Bonilla threatened Klapisch ("I will hurt you"), and threatened to "show you the Bronx," Bobby's home borough. The implication wasn't a guided tour of the Botanical Garden.

Emblematic of the advance hype from Bonilla's first year as a Met, Bobby didn't deliver as promised early in his second—no metaphorical Bronx for Klapisch, not even a trip to Staten Island. Whatever good feelings were generated by his sparkling opening day rapidly dissipated, and the season was only five days old. The Mets were losing and becoming hard to root hard for. A tone was being set. The Mets hit the road for Colorado, where enormous crowds saw them take two of three, and Cincinnati, where they won on a Friday and Saturday. That pair of wins raised the 1993 Mets' record to 6–4.

It was the statistical high point of the season. On Sunday, April 18, the Mets lost their series finale at Riverfront Stadium, 3–2. Eddie Murray and Jeff Torborg were each ejected. Saberhagen, the losing pitcher, called the team "angry." The Mets didn't take their anger out on their opponents when they returned to New York. They dropped two of three to the Giants, two of three to the Padres (catcher Todd Hundley was ejected from that finale after nearly coming to blows with batter Gary Sheffield) and, with their record having dipped below .500, welcomed the Dodgers to Shea.

Mike Piazza and the Mets were about to meet for the very first time.

Neither team was in as good a shape on April 27 as when they got done with their opening set of dates with the expansion teams. New York, despite the grumbling and fumbling, actually had the better mark. L.A. came to town 6–13, a half-game behind the Rockies and seventh in the seven-team National League West. The 8–9 Mets were only sixth in the East, or next-to-last. As an anonymous Mets voice was quoted in the *Times*, "At least we're better than the Marlins."

A titanic clash this was not, despite the Tuesday afternoon matchup that still carried, in theory, the aura of glory days. The Dodgers started Hershiser. The Mets countered with Gooden. In a baseball sense, that was a pretty good story. In a 1993 Mets sense, baseball was only part of the story. Gooden was the focus of another media maelstrom after amateur duffer/professional outfielder Vince Coleman hit him in the right shoulder blade with a golf club. It wasn't intentional (golfers have been known to practice their swings in clubhouses), but it was also kept officially quiet, which rarely/never works in New York. "Something happens and it becomes a big deal," Torborg lamented, as if he hadn't grown up in North Jersey and coached on a fairly well-covered Yankee club. When the press found out why Doc was mysteriously scratched from his projected Monday start that wound up rained out anyway, the Mets found themselves answering more questions that had little to do with why they were playing the way they were playing.

The way they were playing wasn't helping. Gooden, having absorbed a bit of soreness from inadvertently appearing as a hazard on Coleman's imaginary course, was up to the Hershiser challenge. Doc went eight innings, and allowed only two hits, or one fewer than Orel gave up (one of them a double to Gooden) in nine. For the first seven innings, it was a duel that would have fit snugly within the narrative of 1985 or 1988. The only interruption to the esteemed aces' string of zeroes was injected by a catcher who had never played at Shea Stadium before, but wasn't wholly unfamiliar with the inner workings of the park. The Lasorda connection—Tommy was Mike's godfather, even if Mike wasn't technically Tommy's godson (but, the manager explained, "our families are so close, that's what we call it in Italian, godfather")—had brought Piazza to Shea in his teens as a member of the Dodgers traveling party. He lived outside of Philadelphia and had served as the Dodgers' batboy at the Vet. Queens wasn't that far from home, so he took a trip with the team up the turnpike. Piazza could remember watching Darryl Strawberry take batting practice and the Dodgers gather around a TV in their clubhouse. Video to prepare them for that night's Mets pitcher?

Nope. They were "watching a porno film" in Mike's recollection. "I have to admit, coming from the straitlaced, deeply Catholic background that I did, it was a little unsettling. I didn't tell my mother."

Not everything that happens in New York stays in New York. Just as word of Coleman's itinerant golf swing leaked out, what Piazza did the first time he put on a Dodgers uniform for keeps at Shea made all the newsreels. Mike stepped in against Doc with two out in the second inning of a scoreless game and, on the fourth pitch he saw, did something: hit a home run off one of the biggest names in baseball. It was his third of the season, the fourth of his burgeoning career. No disrespect to previous victims, Steve Reed, René Arocha, or Dave Otto, but this was Dwight Gooden. Mike had just taken the Doctor deep.

It was a more impressive swing than Coleman's—"a *long* one," vaunted slugger Ralph Kiner described the homer as it sailed to the back of the Shea left-field bleachers—and did its own kind of damage to Gooden. Doc was down, 1–0. There'd be no more scoring until the eighth, when Gooden walked Piazza and was subsequently undermined by two Mets errors, the second of them on a liner to right mishandled by Bonilla (it was scored an error, with no protest to the authorities lodged). That ball, which led to L.A.'s third and fourth runs, had been struck by Strawberry, batting against Gooden for the seventh and final time in his career. Strawberry and Gooden weren't done being linked in the public consciousness, but the atonal free agency-wrought interlude in which they were listed on opposite sides of the same box score was over. Darryl was a lifetime .167 hitter versus his old teammate . . . and batting .175 for the Dodgers twenty games into the 1993 season.

Gooden was done after eight. Hershiser was nicked for an unearned run in the ninth (instigated by a Strawberry error) and nailed down a 4–1 victory, the first complete game win caught by Piazza on the year. Because of the Monday night rain, the Dodgers' sojourn to Shea amounted to a one-game series, but it was a successful New York debut, the kind of performance a straitlaced kid of any background would be proud to write home and tell Mom about.

* * *

The 7–13 Dodgers and 8–10 Mets each left town, Los Angeles heading home, New York visiting San Francisco. The Mets continued to lose. By the second game of their road trip, they could no longer take comfort in their position relative to the Marlins. The Mets fell into seventh place, where they'd stay for the rest of 1993. Fernandez, the great shortstop upgrade, was scuffling to hit .200 while battling kidney stones, another situation the Mets attempted to muffle. When they took their show to San Diego, there was more of the same. The opener at Jack Murphy Stadium was lost, 7–6. It was the Mets' sixth consecutive setback, Anthony Young's 17th in a row. Anthony had won his first two decisions of 1992, then lost 14 straight. The new year wasn't treating him any better.

The final California stop for the Mets was Dodger Stadium. The Dodgers entered as a last-place team themselves. Once they swept Mets a two-game set on May 4 and 5, they were out of the cellar for good. Piazza collected three hits, drove in three runs, and raised his batting average to

.322. The Mets flew to New York two games behind Florida, 9 1/2 behind front-running Philadelphia and on the verge of early extinction. The season was exactly a month old and 1993 felt all but over in Flushing. Self-esteem was briefly boosted when Gooden and Saberhagen threw shutouts against the Marlins (bracketing a pair of losses to the expansion club), but then the road and more cruelties beckoned. Two losses in three dates at St. Louis were followed by a three-game sweep at the hands of the Expos in Montreal, which ended with Young 0-for-4 and Bonilla batting .214.

Back to Shea for more punishment in what became General Torborg's last homestand. On May 19, after two more losses, bringing the current streak to five, the Mets rallied for three runs in the ninth to tie Pittsburgh at four. In the bottom of the tenth, Bonilla capped the comeback with a two-run homer to beat Blas Minor, 6–4. For other teams, it would have been cause for celebration. For the 1993 Mets, it was a prelude to dismissal. Following their first walk-off win of the season, the front office fired Torborg.

Maybe it was a cause for celebration. Fans had taken to chanting "Jeff Must Go," and Torborg never looked nor sounded particularly happy trying to explain what had just gone wrong in the latest loss. He had come to New York one year removed from Manager of the Year honors in the American League and left the Mets with an 85–115 National League record. It couldn't have all been the lack of a designated hitter flummoxing him (though at one point he admitted having his pitcher due to bat at least once every three innings presented him with a challenge). Injuries had indeed piled up in his first season at the helm, but on this second go-round, he had Coleman, Murray, Saberhagen, and Bonilla . . . maybe that was part of the problem. The big-ticket acquisitions failed to mesh, while the holdovers and reinforcements provided little ballast. Plus lady luck never renewed her season tickets.

Torborg had to go. So did most of the Mets, but an organization could do only so much at once. For the time being, they enlisted Dallas Green, lately a scout for the Mets, famously the pilot who steered an underachieving Phillies team to its first world championship in 1980. It was a switcheroo as old as baseball itself: if one type of manager isn't getting it done, find another type. Torborg was considered cerebral, which is code for he wore glasses. Green's calling card was bombast and bluster. He was going to clean up this town.

It worked for about a minute, at least if you were grading on a curve. The Mets won five of their first twelve under Green. That's a losing pace, but a much better one than was being set on Torborg's watch. Then another bottom fell out and continued to plummet. Between June 4 and June 27, the Mets played 23 games and lost 20 of them. Young pitched right in step with the program, escalating his losing streak to 24 at the end of this nightmare stretch to set a new National League record for sustained futility. The Mets also lost Fernandez, albeit gladly, when they shipped him to his original club, the contending Blue Jays, in exchange for outfielder Darrin Jackson. Fernandez never got it together after his kidney stone trouble, and the Mets figured they were just as well off with rookie Tim Bogar and his .200-ish batting average. Jackson, meanwhile, would be waylaid by Graves' disease, the same thyroid condition that had plagued former first lady Barbara Bush. The executive who sent Tony packing, GM Al Harazin, removed himself from Shea within a couple of weeks himself. He was replaced by his former fellow Frank Cashen deputy, Joe McIlvaine.

While sorting through myriad shortstops, scandals, field managers, general managers, team losing streaks and individual losing streaks, these Mets hadn't strung together back-to-back wins since that long-ago April day in Cincinnati when they upped their record to 6–4. They arrived in Miami at 21–52, one game worse than the 1962 Mets at the same juncture and more than a dozen games worse than the infant Marlins. Florida, 34–40, wasn't lighting the league on fire, but they had the good sense to debut in a year when being an expansion team was neither the most helpless nor hopeless thing you could be.

Nevertheless, the guppy Fish poured their elders just a touch of teal tonic, somehow losing twice in a row to the Mets on June 29 and 30. The first game encompassed a rain delay in which the Joe Robbie grounds crew fought the tarp and the tarp more or less won; a seven-run Marlin seventh that erased a 6–1 Mets lead; a three-run answer from the Mets in the eighth; a tying run off John Franco in the bottom of the ninth; and Jeromy Burnitz, who had earlier blasted his first major-league home run, scoring the ultimate winner in the 12th to tilt the see-saw to the Mets, 10–9. Thus inspired, the visitors quelled the home team more easily the next night, 7–1. They now trailed sixth-place Florida by 10 1/2 and first-place Philadelphia by 28.

The momentum didn't last, but the season refused to end.

IT'S A FAMILY AFFAIR
July 8, 1993–July 13, 1993

The 1988 amateur draft had become legendary by the time the Dodgers returned to Shea in July, thanks to their last and loudest pick, that of the junior college first baseman chosen in the 62nd round as a what-the-heck favor to their manager. Mike Piazza's breakthrough was accompanied by the tale of his relationship with his brother's godfather, Tommy Lasorda, and how sometimes a little nepotism is the best policy. Mike was hitting everything he saw, including the cover of *Sports Illustrated*, where he was hailed as the "Blue Plate Special," carrying on in the tradition of "stellar Dodger rookies." Inside, under the headline, "A Piazza With Everything" (the pronunciation of Mike's last name now widely comprehended), the emphasis was on his longstanding relationship with the longtime Los Angeles pilot; how Lasorda was best buds with Mike's father, Vince; and the critical role Tommy played in making sure Vincent's boy got a shot in Dodger blue.

The offensive numbers posted to date attested to Piazza's breakout being legit. Nobody's father, godfather, or friend of the family could arrange his kind of stats. As *SI* went to press, the 1,390th pick overall from five years before was batting .331, slugging .556, and generally conceded the National League Rookie of the Year award. His monstrous first three months of 1993 all but anointed Mike as the freshman most likely to succeed his fellow 1988 Dodger draftee, '92 ROY Eric Karros, in attaining the distinction. Once Mike's ticket was formally gold-stamped by the BBWAA, he'd become the thirteenth Dodger so recognized, dating back to the award's inception in 1947, when Brooklyn's Jackie Robinson was voted the inaugural honor. Having generated so much momentum, it was no wonder a spot in the

All-Star Game awaited Mike in Baltimore. Piazza was chosen to back up the Phillies' Darren Daulton. Though new on the scene, Mike finished third in the fan voting, trailing only Daulton and the Marlins' impeccably credentialed Benito Santiago, the previous NL catcher to have won the rookie prize, in 1987, the same season Major League Baseball renamed the award for Robinson.

Peter O'Malley's Dodgers really knew how to keep these trinkets in the family. Modernity's inevitable nudges notwithstanding, baseball's instinct was to embrace tradition. Piazza the Dodger following in the footsteps of Robinson the Dodger (not to mention Karros, Fernando Valenzuela, and nine other notables) provided an ideal grace note to this rookie's rise, assuming Mike kept up his hitting in the second half.

"Tradition!" Tevye from *Fiddler on the Roof* could have been commissioner of this sport. Nobody else was, officially, what with the Lords of Baseball having banded together to effectively bounce Fay Vincent from office the previous September. Since they were looking out for their own interests first and foremost, it could be said they, too, were upholding tradition. Milwaukee Brewers owner Bud Selig served as acting commissioner. If the late Bart Giamatti was Zero Mostel, and Vincent was at least Topol, Selig was the unassuming understudy thrust into the spotlight, albeit supposedly temporarily.

* * *

Like the Great White Way, the Midsummer Classic may have been a bit of an anachronism, yet it still made for a grand and perhaps theatrical showcase. The 1993 edition, which marked the All-Star affair's 60th anniversary, seemed to exude particular promise and potential. Its starriest attraction was the Mariners' Ken Griffey. At twenty-three, Junior was in his fifth season and fourth such game amid a prime that was ongoing and presumed never-ending. He stole the All-Star preshow, its usually overwrought Home Run Derby, by flipping his cap around and belting the first ball to ever kiss the B&O warehouse, the fifth-of-a-mile-wide, red-brick edifice that backdropped the perfectly set Camden Yards, itself in only its second season of operation. Major League Baseball couldn't have asked for a better portrayal of the best it had to offer.

A veritable kid called "The Kid," who—as the offspring of Cincinnati right fielder Ken Griffey Sr.—grew up literally running around the clubhouse of that dynastic contraption known as the Big Red Machine—was messing around on natural grass, uncorking blast after blast, having himself a blast and drawing oohs, aahs, and torrents of applause. To a nation checking in on its nominal pastime and getting a gander at not just its flagship player but the throwback ballpark winning raves as a real-life field of dreams, Griffey and Camden Yards embodied contemporary, yet classic, hot fun in the summertime.

America was parked between the Chicago Bulls capturing a third consecutive NBA title and the firing up of NFL training camps, when twenty-seven franchises would gather their respective forces to try to figure how to stop a twenty-eighth, the Dallas Cowboys, from repeating as Super Bowl champs. Baseball needed all the vibrant help it could get. It didn't have Michael Jordan, though he did drop by for a celebrity home run-hitting contest, and it didn't have America's Team (not the primary one, anyway, no matter what the Atlanta Braves called themselves). But for a couple of days, it had a transcendent star on loan from the relative obscurity of the Pacific Northwest—where every game started too late for its score to appear in half the country's morning papers—and it had, after three depressing decades of artificiality and multipurposeness, a beautifully crafted jewel box in which he could display his excellence. It was certainly a cheerier place than the Kingdome.

Griffey wasn't exactly a secret in this age of *SportsCenter*, where several times a day an ESPN viewer could catch his highlights. His rookie card from 1989 was the centerpiece of the Upper Deck portfolio. His gigantism (from an overdose of nerve tonic) was perhaps the most adorable malady to befall the ringers Mr. Burns brought in to play on the Springfield Nuclear Power Plant softball team in 1992's *The Simpsons* episode "Homer at the Bat." Even Jordan was animated enough by Junior's presence to request an autograph.

Co-All-Starring at Oriole Park at Camden Yards (OP@CY in the electronic bulletin board parlance that was beginning to be spoken wherever baseball fans were suitably wired) was Barry Bonds, twice the MVP of the National League in the previous three years. Junior's senior circuit counterpart in talent and totals if not charisma was somehow experiencing a career renaissance despite the fact that he was already a certified superstar. Having departed the Pirates to sign with his childhood team, the Giants, in the offseason, Bonds was singlehandedly resurrecting baseball in San Francisco.

The Giants had come perilously close to leaving town the year before; Lasorda and Vince Piazza—who had done well as a suburban Philadelphia car dealer—had been linked to a potential ownership group that seemed destined to relocate the old New York Giants to St. Petersburg. The Tampa Bay done deal fell through, though, and a transplanted Manhattanite, Peter Magowan, previously best known as CEO of the Safeway supermarket chain, swooped in and whisked *his* childhood team through the express lane, leading a new ownership group that eschewed St. Pete for San Fran. San Francisco not only retained its baseball team but adopted as its own the son of Bobby Bonds (a.k.a. the next Willie Mays), not to mention the god-son of Willie Mays (a.k.a. the only Willie Mays). Amid the coziest of West Coast homecomings, Barry had the Giants well out in front of the defending NL champion Braves in the Western Division and another Most Valuable Player trophy on order.

Bonds, Griffey, Piazza . . . everybody of stature was related to somebody. Magowan wound up in San Francisco in the late 1950s because his father had lately moved the family out there from New York. It was great, if coincidental, timing. The elder Magowan was at the Polo Grounds on October 3, 1951, rooting for the Giants. The son was in fifth grade, listening to Bobby Thomson driving Russ Hodges to distraction on the radio, courtesy of a very understanding teacher. While New York's abandoned Giants fans had to figure out how to keep tabs on their beloveds (or ruefully wait for an expansion team to take their and the Dodgers' place), Peter followed his team across the country. Some three-and-a-half decades later, he kept them from moving again, adding Bonds for six years at a record-breaking $43.75 million to assure the Bay Area everything was gonna be OK.

* * *

Even where there were no bloodlines or old compadres woven into the narrative, feel-good stories abounded at the All-Star Game. John Olerud, who coped with the aftereffects of a brain aneurysm by wearing a batting helmet (minus the earflaps) in the field, was flirting with .400

for the first-place Toronto Blue Jays. He was the American League starting first baseman. The National League's version of Olerud, in position if not demeanor, was John Kruk, the scruffiest of the preternaturally scruffy first-place Philadelphia Phillies. Kruk was rapidly becoming a sport-wide cult hero for dispensing bon mots like "I ain't an athlete, lady, I'm a ballplayer." His batting average wasn't as stratospheric at the break as Olerud's (.350 vs. .395), but nobody touched "the Krukker" for personality.

The 1993 All-Star Game would be less remembered for the AL's 9–3 victory—Piazza struck out versus the Jays' Duane Ward to end it a day after going dingerless in the Derby—than it would the lefty-batting Kruk bailing out against Griffey's Seattle teammate, Randy Johnson. Lefties generally didn't bat let alone connect against the intimidating southpaw. The Big Unit sent a scowling message, firing his first pitch about a warehouse-width above Kruk's head. The Phillie theatrically but sincerely patted his chest, checking to see if his heart was still ticking. He tried a couple of swings, missing, but surviving. It wasn't the most competitive of at-bats, but the game didn't count. Only a curmudgeon couldn't laugh along with Kruk.

So much frivolity and festiveness emanated from Camden Yards that it only served to remind fans of the hands-down worst team in baseball that they weren't a part of the fun. Technically, a Met was on hand. All teams had to be represented, and there was a man in a Mets uniform introduced among the National League All-Stars, the same man who played left for the final three innings and singled off 1986 Met Rick Aguilera in the eighth.

New York's NL All-Star was Bobby Bonilla. Somebody had to be picked. Given a choice, Mets fans might have RSVPed their regrets.

* * *

Bonilla's stats were ample for a seventh-place ballclub: 20 home runs and 55 RBIs in 87 games. But in no way, shape, or form was Bobby Bo the people's choice. The embodiment of *The Worst Team Money Could Buy* couldn't overcome his fabulous first impression once his attempt at intimidation ("I'll show you the Bronx") fell a few levels below Randy Johnson's, while the snarl that defined '92 in Flushing never curled upward within the Metsopotamian mind. Bonilla hit better in 1993 than he had in his first year as a Met, but his image never recovered . . . and his team just kept getting worse.

The last opponent the Mets saw before Bonilla traveled to Baltimore and the other twenty-four of them scattered for a three-day vacation was the Dodgers, into Shea for five games in deference to having been rained out once in April. This was the first year of paid attendance being reported as tickets sold as opposed to fans using tickets bought. The crowds reported at shvitzy Shea (temperatures in the city reached triple-digits three days running) appeared to be the product of a heat mirage on the official scorer's part. It was emptier than the agate would indicate, and if the humidity didn't get you, the standings did.

Nevertheless, the Mets held their own, in their 1993 way. Well, not in the first game of the Thursday July 8 doubleheader, started and lost by rookie Dave Telgheder (4 IP, 8 ER). The Dodgers won, 11–8, with Piazza going 3-for-5 and topping off the Dodger scoring on a two-run homer off yet another neophyte, Rule 5'er Mike Draper, in the sixth. The Mets won the nightcap, as the visiting star catcher sat and Bonilla hit a game-ending tenth-inning home run. The next steamy night, Friday, Piazza homered again, another two-run job, this one off a veteran, forty-year-old Frank Tanana (threw in the 90s in the '70s, and in the 70s in the '90s, as the line went) and the Dodgers prevailed. On Saturday afternoon, it was the Mets' catcher who did all the slugging. Todd Hundley homered in the first, grounded out productively in the third and doubled off Roger McDowell in the eighth, totaling four runs batted in the Mets' 7–6 win. Hundley owned the day, but his average rose only to .233, or 84 points beneath Piazza's.

Sunday night, an ESPN presentation, pitted an aging fastballer versus an older knuckleballer, Dwight Gooden for the Mets taking on Tom Candiotti of the Dodgers. Doc was also holding his own in this, his tenth season in the big leagues. Gone was the K Korner and the accoutrement of super-stardom, but he was still as much of an ace as the Mets had. Entering the evening, Gooden was a .500 pitcher for a team wallowing 32 games below break-even. His ERA was a respectable 3.40, though it had been trending upward since mid-June. Still, a poll of Mets fans probably would have nominated the diminished Doctor as their All-Star over Bonilla.

Old Doc (baseball-weathered as he was, it was sometimes hard to remember Gooden was only twenty-eight in people years) acquitted himself admirably for a team that inspired so little admiration. He nursed a 1–0 lead through five before allowing consecutive singles to Piazza, Eric Davis, and relocated Expo nemesis Tim Wallach. Piazza crossed the plate to tie the game. It stayed tied until the eighth when Gooden gave up a solo homer to Davis. Candiotti had done all right himself, but Lasorda lifted him for a pinch-hitter in the sixth. The Mets, having absorbed an eyeful of Piazza since Thursday, now had the pleasure of facing another Dodgers freshman with a telling family tie.

Pedro Martinez was on to pitch. He was twenty-one years old and better known as the younger brother of Ramon Martinez than he was as a comer in his own right, but at Shea his last name could have been Smith, Jones, or Shlabotnik. It didn't matter. Like Mike, Pedro was succeeding on his own abilities. The Mets didn't touch him in the sixth. Jeff Kent led off with a walk in the seventh, but Martinez picked him off immediately, then retired the next two hitters. The Dominican rookie collected one more out in the eighth, finally gave up a single, and was double-switched out of the game in favor of Dodgers closer Jim Gott. The Mets went on to lose, 2–1.

Save for Bonilla, the 27–60 Mets charitably removed themselves from public view for the next few days. Piazza was the only Dodgers player going to Camden Yards, but they were in far better shape for when baseball resumed for real. Maybe not good enough to catch the Giants, but at 46–41, they were making up for their miserable 1992, at least. They, unlike the Mets, were getting better. They, unlike the Mets, were fortifying their over-the-hill gang with young talent: Martinez, Karros, Piazza. Pedro, as was the case with Latin players, wasn't subject to the amateur draft, but L.A. came up big twice in 1988, snagging the reigning Rookie of the Year, Karros, in the sixth round, and the surefire next one in the 62nd.

Piazza may have arrived in unorthodox fashion, but he had surely arrived. He made the most out of that courtesy pick. He converted himself from first baseman in junior college to a catcher in the pros. He embedded himself at the Dodgers' Dominican academy, a place intended to cultivate the careers of youngsters from Latin America, not the son of a big-time car dealer out of Pennsylvania. Vince Piazza not only knew Tommy Lasorda (who compared young Mike's power to that of Ralph Kiner), but Tommy indirectly gave him an in with Ted Williams. Teddy Ballgame once came over to the house and watched Mike hit in Vince's homemade batting cage.

The Greatest Hitter Who Ever Lived gave the teenager his blessing. Piazza persevered. A break here, a break there, but ultimately young Mike made his own breaks, shaking off setbacks at the University of Miami, giving it another go at Miami-Dade, later leaving his home country, not speaking the language in the Dominican Republic, overcoming internal perceptions that he was nothing more than Tommy's boy as he scaled the Dodgers system. Now, in 1993, the kid who made the 1988 draft the stuff of legend was as much the toast of baseball as anybody else . . . a different kind of toast than the Mets already were by midseason.

ENDLESS SUMMER
July 24, 1993–August 15, 1993

You want a brood for whom Southern "Californee" was the place they shouldn't be? With all due respect to the Clampetts of *Beverly Hillbillies* fame, load up the plane and meet the 1993 Mets. L.A., as much as any place on the unkind National League map, was their Waterloo. Perhaps not in the standings, for the standings were already a lost cause. No, their reputation was beaten into submission once and for all in 1993 in Los Angeles. They might have slipped into last-place obscurity had it not been for the second of their two trips to take on Mike Piazza and the Dodgers.

Saturday afternoon, July 24, was the day "blow up the Mets!" became the franchise's rallying cry. The Mets had lost on Friday night, Piazza crushing his 20th homer of the season off Tanana (before being rested during the subsequent day game after the night game), but were making a valiant effort at staving off a losing streak. Trailing by three in the seventh, Eddie Murray and Bobby Bonilla each drove in runs against Pedro Martinez. In the eighth, utilityman Jeff McKnight delivered a sacrifice fly off Pedro to knot the game at four. Vince Coleman then grounded out to end the inning and facilitate Dallas Green's next move. He double-switched Coleman from the game and brought in Anthony Young to pitch the bottom of the eighth.

It worked, for a spell. AY allowed a runner as far as third, but got out of it. He retired the Dodgers in order in the bottom of the ninth after Jim Gott did the same to the Mets. Gott took care of the Mets in the top of the tenth as well. Anthony, though, left his rabbit's foot back at the hotel. Jody Reed reached him for an infield single. Henry Rodriguez got him for an outfield single. Brett Butler sacrificed them each up a base. Jose Offerman was intentionally walked to fill the bases. Eric Davis lined out to Jeff Kent. If Young could just take care of pinch-hitter Dave Hansen . . .

They may make situation comedies in Los Angeles, but not every one of them is filmed before a live audience. Cruelty thus cued the laugh track when Young walked Hansen, forcing in Reed. The Mets lost, 5–4. It was their second straight defeat, Young's 27th. The major-league record for individual pitcher futility continued unabated.

That very same day, a new standard for recklessness by a big leaguer was established out in the Dodger Stadium parking lot where Coleman, hitching a Jeep ride from Davis (with Bonilla in tow and Young in another car; the four were heading to the Dodger's house for a cookout), tossed a powerful firecracker in the direction of some autograph-seeking fans for whom he and his pals weren't signing. It was supposedly done in fun. The result grew into serious business. Authorities described what Coleman tossed as "an explosive opposed to a firecracker," a veritable "quarter-stick of dynamite" that could do real damage.

It did. A two-year-old girl sustained injuries. The Mets—Coleman, all of them—sustained a public relations black eye, something that somehow transcended their horrendous record and previous sketchy behavior. By the time the Los Angeles County District Attorney's office filed felony charges, Coleman had played his last game as a Met. Co-owner Fred Wilpon soon promised there'd be no more Vinny from Queens, and he made good on it, despite the money and time remaining on his four-year contract.

Coleman's compulsion to play with matches overshadowed one of the few upbeat moments of 1993, probably the first time the sight of somebody associated with a Mets uniform inspired positive vibes since Opening Day. On July 28 at Shea, against the Marlins, the streak that wouldn't stop at last ended. Anthony Young became a winning pitcher. It wasn't easy (it couldn't be; it was 1993). Young entered a tie game in the ninth. Benito Santiago singled. Todd Hundley fumbled a sacrifice bunt from Darrell Whitmore. Walt Weiss bunted his way on. The bases were loaded for Rich Renteria, who grounded to Bonilla, who was moved to third base the same weekend Coleman found infamy at Chavez Ravine and never played right field for the Mets again. Back at his old Pirate position, Bobby Bo started a 5–2–3 double play, cutting down Santiago at the plate in the process.

One more out would save Young's bacon, but his luck had yet to sizzle. Ex-Met Chuck Carr, a speedster who was on his way to winning the National League stolen base title, bunted. Not only was he the third Marlin to bunt in the inning, he was the third to reach base. Whitmore came home with the go-ahead run to put Florida ahead, 4–3, and Young in the hole for what was verging on the 28th consecutive time.

Not so fast, fate. Pity was about to be taken from above, or at least from Anthony's teammates. Against Bryan Harvey, with 29 saves already in his portfolio, the Mets got going. McKnight, pinch-hitting for Tim Bogar, led off with a single. Dave Gallagher bunted him to second. Ryan Thompson blooped a ball between first and right that eluded three Fish fielders. McKnight galloped home with the tying run to unhook Young from the loss. One out later, Eddie Murray, whose first run batted in sixteen years earlier off Bert Blyleven helped Jim Palmer secure a win, lined a double down the right-field line. Thompson took off from first and didn't quit running until he crossed the plate. The Mets won, 5–4.

A man named Young had aged 465 days between wins, but a feeling so rare as having a W placed next to one's name, even if it signifies a won-lost mark elevated to 1–13, never gets old. The Mets were happy. Mets fans were happy. Young was delighted to be famous for something other than losing. He was thrilled to accept an invitation to fly back to L.A. on an offday in August and appear on *The Tonight Show with Jay Leno*. Losing 27 straight had made him a celebrity. Winning one at last allowed him to talk about it with a smile on his face.

* * *

Like most good news in Metland in 1993, it was over by the commercial break. Coleman's felony charge made the bigger Mets headline to come out of Los Angeles in early August, and in between, Saberhagen inflicted himself upon the news, or to be more specific, the news media. He had sprayed bleach at reporters in the Mets clubhouse through a Super Soaker water shotgun (oh, and he had already messed around with his own round of firecrackers for the heck of it, also to playfully harass the working press). It wasn't quite the scandal wrought by Coleman—whose firecracker toss "was the most accurate throw he has made all year," according to Leno—but it wasn't a good look. A five-game suspension was eventually sent Saberhagen's way. It wouldn't be served until the beginning of 1994 because, in that way the Mets world turned, Bret would be out for the season post-bleach, requiring arthroscopic surgery on his left knee.

Coleman, meanwhile, was detached from the ballclub that saw him as a transformative figure upon signing him in advance of the 1991 season. The Mets certainly transformed during Vince's stay. They had been a contender when he alighted and they were a laughingstock as he departed. He eventually accepted a one-year suspended sentence for his actions in Los Angeles. In New York, the Mets put him on administrative leave. His Mets playing career was over after 235 games spread across three seasons. He stole 99 bases as a Met, one shy of 100, which made a certain amount of sense. Vince Coleman's addition to the Mets never did quite add up to what you wanted it to be.

The Mets kept playing without Coleman, without Saberhagen, soon enough without their highest-profile attraction of the summer. Did a smidge of success spoil Anthony Young? After that one win against Florida (which was about to be a loss, but let us not detract from that which felt ever so temporarily good), AY gathered a couple more saves, but returned to form in Philadelphia. On August 13 and 15, he was charged with losses that indicated the plug was ready to be pulled from his summertime variety hour, which was days from being relocated to Triple-A Norfolk. The first loss after his history-halting win said all that needed to be said about the kind of season it was for the Mets and the pitcher. Called on in the ninth to a one-on, two-out situation against the Phillies at the Vet, Young allowed a walk, was undermined by a game-tying error, issued an intentional walk to load the bases, and surrendered a game-losing grand slam to Kim Batiste.

Before Anthony could blow the save on the fifteenth and drop his team's record to 40–77, the Mets experienced a fairly nice night on the fourteenth, winning a game behind a youthful right-handed pitcher from Fresno, California. You couldn't blame Mets fans for squinting hard and trying to see the second coming of Tom Seaver. Despite the biographical similarities, twenty-three year-old Bobby Jones wasn't projected as Franchise 2.0, but seeing as how 1993 was on pace to be the Mets' first 100-loss season since Seaver's rookie year of 1967, any resemblance to a silver lining was welcome.

Jones evoked another Mets legend, for he was chosen with a free agent supplemental compensation pick as the bounty awarded to the Mets for their having lost Darryl Strawberry to the Dodgers. Straw's departure more or less begat Coleman in Flushing. These days, Darryl was as much a non-factor in L.A. as Vince was in New York. A lingering back injury had kept Darryl out of action since the middle of June. If Jones was the literal compensation for the still-missed superstar leaving for Los Angeles, then here was the chance to fill a Strawberry-shaped void at Shea. Coleman couldn't do it with speed. Bonilla couldn't do via slugging. Maybe Jones could do it from the mound.

Bobby's first start was a potential harbinger of things to come if you chose to see it that way (and if you were squinting to see Seaver, why wouldn't you so choose?). The numbers didn't look Terrific—6 IP, 7 H, 5 R—but only one of the runs was earned and, besides, the Mets hit for the rookie more in a night than they did for good old Young in a month. The game wound up 9–5 in the Mets' favor, led not only by Jones, but freshman Bogar. Playing second this Saturday night, Tim went 4-for-5: two doubles and two homers, the second of those an inside-the-park trip. At twenty-six, he was enjoying the game of his life.

Talk about a highlight . . . and talk about how Mets highlights always seemed to be filtered through shades of gray. When the infielder slid head-first into home in the ninth inning, he tore the ligaments in his left hand, shelving him for the remainder of 1993. Just as Tim Bogar was heating up, he was definitively doused.

Philadelphia was not located in Southern California, but goofball sit-com plot devices were determined to follow the Mets wherever they went, even if hilarity rarely ensued.

A LONG SEPTEMBER
August 29, 1993–October 3, 1993

Mike Piazza's big-league career approached its first anniversary with two to grow on: two home runs to help Orel Hershiser beat the Cardinals at home on Sunday, August 29, 8–3. Mike's numbers in his official rookie year were up to 27 home runs, 84 runs batted in and a .316 batting average. All those figures were stunning, even if Orel did have him beat on the last one, raising his own average to a DH-shaming .424—great stats and a great time for a team whose season was decidedly so-so.

The Dodgers left last place behind in May, but rose as high as second only for a couple of days in mid-June. As September approached, they hovered a few games above .500, stuck in fourth place. It was a better situation than the one Piazza entered fifty-two weeks earlier, but it wasn't what you thought of when you contemplated the Dodger way.

Darryl Strawberry was not only done for the season—out since the Dodgers vacated second place on June 16 with his bad back and .140 batting average—he didn't generate any internal fondness by missing a physical rehab appointment. For that, he was fined a day's pay. Darryl's missteps took a more serious turn on September 4 when he was arrested for allegedly striking Charisse Simons, the woman with whom he was living. Simons declined to press criminal charges and the two married in the offseason. Fellow Los Angelino Eric Davis hadn't helped lift his hometown team, either. About a month after he gave Vince Coleman and his exploding paraphernalia a lift through the Dodger Stadium parking lot, L.A. traded him to Detroit. One of the great five-tool hopes of the 1980s was sent out of town, the other lingered inactive on the books; Straw had a year remaining on his contract.

The Dodgers were literally wearing their most painful wounds of 1993 on their sleeves. A patch on their uniform's left sleeve commemorated No. 52, reliever Tim Crews, who died in a Florida boating accident in spring training, a tragic mishap that also took the life of Cleveland Indians teammate Steve Olin and severely injured ex-Met and -Dodger Bobby Ojeda. Before signing with the Tribe, Crews had spent six seasons as a Dodger. His catcher of record in the last major-league game he ever pitched was Piazza.

More sad news for the Dodgers family came in midseason, necessitating another patch for the right sleeve. Nos. 39 and 52 were sewn on following the week-apart deaths of Hall of Famers Roy Campanella and Don Drysdale. Each man was a Dodgers legend whose continued association with the club was a continuing reminder of the franchise's Brooklyn roots. Campy, who lived to seventy-one, and Don, fifty-six, may have gotten to enjoy extended post-playing lives, but like Crews, who died just short of his thirty-second birthday, they were mourned as having been gone too soon.

The Dodgers soldiered on and Piazza continued earning his stripes. The first of his two home runs against St. Louis at the end of August set an L.A. rookie record, eclipsing that set by Joe Ferguson twenty years before. Ferguson, a catcher, was now a Dodgers coach. Like Campanella in his final Vero Beach spring, Joe worked to bring Mike's defense along. His hitting didn't need much help. "He always could hit," the coach had said of the prospect he helped shepherd to a starting role.

One year into a career that had earned so many raves, Piazza certainly knew how to talk the talk, which is to say you don't say much of anything about yourself if your team's performance doesn't speak for itself. "If your team isn't winning," the rookie said after his two homers broke a three-game losing streak, "you really don't have much to celebrate."

* * *

By late September, the only division with no cork popped was the National League West, which you wouldn't have bet would go uncelebrated for so long had you checked the standings on July 22 and noticed the Giants holding a 10-game lead over the geographically miscast Atlanta Braves. Figuring they had too much pitching to consider themselves done—tri-aces Tom Glavine, John Smoltz, and Steve Avery had been joined if not trumped in the offseason by 1992 Cy Young winner Greg Maddux—the two-time defending NL West champs traded for slugger Fred McGriff on July 18, cast off by the perpetually salary-shedding Padres.

It was a nice gesture toward contending, but Barry Bonds, Matt Williams, and the rampaging Giants didn't appear to be giving any ground. Even an omen to come smoking out of an Atlanta Fulton-County Stadium luxury box—a pregame fire coinciding with McGriff's Braves debut, which itself flipped an 0–5 deficit to an 8–5 win (with the Crime Dog homering)—didn't much impede San Francisco's march toward the postseason. Atlanta heated up, but San Fran didn't cool off. From the night McGriff set a spark to the Braves offense, though, Hotlanta won twelve of eighteen.

Eventually, the race tightened. The Giants and Braves emerged as the best teams in baseball by a long shot, yet one of them would go home when the regular season ended. In 1994, Major League Baseball planned to break each league into three divisions apiece and add a wild card to the mix. It was impossible to conceive of a 100-win team ever again not making the playoffs. In 1993, it was going to happen, and the hardest-luck loser the National League would ever know in the divisional era was about to emerge on the season's final day. The Braves and Giants arrived on Sunday, October 3, tied at 103–58. For now, they were each other's fiercest foes. For eternity, however, the Giants had only one true archrival, and that was whose stadium they were visiting with their season on the line.

While Atlanta caught a scheduling break and was hosting the Rockies on the final weekend, the Giants found themselves taking on the Dodgers in L.A., an echo of so many endings in National League history. Like 1951, when Bobby Thomson and New York stuck it to Ralph Branca and Brooklyn. Like 1962, when the best two-of-three sudden-death script shifted to California yet ended with the same tale of Giants joy and Dodgers doom. Like 1991, when it was Darryl Strawberry and the Dodgers who were caught from behind by the then-burgeoning Braves. Only two years before, Los Angeles and Atlanta were tied for first with three games to go. The Giants welcomed their cousins into Candlestick. Two wins over Dem Bums, combined with two Brave wins three time zones east, handed the Western Division to the team from Georgia.

These definitive Giants-Dodgers tilts tended to tilt one way. L.A., like Brooklyn, had been the more successful franchise by almost every measure for a half-century, but the team from Coogan's Bluff and its Northern California descendants had a knack for getting in the last lick. It stung everyone who bled Dodger blue, just as it validated the existence of those who saw the world in black and orange.

Unlike 1991, the spoiler shoe was on another foot. Like the Giants two years earlier, these Dodgers were long eliminated. Like the '91 Giants, the '93 Dodgers didn't notice. If one archrival was in a race, the other was in no way playing out the string. Sunday, October 3, was the forty-second anniversary of the Shot Heard Round the World and the thirty-first anniversary of its sequel, San Francisco's first pennant clinched at Los Angeles's expense. If you liked omens that didn't threaten to burn down stadiums, you had to like what the date meant to the Giants.

But you couldn't underestimate what the rivalry meant to the Dodgers, who had a touch more motivation on top of ruining the Giants' season embedded in their also-ran record. They entered Sunday at 80–81. It represented a great leap forward from 63–99, even if all it got them was fourth place. Still, 81–81 looked so much better to everybody in Los Angeles than 80–82. Unlike so many last games in which somebody has no chance to proceed any further, no feet were on planted on any buses. Tommy Lasorda and general manager Fred Claire each delivered a little pep talk prior to first pitch. If you saw it in a baseball movie, you'd call it unrealistic.

The time difference meant Atlanta took the field while it was barely past nine in the morning in California. The Rockies threw their opening day starter, David Nied, at the Braves. Nied had a promising future in Georgia, going 3–0 after being called up the previous September, but a team with as much pitching as the Braves had couldn't protect everybody from the forthcoming expansion draft. Colorado took him first. Atlanta battered him last. The youngster didn't last four innings. Just as Nied faced a Cy Young winner on opening day in Dwight Gooden, he was seeing another on closing day in Tom Glavine . . . and who wouldn't trust Glavine in a do-or-die Game 162? Tom pitched into the seventh, holding off Colorado and gaining his 22nd victory of 1993, tied with the Giants' John Burkett for most in the NL. The Braves beat the Rockies, 5–3, and finished their officially sanctioned allotment of baseball with a 104–58 record.

It might not be enough, just as 162 games weren't enough for the Giants and Dodgers of 1962 and 154 didn't do the trick for the pair in 1951. If the

Giants could sweep the Dodgers, they, too, would finish 104–58 and there would have to be a 163rd game of the tie-breaking variety, the kind of winner-take-all affair not removed from its "Open Only in Case of Emergency" glass compartment since 1980, when the Astros needed one extra game to quell, yup, the Dodgers.

The Giants' pitching wasn't as high profile as the Braves', but their lead duo of Burkett (22–7) and Bill Swift (21–8) were a match for anybody. Unfortunately for San Francisco, neither of them was due on the hill on Sunday. Dusty Baker was going with Salomon Torres, a well-regarded prospect with exactly seven starts in his major-league career. The eighth was intended to settle the National League West. The Dodgers countered with veteran Kevin Gross and nothing to lose.

For a while, it was a game. Scoreless after two, then 2–0, L.A., after three. It was 3–1 in the middle of the fifth, once Torres (3.1 IP, 3 ER, 5 H, 5 BB) was gone and the Giants scratched out a run. Then, in the bottom of the fifth, it began to slip once and for all away from San Francisco.

Who should pull the rug but the impending Rookie of the Year, the darling of Chavez Ravine, the blossomed, never mind budding, superstar of Los Angeles? From that last Sunday in August when he strafed the Cardinals to this first Sunday in October when the Giants were tiptoeing on coals, Mike Piazza had been as hot as any faultily wired luxury suite anywhere. The blaze wasn't about to be put out by Dave Burba, Baker's third pitcher of the afternoon.

Mike led off the home fifth with a home run, "a high drive into right field," as called by Vin Scully. Dave Martinez looked up at the track, but a blue fence wouldn't let him follow the flight of the ball any further. It was "gone!" by Scully's understated reporting, and with it, much of the Giants' hope. Cory Snyder came up two batters later with a man on and did to Burba pretty much the same thing Piazza had. In the sixth, an Eric Karros RBI single made it 7–1.

The Giants' season was all but over by the eighth, but there's always room for punctuation. Like punch, it was provided by Piazza. Dave Righetti was pitching for San Francisco. With one out, Jose Offerman walked and Tim Wallach singled. Mike stepped up for his last at-bat of 1993. Scully observed what happened next:

"He hits a high fly ball to right field . . . back goes Martinez . . . to the wall . . . it is gone! Miracle upon miracles, he's hit another one!"

Yet, Piazza homering twice wasn't really so miraculous on the face of it. October 3 was the fifth game in 1993 in which Mike homered twice . . . and the fourth time since August 29. From that day forward, Piazza had put on the fiercest of finishing kicks: 10 home runs, 31 runs batted in, a .336 average, a .664 slugging percentage and a heaping helping of revenge for 1951, 1962, and 1991 on behalf of blue-bleeders from coast to coast. To paraphrase what Scully said when Kirk Gibson took a trip around those same Dodger Stadium basepaths five years earlier, in a month that had been so incredible, the relatively predictable had happened.

Nevertheless, that last home run he hit—last of the game, last of the stretch drive tear, last of the season for him—did demonstrate a flair for the breathtaking. True, the Giants were already on their last breaths as it was, but the way Piazza went to the opposite field a second time to, as Scully described it, "put a fillip to one of the more dramatic moments of the year," left an impression. Just as no other broadcaster would use "fillip" (an explosive flourish, more or less) to emphasize a point, not too many hitters extant seemed capable of going out with that kind of bang.

Mike's second Sunday home run elicited a second curtain call (*"they are going wild at Dodger Stadium"*) and revved the engine on the Giant bus. They lost the game by a score of 13–1 and finished second with a record of 103–59. Los Angeles was a .500 team. Piazza, with his last swing closing the latest chapter in the Dodgers-Giants feud, was a .318 hitter, with 35 homers (as many as his predecessor, Mike Scioscia, hit in his first nine seasons) and 112 ribbies. He was a Silver Slugger in waiting—he won the award at catcher, while Hershiser's .356 earned Orel the prize among pitchers—and the Rookie of the Year by universal acclamation.

A vote was taken. It was a formality. Piazza was listed first on all twenty-eight ballots. He was the first unanimous Rookie of the Year in the National League since Benito Santiago in 1987. Mike finished a distant ninth to Barry Bonds (46 HR, 123 RBIs, .336 BA) in MVP voting, though if you exclude all Phillies, Braves, and Giants—that is, everybody who didn't win a division or compete like hell right down to the wire for one—only Marquis Grissom of the second-in-the-East Expos outpointed Piazza. No other Dodger showed up among the Most Valuable candidates, and no Dodger generated any Cy Young support. Pedro Martinez received a couple of runner-up points way down in the Rookie ranks, but otherwise, the 1993

campaign in L.A. boiled down to Mike Piazza essentially making the difference between 63–99 and 81–81.

A team could do better. But a team could do a whole lot worse.

* * *

While Piazza was firing one fillip after another over the final five weeks
of the season, the New York Mets and their decided lack of MVP candidates
were getting their heads bashed in on a regular basis. Figuratively speaking,
of course, though after 130 mind-numbing games, could anybody in the
contracting universe of those who cared about the Mets tell the difference?

August 29 at Shea Stadium was Banner Day, a tradition for the team
since it was invented at the Polo Grounds in 1963. The Mets were on their
way to losing 111 games in the franchise's second season, but fans were
thrilled to have a chance to express their standings-impervious affection for
their team. Banners started showing up almost immediately in 1962. Not all
of them were complimentary, and management wasn't prepared to embrace
them (the organization was run by M. Donald Grant, not exactly a man of
the people), but after a fashion, the higher-ups figured they should get out
in front of the parade.

Thus was born the Banner Day procession, an annual highlight wedged
between games of doubleheaders in good times and bad until doubleheaders went the way of the Polo Grounds. Banner Day hung in there like a bedsheet billowing in the wind despite its natural habitat being crossed off the
pocket schedule. In 1993, it was a pregame affair. So while Mike Piazza was
across the continent preparing to swing his cudgel against Allen Watson,
and 21-season veteran Frank Tanana was in the clubhouse trying to psyche
himself up for a showdown with Rockies rookie Lance Painter, Mets fans
were doing what Mets fans always did.

They were telling the world that they hadn't given up. Hundreds upon
hundreds of banners flooded out from beyond the center-field gate. They
could be a little jaundiced in their perspective (WE BOUGHT SEASON
SEATS; WHY ARE YOU HERE?), but many praised these 45–84 Mets just
for being Mets. They showed faith that 1993 wasn't what the Mets were
going to be forever. They gave love to a version of the Mets even original owner Joan Payson would have had a hard time hugging. METS, one

preternaturally forgiving entry insisted, YOU'RE NOT LAST. WE'RE BEHIND YOU. Another punned and peered ahead: WITH 'GOOD YEARS' AHEAD & 'SCORES' TO SETTLE, LET'S POWER THE PEDAL TO THE MET-AL. A third, after 129 games to the contrary, declared, THEY WEEBLE, THEY WOBBLE, BUT THEY WON'T FALL DOWN/IN 1994 WE'LL BE THE BEST IN TOWN.

Paeans were painted for an edition of the Mets that on this Sunday would trot out a lineup of Ryan Thompson, Charlie O'Brien, Eddie Murray, Bobby Bonilla, Jeff Kent, Dave Gallagher, Chico Walker, and Kevin Baez in support of Tanana. Frank's third major-league start, two decades prior, came on the same night Dave Augustine of the Pirates lifted a deep fly ball to left field in this very stadium. Instead of clearing the fence, it struck its top and bounced back into the glove of left fielder Cleon Jones, who fired to short-stop Wayne Garrett, who relayed to catcher Ron Hodges, who tagged the blessedly slowest baserunner Pittsburgh could send from first base, Richie Zisk.

It was the top of the 13th inning, a 3–3 game desperately needed by the Mets who were making a pennant run so impossible that it made hobbled Kirk Gibson and his depleted Dodgers appear behemothic by compari-son. Yet the impossible became the probable on September 20, 1973, the night the Ball off the Top of the Wall play entered into Mets legend and the phrase "You Gotta Believe" cemented itself in the Mets' vocabulary. The Mets won that game (rookie Hodges, by no means a Piazza '93 prototype, driving in the deciding run) and kept winning until they almost won the World Series.

Mets fans never forgot. One of the few cheery evenings at Shea in 1993 was the twentieth-anniversary gathering of 1973 Mets. Tom Seaver, Willie Mays, and Yogi Berra all managed to miss it—and, of course, the 1993 Mets lost the game that followed the ceremonies—but it was still an evocation of how much fun it could be to be a Mets fan when everything that could go right did go right. Nineteen seventy-three, maybe more so than 1969 and 1986, is what drove otherwise mentally sound souls to apply marker to poster board and exclaim a desire to keep Believing in this team. You hadta.

Banners that suggested all hope wasn't forever lost finished their route around the warning track. A warm round of applause was offered for all that trademark faith. Then the audience turned its attention to the Mets and Rockies, finishing their second Shea series, their first since the Mets jumped to a 2–0 start. That was less than five months, or a thousand experiential light-years before. On April 5, you couldn't imagine the Mets losing to a first-year ballclub. On August 29, no indignity seemed beyond the reach of the seventh-place Mets.

The Mets lost, 6–1, to fall to 45–85, on the off chance that anybody was still keeping track. Bobby Bo's first-inning triple plated Murray to stake Tanana to a 1–0 lead. Vinny Castilla, another ex-Brave on whom Colorado was building its foundation, homered to start the third. Shea grew quiet as the game grew sleepy. Neither could be nudged awake until Jerald Clark hit a three-run bomb off Tanana to basically end the competitive portion of the Mets' day. From the second through the eighth, the Mets notched two hits and no runs versus Painter. In the ninth, already ahead, 5–1, Colorado built an insurance run against John Franco after two were out on an infield single, a wild pitch, another wild pitch on a third strike that allowed the batter to reach and another single (to the opposing pitcher). One more wild pitch was thrown for dreadful measure. Then the Mets went down in order in the ninth, all at the hands of Painter, a winner for the first time in his big-league career.

Five hits and no walks in nine innings against a pitcher who wasn't attracting any Rookie of the Year interest. Forty games below .500. A season-split with the expansion Rockies. The Mets had been mathematically eliminated the previous Wednesday. Nobody who hadn't drawn up a starry-eyed banner doubted all spirit had escaped them far earlier, and their second manager of the season, Dallas Green, wasn't about to issue an institutional pat on the back. Phrases he threw around postgame included "defeatist, dead-butt approach," "we've had enough fear," and "they just don't care because they think the season is over."

The winning banner suggested AN APPLE A DAY KEEPS THE LOSSES AWAY, yet the Mets didn't raise Shea's home run apple at all. Not a banner day for the 1993 Mets, but a typical one. September's dawn meant a potential influx of new bodies if not an infusion of vigorous blood. If Green wasn't excited about his veterans, he tamped down his fervor to try out any stray newbies, not that he wouldn't play them. "Hey," he reasoned, "we can lose with anybody."

* * *

Never has a manager demonstrated such prescience. Onto the Mets roster arrived Mauro "Goose" Gozzo, Tito Navarro, and Butch Huskey. They
were melodious enough to please Terry Cashman should he have been
moved to update his Mets-specific version of "Talkin' Baseball," but "Huskey, Tito, and the Goose" notwithstanding, it was the same old song.

Except for a riff that hadn't been heard in a Mets game for eighteen
years. On September 8, four days after Jim Abbott's one-armed no-hitter
at Yankee Stadium captivated baseball fans everywhere, the Mets partook
in something that couldn't have possibly surprised anybody. They were no-
hit. Stifling a Mets lineup hitless for the first time since Ed Halicki accomplished the feat in 1975 was Houston Astro Darryl Kile inside the Astrodome. Sooner or later, a team led by a manager who keeps reminding them
how abysmal they are will live down to basest expectations. The final was
7–1, the Mets' run achieved on a walk, a wild pitch that Kile's catcher Scott
Servais misinterpreted as a hit-by-pitch, an errant throw from first baseman
Jeff Bagwell who realized it was no HBP and acted to retrieve it, and admirable hustle from Jeff McKnight. The utilityman was the guy who walked
and then kept running once he saw the pitch get away.

One in the "run" column, zero in the "hits" column. You could say the
Mets didn't even know how to get no-hit correctly.

Kile's gem (no other walks, nine strikeouts, including three of the debut-
ing Huskey) raised his record to 15–6. Symmetrically, Tanana, being at the
opposite end of history, dropped his to 6–15. That he would survive 29
starts as a 1993 Met while maintaining a functioning left arm, never mind
functioning mental faculties, had to make him that much more appealing to
the pitching-desperate Yankees. Usually the New York teams avoided trading with one another lest one team eventually be embarrassed by the outcome. Once your players are led into battle to the cry of "defeatist, dead-butt
approach," your team is probably immune to further embarrassment. The
Mets accepted minor leaguer Kenny Greer as payment and sent Tanana to
what was left of the AL East pennant race. Frank could give George Steinbrenner a post-World Series parade pedicure in Macy's window and it
wouldn't make the Mets appear or feel any worse.

If their record and their skipper weren't rubbing it in enough, there was
always television's most talked-about star. On August 30, one night after the
paraded banners had been folded lovingly in drawers (or flung angrily in

Dumpsters), David Letterman began his new show on CBS. Unlike Butch Huskey, he was no neophyte in his medium. Dave had been on NBC for more than a decade at 12:30 A.M. It was an enormous deal that he was getting the 11:30 slot at CBS, especially after the industry intrigue that surfaced when Jay Leno, and not Letterman, succeeded Johnny Carson as host of *The Tonight Show*.

While Jay was finding his footing in Burbank, inviting on guests like recent 27-consecutive-games-loser Anthony Young, Dave made himself at home on Broadway with an irresistible comedic target: Anthony's team. As AY faded from view (he came back from Norfolk, took one more loss on September 11, and five days later submitted to surgery on his left thumb), the losing continued for the Mets ... which probably seemed kind of funny if you weren't the type to instinctively scrawl YOU GOTTA BELIEVE MORE IN '94 on the next bedsheet you could dig out of your linen closet.

On September 7, 1993, during the seventh episode of *The Late Show with David Letterman* and less than twenty-four hours before Kile's no-hitter, the Mets made their first Top Ten appearance. At No. 6 on the Top Ten bad things about living longer was, "If you're a Mets fan, you'd rather go early."

The losses kept mounting. The desk pieces wrote themselves. The Mets earned their very own Top Ten list by September 23: Top Ten New York Mets excuses. At least half were highly specific.

10. All those empty seats are distracting.

9. Part of a grand plan to make Florida Marlins overconfident next year.

7. Two words: Guaranteed contracts.

4. Baseballs harder to throw than explosives.

1. No one named "Mookie"

A month later, after baseball's postseason was done, Dave's writers issued a "Generic Top Ten List." Its penultimate item, at No. 2?

"The Mets suck."

It was a suck that transcended the borders of time, space, and sports seasons, but as was the case in 1973, it wasn't over until it was over. The second half of September and the first tenth of October still had Mets games dotting their calendar pages. The playing continued, if not by popular demand.

* * *

The Mets' final engagement of 1993 came Sunday, October 3, at Joe Robbie Stadium. They landed there on a mysterious five-game winning streak, highlighted by Greer pitching the 17th inning of a 17-inning 1–0 win at Shea against the Cardinals. It turned out to be Greer's only inning of work for the Mets ever. They were buried in last place, but were on the verge of avoiding one final indignity. If the Mets could win a sixth consecutive game and finish no worse than 59–103, they wouldn't set the standard for worst record by a non-expansion team in an expansion year, held for thirty-one years thus far by the 1962 Chicago Cubs, who might be remembered as worse had it not been for the 40–120 1962 Mets. Talk about small favors.

On the same day Tom Glavine was disappointing the Rockies and Mike Piazza was devastating the Giants, Dwight Gooden did something utterly unexpected. In the top of the ninth, with the Mets nursing a 4–2 lead, Ryan Thompson doubled. Green sought a pinch-hitter for Pete Schourek. *What the hell*, he figured, calling on Gooden, who had been too hurt to pitch over the final month but was still technically active. Gooden grabbed a bat.

That Doc enjoyed hitting was no secret. He talked about it as pitchers were prone to. He also walked the talk, as it were. Gooden's seven career home runs, including two in 1993, were the most ever slugged by a Mets pitcher. In 1985, when every one of his outings was an event, the 24–4 pitcher swore, "I'd take a home run over a no-hitter every day." Reflecting on his non-pitching prowess on the thirtieth anniversary of the 1986 world championship, Doc made no bones about it: "I used to love to hit."

When Doc was young and he was the center of the Mets universe, his bat was a bonus, but his arm was to be protected at all costs. Gooden wanted to bat left-handed, his natural side, but the Mets wouldn't allow it. It would expose his right elbow, the most valuable joint in baseball. If the Mets found themselves short of hitters, they hesitated to let Doc have at it. Rick Aguilera? Sure, fifth starter, let him pinch-hit. You don't mess around with the future of Dwight Gooden.

In 1993, the future of Dwight Gooden was as murky as anything else attached to the Mets. What was clear was that he no longer enjoyed that kind of golden status, the blend of youth and talent you wished bubble-wrapped for safekeeping. That was the kind of care dedicated these days to a Griffey in Seattle or a Piazza in Los Angeles. The Mets of New York had nobody remotely like that.

Thus, Gooden in Miami was told go ahead, hit. It's unlikely anybody was worrying about which elbow Doc had pointing toward the pitcher on this, the last day of his tenth year as a Met. He batted righty anyway.

And he tripled. Doc Gooden pinch-hit a triple off Richie Lewis of the Marlins. It was the "go figure" moment of the go-figurest year the Mets had ever endured. It scored Thompson from second, increased the Mets' margin to 5–2 and set the stage for one last wave of Mets offense . . . or approximately the third they'd unleashed all season long. Joe Klink, an ex-Met farmhand, relieved Lewis. Navarro ran for Gooden. Joe Orsulak singled Tito home. Kevin Baez singled Orsulak to second. Another Marlin pitcher, Matt Turner, threw a wild pitch that advanced them both. Murray placed a grounder on the right side of the infield. In the first inning, Murray doubled for his 99th run batted in of 1993. Here in the ninth, his productive out plated Orsulak for No. 100.

Say what you would about Murray—co-owner Nelson Doubleday dismissed him as a designated hitter who belonged in the American League—but he knew a milestone when he saw it. With eight runs batted in across his final four games, he made himself a 100-RBI man for the sixth time in his career and for the first time since 1985. If nothing else, it would look terrific on the open market.

The Mets weren't quite done with their barrage. Jeromy Burnitz's sac fly brought home Baez, and Chico Walker, who had been notified of his impending release prior to the game, made his last swing as a Met count. Chico homered, putting his signature on a Mets season for the second time in an otherwise low-key career. Seven years earlier, on the night the inevitable became a reality, it was Walker who grounded to second baseman Wally Backman for the final out of the first Mets division clincher since 1973. He was, in his own way, part of the 1986 world championship. He was now the last good thing about the 1993 denouement.

Because this season was the embodiment of into every life a year of rain must fall, Chico and the Mets couldn't make a clean break from Game 162. Mike Maddux came on to pitch the bottom of the ninth. He had a 9–2 lead. Orestes Destrade led off with a single. Alex Arias was due up next. Nobody pinch-hit for him. It simply started to pour so heavily that the umpires decided it could not go on, even if it couldn't just go away. The tarp was ordered. The Joe Robbie grounds crew had learned to unroll and spread it properly since June.

The rules said the teams must wait. So they waited. For seventy-five minutes, with nothing on the line except flights out of Miami, Fort Lauderdale, or perhaps West Palm Beach, the Mets waited. The rain paid them no mind. Once the minimum weather delay of one hour and fifteen minutes was ticked off the clock, the umps did what Green implied the Mets had done by the end of August. They gave up. It was an official ballgame, 9–2, the 59–103 Mets were granted their sixth consecutive victory to end 1993 on a wet, modestly high note. They took nine of thirteen from the 64–98 Marlins, the only season series they won, and finished 38 games out of first place.

The 1993 Mets wouldn't be worse than the 1962 Cubs, which wasn't exactly on a par with avenging the 1962 Dodgers, but when the heavens tell you in so many words, "Don't fuss with the final three outs, just head for the airport," then you take the hint, you pack your bags, and you board a flight bound for some other season.

PART III
THE BIG DIG

WHAT REALLY HAPPENED
TO THE CLASS OF '93?
April 4, 1994–October 28, 1995

Two of the most dynamic players in the extraordinarily dynamic 1993 World Series were the opposing leadoff hitters, the Phillies' Lenny Dykstra and the Blue Jays' Rickey Henderson. In the sixth game at Toronto, with the Phillies needing a win to force a winner-take-all showdown, Lenny—a little guy by most measures, but bulked up since he sparked the 1986 Mets to their championship—launched a three-run homer off Dave Stewart in the seventh inning. It keyed what became a five-run rally that continued versus Danny Cox and Al Leiter and gave the Phils a 6–5 lead they held going to the bottom of the ninth.

But the Blue Jays had the leadoff man to top all orders, Rickey Henderson. He hadn't had much of an October to date, but with Mitch Williams pitching, Rickey drew a walk to start the most crucial half-inning of them all. One hard-earned out later, Williams gave up a hit to Paul Molitor and then, to Joe Carter, the first walk-off home run to end a World Series since the one hit by Bill Mazeroski in 1960. Carter became the toast of a nation, his shot heard round Canada echoing forever more thanks to Jays radio announcer Tom Cheek's encouragement to "Touch 'em all, Joe, you'll never hit a bigger home run in your life!" Molitor, who hit .500 in the Series, was the worthy MVP recipient. Henderson collected only five hits, but worked out five walks and scored six runs. If Rickey scored, the Jays won.

The Mets thought they had a leadoff hitter of that ilk in Vince Coleman. They didn't. What they had was an albatross. Fred Wilpon swore Coleman was done with the Mets, even though the Mets weren't done having to pay him. Would anybody take Vinny off their hands and out of Queens?

Yes, as it turned out. The Kansas City Royals agreed to accept Cole-man's contract as long as the Mets took back an outfielder they didn't want any longer—Kevin McReynolds . . . the same Kevin McReynolds the Mets unloaded with Gregg Jefferies two winters earlier for Bret Saberhagen (and utilityman Bill Pecota, whom Jeff Torborg said New York was going to love; Pecota, like Torborg, was long gone from New York). Done, the Mets said.

McReynolds hadn't been noticeably missed at Shea Stadium, but at least he hadn't been part of 1993. The Mets tiptoed into 1994 wanting to put the year before behind them. Coleman was gone. Eddie Murray left to sign with Cleveland and was replaced by a less accomplished former Oriole first baseman, David Segui. Anthony Young was sent to the Cubs for short-stop Jose Vizcaino. Stray Braves starter Pete Smith landed in a Mets uniform as well. Dallas Green pushed the slow-to-develop Todd Hundley by pro-moting another young catcher, Kelly Stinnett. It didn't much matter who the Mets brought in. Management simply yearned to look less dreadful.

The 1994 Mets could have used a mental health year. If they couldn't convince their fans they were building a much better team right away, they could at least put on a better face. The best face they had belonged to Mr. Met, the old team mascot who had been in mothballs for the previous cou-ple of decades. Mr. Met was reanimated and roamed the field at Shea. So did kids who went to specially marked games that allowed them to run the bases afterward. The DynaMets Dash, it was called, a friendly distraction from whatever the Mets were doing during games. And if the games were too much to bear, there was another attraction/distraction installed at Shea in '94: Nickelodeon Extreme Baseball, a miniature amusement park planted on the other side of the outfield fence. Green slime (no relation to Dallas) would be in abundance. If the Mets couldn't be good, at least they could dispense goo.

* * *

Without warning, the 1994 Mets played better baseball than could have been dreamed. After a celebrity with Illinois ties—First Lady Hillary Clin-ton, who grew up in nearby Park Ridge rooting for Ernie Banks's Cubs—threw out the ceremonial first pitch in Chicago, Dwight Gooden withstood three home runs from Tuffy Rhodes to win on Opening Day at Wrigley.

The Mets played three and swept that first series. Segui and Vizcaino indicated they were solid additions. Jeff Kent did his best Mazeroski of 1960 impression, at the plate at least, knocking in 23 runs in the Mets' first 14 games and batting .421 to start the season. When Jeff brought his hot bat along on the Mets' first West Coast trip, he was far outdoing 1993's and, for that matter, 1983's Rookie of the Year.

Mike Piazza, after sharing the *Sports Illustrated* baseball preview cover with Ken Griffey Jr. ("So Good . . . So Young"), was off to a slow start. When the Mets alighted in L.A. on April 20, his batting average dropped to .213. Darryl Strawberry, meanwhile, hadn't batted at all nor would he. As the season was starting, Darryl announced he was battling a substance abuse problem. Tommy Lasorda dismissed Darryl's disease as personal weakness. Strawberry checked into a rehab clinic. He was done as a Dodger. In May, he and the team reached a financial settlement. In June, he signed with the Giants.

Kent couldn't keep up his extraordinary stats forever, and the Mets had a tough time remaining competitive. They peaked at four games above .500 on May 10 and steadily declined over the ensuing seven weeks. Yet bright spots emerged here and there, none brighter than Saberhagen, who settled in and became an absolute control freak, going 47 2/3 consecutive innings without issuing a walk. Alas, not every former Cy Young Award winner was having such a wonderful 1994.

Gooden never fully found his form on the mound or, more critically, off it. The pitcher who electrified New York in 1984 and 1985, helped bring it a world championship in 1986, and disappointed it greatly in the spring of 1987 when he tested positive for cocaine, was caught again. A disease, not weakness, ensnared Doc in late June of 1994. But it wasn't an illness that could be waited out on the DL. Major-league rules mandated he be suspended, so he was. The banishment covered the length of his contract, scheduled to run out at the end of the season.

With heads shaking and nobody applauding, the last of the 1986 Mets was finished as a Met. Over the winter, Howard Johnson had signed with Colorado and Sid Fernandez had moved on to Baltimore. Doc was the sole connection to the team that won 108 games, a pennant, and a World Series. Now that connection was severed.

The season went on. It always does, doesn't it? A rookie lefty named Jason Jacome took Gooden's place in the rotation. He looked good, as did second-year starter Bobby Jones. Rico Brogna, an under-the-radar spring pickup, filled in for the injured Segui at first and Wally Pipped him. Brogna was practically a modern-day Lou Gehrig from late June to early August if you didn't mind hyperbole.

The Mets, though nowhere near the first-place Expos or any of the contenders for the wild card in the newly configured three-division National League, were cobbling together a respectable season. Saberhagen was named their All-Star representative. He didn't pitch in the game in Pittsburgh—where Piazza, who shook off his early-season doldrums, started by fan vote—but at least Mets fans didn't have to feel so isolated from the good vibes surrounding baseball this midsummer. The new divisional format was stoking interest as was a rise in home run production. Matt Williams of the Giants appeared to be seriously challenging Roger Maris's single-season record of 61. The Padres' Tony Gwynn was evoking memories of Ted Williams's 1941, batting close to .400. Montreal, buoyed by the offseason acquisition of young Pedro Martinez from the Dodgers, appeared too overwhelming for realigned Atlanta to catch unless Fred McGriff's team caught fire again. A barnburner of a race had developed in the NL Central between the Reds, managed by old friend Davey Johnson, and the Astros, skippered by relatively unknown Terry Collins. Piazza and the Dodgers dueled Strawberry and the Giants in the West.

The 1994 Mets, just by virtue of not being the 1993 Mets, represented a low-key triumph, resonating for their hardy band of supporters who weren't swayed by a renaissance in the Bronx (the Yankees were in first place) and weren't concerned with Nickelodeon-branded slime. These Mets recovered from their May and June blahs and were flirting with .500 a year after finishing 44 games under it. They'd lost Dwight Gooden, but they'd discovered Rico Brogna. Life went on. Baseball went on. It wasn't extreme, but it wasn't at all bad.

Then it wasn't at all. Baseball went on strike. The owners—that same marvelous class of folks who gave fans of all stripes the 1981 split season, the 1984 compensation pool, and 1987 collusion—were now maneuvering to implement a salary cap. Bystanders by no means as well-versed in the issues as Players Association chief Donald Fehr or his predecessor Marvin Miller could figure out this was a cry for help. *Stop us before we pay you again.* Not surprisingly, the players balked at the notion. Bargaining was futile. On

August 11, with nearly a third of the schedule yet to be played, the players resisted the owners with the only weapon they had: their skills. They went out on strike. The season stopped. Then it was cancelled. There'd be no division winners, no playoffs and, for the first time since 1904, no World Series. It was bad news for the Expos and fans of every team that fancied itself a legitimate contender.

For Mets fans, it was no fun, either. Mr. Met, the DynaMets Dash, and Nickelodeon Extreme Baseball all closed up shop early. Dallas Green's charges won 55 games, lost 58, and finished in third, way behind Montreal and Atlanta, a little ahead of Philadelphia and Florida. The sample size was stunted, but the evidence was compelling.

The Mets, David Letterman's random pronouncements notwithstanding, no longer sucked . . . that much.

* * *

Unfortunately, if baseball wasn't going to be played, the Mets were, for all intents and purposes, no longer anything. Nineteen ninety-four became 1995 and the players and owners remained ensconced in opposite dugouts, nowhere near accord. The owners—led by one of their own, head Brewer Bud Selig, who replaced an elbowed-aside Fay Vincent a little more than a month after Vincent presided over Tom Seaver's big day at Cooperstown and continued to serve as "acting" commissioner more than two years later—decided the season would start on time anyway.

For their latest trick, the owners introduced replacement baseball. Fans, they figured, rooted for the uniforms more than any of the individuals filling them, so why not hire whoever would wear them and call them Braves or Expos or Phillies or Marlins or Mets?

It was an idea antithetical to sports loyalties. Even in the age of accelerated player movement, there is an organic quality to change. Turnover is expected, sometimes desired. Wholesale churn instigated by one party, the one that decided negotiating labor peace was too much of a hassle, landed more weirdly on the brain than the notion that Michael Jordan was playing baseball (which he tried briefly, in the minors for the White Sox, but gave up to go back to basketball). Baseball teams—minus the Orioles, who were run by labor lawyer Peter Angelos and had Cal Ripken's Gehrig-nearing consecutive-games streak to think about—poked around for lesser-known names to fill their laundry in Arizona and Florida in what became the false spring of 1995.

At Port St. Lucie, minuscule crowds stepped reluctantly up to meet the ReplaceMets, as they were called in the papers. If the 1994 Mets of Rick Parker, Shawn Hare, and Jonathan Hurst tilted to the relatively obscure, these would-be 1995 Mets were literally unheard of before they donned their MLB-issued shirts and pants. Bubba Wagnon was a landscaper before he decided to try his hand at the infield. Chris Walpole was signed on the strength of his experience as a third baseman for the Thunder Bay Whiskey Jacks . . . except Walpole made up that line on the back of his imaginary baseball card and there was no Baseball-Reference to check his claim against. Yet for a surreal February and March, Wagnon the lawn guy, Walpole the fake Jack, and a bundle of unrecognizables who didn't mind wearing the replacement player (or, more unkindly, "scab") label for the chance to wear a Mets uniform and draw a Mets paycheck constituted the Mets. They were joined by a handful of not-yet-unionized low-level minor leaguers, a smattering of retired major leaguers who figured they had nothing left to lose (1986 Met Doug Sisk among them), and a cadre of former farmhands familiar mostly to those who took the "Future Stars" page of the official yearbook seriously. Shawn Abner, the No. 1 overall pick of 1984 draft and part of the package the Mets sent to San Diego to acquire McReynolds in the first place, was granted a second St. Lucie chance.

Green had to manage the ReplaceMets and was characteristically not thrilled by the task. Dallas believed "dressing up subpar players in major-league uniforms would make a mockery of the game," and within that mockery, these Mets were the worst in the Grapefruit League, starting their exhibition slate at 0–9. Fortunately, before anybody could play a replacement game that counted, US District Court Judge Sonia Sotomayor issued an injunction against the owners and effectively ended the strike. Bob Stoddard, who'd pitched more than 400 innings in the majors, but none since 1987, was going to be Green's opening night starter in Miami one year after Gooden was his man in Chicago.

Instead, most of the ReplaceMets were sent away and the "real" Mets arrived in St. Lucie. They'd have a few weeks to get their act together before flying to Denver to help the Rockies with another first in their franchise history, the opening of Coors Field, the National League's first answer to Camden Yards. The Mets went about replacing their 1994 selves in a more traditional manner, inserting Long Islander Pete Harnisch into their rotation after a trade with Houston and penciling in ex-Dodger Brett Butler as their leadoff hitter once they signed him as a free agent. Butler was on the market the same winter the Mets opted for Coleman. Brett seemed a better Met bet. Now, four springs later, the thirty-seven-year-old sparkplug could show if hindsight was a winning wager.

These authentic Mets arrived in snowy Denver, Butler batted first at Coors Field, and his new team scored nine runs to commence the 144-game season on April 26. Brogna blasted the new park's first home run, Hundley its first grand slam. Problem was the Rockies baptized their playpen with 11 runs, including five off Mets starter Bobby Jones—more Stoddard than Gooden at mile-high altitude—and three in the bottom of the 14th when Dante Bichette went showily deep off Mike Remlinger. Bichette swung, dropped his bat, fiddled with a batting glove and shook a fist before heading to first.

The Mets were heading to Shea after losing both games in Colorado. What they received was a little less than a hero's welcome. On a Friday night that drew 26,604, their lowest home opener total in fourteen years despite the giveaway of official team yearbooks, their victory over the Cardinals was overshadowed by a reception from a segment of fans who hadn't quite forgotten that they'd been deprived of baseball since the previous August. A common construct of the strike was it was a bunch of millionaires at war with a bunch of billionaires. A pox on both their houses was the message expressed by three young men who stormed the field wearing shirts that said GREED. They tossed an estimated $150 at the players' feet, a dollar at a time, and got as far as second base, where they raised their fists in defiance before being arrested.

* * *

For a while, that was the extent of the excitement at Shea, where crowds were slow to fill the seats and wins were infrequent happenings. Inevitably, Mets fans, locked out by the present, looked forward, enabled to a great degree by those yearbooks given away on opening night or purchased later.

Perhaps understanding that glorifying their major-league players at such a touchy point in time was a tough sell, the 1995 Mets yearbook gave itself over mostly as a preview of all those future stars the organization perennially hyped. The centerpiece of the publication was a feature called "Mets 2000," which presented a Shea bridge to the twenty-first century. It was a lineup premised on the notion that it could be filled only by those who had not yet used up their rookie status entering 1995 . . . and that the Mets' farm system was stocked with so much talent that you couldn't wait for 2000 to arrive in Flushing.

Ladies and gentlemen, your alleged New York Mets of the next millennium:

C–Brook Fordyce
1B–Byron Gainey
2B–Julio Zorrilla
SS–Rey Ordoñez
3B–Edgardo Alfonzo
LF–Preston Wilson
CF–Jay Payton
RF–Carl Everett
LHP–Bill Pulsipher
RHP–Jason Isringhausen

Some of these names were already familiar to fans of the 1995 Mets. Three were 1995 Mets from the get-go, making their major-league or team debuts on opening night at Coors Field. Everett, a Marlin for 70 at-bats the two previous seasons, had seen time in right field, with Bobby Bonilla transitioned into a full-time third baseman (the position he played when he came up with the White Sox), great 1993 hope Ryan Thompson injured, and former future star Jeromy Burnitz traded to Cleveland for three pitchers. Fordyce played in four games as a Met before he was submitted to waivers and snatched up by the Indians. Alfonzo, the "total package," in the wholly unbiased view of the yearbook, was serving as a utility infielder at the outset of the year. The twenty-one year-old from Venezuela—he wore 13 as homage to one of Seaver's old shortstops, Dave Concepcion—made his first impression by whacking an inside-the-park home run at Riverfront

Stadium on May 6. Edgardo helped the Mets build an 11–4 lead and was an innocent bystander as the Reds stormed from behind to win, 13–11.

Scoring myriad runs wasn't much working for the 1995 Mets, but give them five years and they'd figure it out. By the yearbook's reckoning they'd have a "legitimate, middle-of-the-order run producer" in left from Wilson, still better-known as Mookie's stepson three years after the Mets drafted him first, and "a sweet swing, excellent speed and Gold Glove-type potential" in center courtesy of Payton, a supplemental first-round pick in 1994, compensation from the Orioles for signing Sid Fernandez.

The shortstop in the hypothetical lineup was "already a defensive legend." Ordoñez was a Cuban defector, awarded to the Mets in a special lottery in 1993. A special lottery was held in 1966 and resulted in Seaver being assigned to New York, and that turned into something legendary, so if you took your guidance from signs rather than the draft, you were entitled to project Ordoñez joining Alfonzo on the left side of the Mets infield before the current century elapsed.

The rookie names that gripped the Mets fan imagination the most in 1995 were the two pitchers listed. The Mets were, after all, famous for their pitching, starting with Seaver, running through Gooden and soon, if the buzz was accurate, Isringhausen the righty and Pulsipher the lefty. With the Mets going nowhere, the drums were beating for the prospects who had yet to be seen. It was suggested, by media and fans alike, that New York get a look at Pulsipher, a.k.a. Pulse. He was promoted in June. Isringhausen—Izzy—got the call in July.

They weren't the immediate answer, but they were promising. And there was another behind them, the No. 1 draft pick in the nation of 1994, Paul Wilson, a righty who could be imagined filling the Tom Terrific/Doctor K role . . . though no sane Mets fan would object to Pulse or Izzy taking on the title of ace. The Mets were famous for *lots* of pitching. Three golden arms were better than one, certainly superior to none.

By August, the future was laying down markers everywhere at Shea. Wilson was at least a year away, but Izzy and Pulse were in the rotation; "Fonzie," as Alfonzo was becoming known, had shown uncommonly professional instincts and abilities wherever he was deployed before a stint on the DL; Everett began to hit for power; and a few of the older youngsters, like Jones, Brogna, Kent, and Hundley—around since 1990, making him second in tenure on the team to John Franco—chipped in. As the trade deadline neared, the Mets ditched entirely the concept of the present and dealt to contenders Butler (back to the Dodgers), Bonilla (the Orioles) and Saberhagen (the Rockies). One of the pitchers picked up from the Tribe for Burnitz, Dave Mlicki, kept improving. Butch Huskey returned from a year in the minors and looked like a formidable slugger. Alex Ochoa, the "five-tool" prize Baltimore sent for Bobby Bo, showed off an incredible outfield arm.

These kids could play. These kids could win. Down the stretch, albeit nowhere near a playoff race, the Mets went 34–18. On the final day of the season, while attention was being paid elsewhere throughout baseball, the Mets were completing a weekend sweep of the East champion Braves. It earned them a second-place tie with the Phillies, even if neither team finished above .500. Details, details—69–75, given the context of 1995, felt as good as anything to Mets fans since it sunk in that 108–54 was no longer available to them.

The 1995 postseason went on without the Mets. Piazza's Dodgers were there, though they'd be swept by the Reds in the first round (a.k.a. the National League Division Series). Mike continued to redefine what a catcher could do with a bat, hitting .346 while homering 32 times. He also caught the sport's latest phenom, Hideo Nomo, who signed with Los Angeles after starring in Japan. Nomo, like Piazza, was a Rookie of the Year winner in waiting, outpointing Atlanta third baseman Chipper Jones. (Izzy placed fourth.)

The Braves wound up winning it all, which wasn't terribly surprising, considering how good they'd been throughout the decade. What was a little jarring, maybe, was how many 1993 Mets frolicked around in October. Vince Coleman was part of the "Refuse to Lose" Mariners who beat the Yankees in the ALDS and took the Indians to six games in the ALCS. Cleveland's offense was fortified by Eddie Murray, who homered in each round the Tribe played, including the battle of enlightened logos they lost to the Braves in the World Series. Atlanta made its way to a championship by first dispatching Saberhagen's Rockies before disposing of Cincinnati. Only Bonilla was absent from this heartwarming postseason procession, but Bobby Bo had already had his moment in the national spotlight.

The erstwhile Bronx tour guide could be found slightly off to the side in the image that defined baseball's 1995 comeback, in the home dugout at Camden Yards on the night of September 6, in the moments after Cal Ripken surpassed Lou Gehrig as the sport's all-time ironman. Once four and a half innings were complete at Baltimore, Ripken could be said to have played in his 2,131st consecutive game, a mark generations believed beyond approach. It was too good an instant to let pass with just a tip of the cap from Cal. So two of his fellow Birds made certain he gave the crowd more. They pushed him out of the dugout and onto the warning track for a gratitude lap.

One of those Orioles doing the pushing was Rafael Palmeiro. The other was Bonilla. The same Bonilla who'd acquired and cultivated such a nefarious image at Shea. Even in '94 and '95, when his production in Queens was robust enough (he was the Mets' lone All-Star prior to being traded), he never really shook his reputation as a player who put himself ahead of his team. Mike Cubbage was still coaching third in 1995 and Bonilla apparently took up Coleman's cause of making the man's life miserable. One May night in Philadelphia, Bobby ran through Mike's stop sign during the game and cursed him out to reporters after it. *That* Bonilla, an anonymous Met was quoted at the time, was "typical." *This* Bonilla, captured by ESPN's cameras thinking foremost of Cal Ripken and Orioles fans, was clearly one heckuva teammate.

The Mets had the only Bonilla on record for most of four seasons. They had Saberhagen, Murray, and Coleman, too. They had them together in 1992, and they became identified as the worst team money could buy. They had them together in 1993, and the team grew even worse. Yet once they got rid of all of them, the four players individually reverted to the form that made the Mets desire them in the first place, before they managed to combine to drag them into last place. Nowadays, shed of their Mets association, they had reestablished themselves as winners.

Was it something in the Flushing water? Probably not, considering the Mets went on a tear once every last one of them was removed from Shea. It was hard to make sense of in 1995. No wonder the Mets urged you to never mind, just lie back and think of 2000.

USED TO BE THEIR TOWN, TOO
April 1, 1996–October 26, 1996

The Mets fell in a forest in 1996. Hardly anybody in New York heard them. Most New Yorkers were too busy obsessing on the Yankees. The wolf that lurked on the other side of the Triborough Bridge, smacking its lips for three seasons, devoured the entire city. The Yankees had contended in 1993, but fell short of the Blue Jays. They led in 1994, but were stopped cold by the strike. They reached the playoffs in 1995, but were cut down by the Mariners. In 1996, nothing could stop them from taking over New York completely and thoroughly the way the Mets had in 1986.

That is to say with 1986 Mets. Dwight Gooden was now a Yankee, heart-warmingly rehabilitated from his second drug suspension and throwing for them what nobody had ever thrown for the Mets: a no-hitter. Darryl Strawberry was a Yankee, too, and a beloved one at that, having publicly beaten back his addictions. There was Doc and Straw and Coney, who became a Met directly after 1986, but whose continued presence in pinstripes was enough to sting the eyes of any Mets fan who stole a glance over the bridge. David Cone didn't leave the Bronx as a hired gun after arriving there as such in 1995. He was one of them for keeps, as was Joe Torre.

Joe Torre? Yes, Joe Torre, the same Joe Torre who broke into managing as a Met in 1977 while still playing as a Met. Torre was Tom Seaver's last Mets manager his first time around. M. Donald Grant hired Torre to replace Joe Frazier on May 31 and traded Seaver out from under him fifteen days later. Torre managed the Mets to one second-division finish after another until 1981 when Frank Cashen let him go. He experienced some success managing the Braves, less running the Cardinals, and was on nobody's obvious short list of pilots-in-waiting when George Steinbrenner did what George Steinbrenner was prone to do and fired Buck Showalter. Showalter had led the Yankees from their fallow period to the postseason, but Ken Griffey scored on Edgar Martinez's dramatic double in the Kingdome to end their playoff appearance and, besides, the only short list that mattered was Steinbrenner's. Joe was George's prime candidate because Arthur Richman spoke up for him.

Richman worked in the Mets' front office for an eternity and, like everybody else, it seemed, drifted to the Yankees by 1996. Don Zimmer, Original Met third baseman, was Torre's bench coach. Mel Stottlemyre, pitching coach under every Mets manager from Davey Johnson to Dallas Green, now aided Torre. So did Willie Randolph, who took his last major-league swings as a Met in 1992. He was Joe's third base coach, standing across the diamond from first base coach Jose Cardenal, who played for Torre's Mets in 1979 and 1980. All that ex-Met karma infused the dormant dynasty with doses of baseball skills, smarts and, in the estimation of some, likeability. These Yankees, it was widely reported, weren't the Yankees you grudgingly respected. These were the Yankees you willingly embraced. That was a matter of taste, but what couldn't be disputed was they won 92 games and the American League East championship.

The franchise that nurtured so many of its components did nothing of the kind.

* * *

The 1996 Mets had their moments and personalities, but not nearly enough of them to maintain the momentum they'd established at the end of 1995. The key to their immediate future was going to be what was dubbed Generation K: Paul Wilson joining Jason Isringhausen and Bill Pulsipher and forging a decade or so of pitching excellence. It didn't happen. Pulse got hurt in spring training and never pitched in 1996. Izzy and Wilson had some good outings, but more bad outings. Vaunted young pitching did not define the '96 Mets, except for the disappointing aspects.

One piece of the Mets' future, as foretold in the 1995 yearbook, did come to fruition. Rey Ordoñez was a defensive legend from his first game, opening day at Shea, April 1. Starting at shortstop, Ordoñez accepted a relay from his left fielder and fired it to his catcher in the seventh inning. Sounds routine enough, except Ordoñez had to do everything very quickly as the opposing Cardinal baserunner was heading for home, so the rookie was forced to make his throw from his knees.

And he nailed the runner, Royce Clayton, ending a St. Louis rally and allowing the Mets to continue a comeback that was already in progress. "Never, ever, ever seen anything like it," new Mets center fielder Lance Johnson insisted to reporters. "I'm still not sure what I saw. I can't wait to go home and see that on the highlights."

On this chilly, rainy April Fool's Day, the Mets did something real and even more spectacular, rallying from the 6–0 deficit Bobby Jones had buried them under and emerging 7–6 winners. Ordoñez was the most pulsating element of the afternoon, but not to be overlooked were the two teammates who were part of the 7–6–2 putout that was about to become a staple of defensive montages everywhere. The left fielder was Bernard Gilkey, like Johnson, a newcomer to the Mets. He homered to helped get the Mets back into the game in the sixth. The catcher, entering his seventh season as a Met, was Todd Hundley. It was his homer that put the Mets on the board in the fourth.

Johnson, Gilkey, and Hundley would wind up the Mets most often mentioned as 1996 unfolded. Ordoñez, too, though as rookie shortstops in New York went, he would be overshadowed by the one the Yankees were breaking in. Rey was an incredible fielder, but a project as a hitter. The other shortstop in town, Derek Jeter, was reasonably handy with the glove, hit really well and, amid a blend of youngsters and veterans, took on a leadership role for Torre's team. He was on his way to American League Rookie of the Year honors as well as the playoffs.

Mets fans didn't have a Jeter in Ordoñez and they didn't have a core to match the homegrown unit Jeter was forming with center fielder Bernie Williams, catcher Jorge Posada, starting pitcher Andy Pettitte and setup reliever Mariano Rivera. They didn't have Cone, Strawberry, and Gooden anymore, either, not to mention Paul O'Neill, Tino Martinez, Cecil Fielder, Wade Boggs, Kenny Rogers, and whatever other names Steinbrenner had gathered. But they did have those three players to keep them unexpectedly occupied while their three anticipated pitchers didn't jell.

Johnson was good for 227 hits, 21 of them triples, setting two franchise records. One Dog's 50 stolen bases were the most by any Met since Mookie

Wilson. Gilkey posted 117 RBIs, tying Howard Johnson's club mark. But when it came to keeping Mets fans' attention in 1996, nobody could touch Hundley. Though there were hints of a breakthrough in 1995, when he batted .280 and went deep 15 times in 90 games, nothing in Todd's prior six seasons as a Met prepared Mets fans for what they were about to see from him in 1996.

It was a year when slugging was becoming all the rage throughout baseball. Mark McGwire of the A's led the sport with 52 home runs, followed by Brady Anderson of the Orioles with a curious 50 (he'd never belted more than 21 before) and Griffey of the Mariners with 49. In the National League, the pecking order was Colorado's Andres Galarraga with 47, Florida's Gary Sheffield and San Francisco's Barry Bonds with 42 apiece, then, as incongruous as it appeared to anyone who'd been waiting since 1990 for him to blossom, Hundley. Todd in a blink became one of the game's elite sluggers, bashing 41 home runs—ten more than he'd combined for in 1994 and 1995—and driving in 112. He, like Lance, was enough of a standout to merit invitation to the All-Star Game in Philadelphia, where he backed up Mike Piazza, who was having his usual bang-up season. Mike received the most votes of any National Leaguer going into his homecoming game and left it with the MVP award in tow. Todd stayed hot after grabbing a bit of the Piazza-dominated spotlight, though, becoming enough of a sensation to spur talk of a pregame home run derby between himself and the Cubs' Sammy Sosa the next time their clubs played. This was in August, when Sosa led the National League with 39 round-trippers and Hundley was second with 36. Cooler heads got involved and kiboshed the proposed contest.

Todd surpassed Sammy, who finished with 40, and outslugged Mike—whose not insubstantial 36 home runs propelled the Dodgers into the playoffs for a second consecutive year. Hundley also inked his name into a couple of record books. With his 40th, Hundley took the Mets' single-season home run record from Strawberry. With his 41st as a catcher (meaning games in which he caught, not those in which he batted while wearing a chest protector and face mask), he passed the total set by Roy Campanella in 1953. It was a big enough deal to lure Campy's widow, Roxie, to Shea for a brief torch-passing ceremony.

The second-most celebrated 41 in Mets history served, five-and-a-half months after Ordonez's opening day fling, as a bright bookend to an otherwise dreary year, a season Mets not named Johnson, Gilkey, and Hundley spent mostly on their knees. "The way the team's been playing," Tim Bogar admitted amid the fuss over Todd's feat, "there's not been much to think about except him hitting that home run." What there was to think about wasn't encouraging. Rico Brogna went down with an injury and didn't play after June 19. Jeff Kent, who, with Thompson, was enough of a package to surrender Cone for four years earlier, was also traded to Cleveland. Jeff and Jose Vizcaino went in late July for Carlos Baerga. Ordoñez's glove had bumped Vizcaino to second, which, in turn, shoved Kent to third. Rey ultimately made them both seem rather superfluous. Baerga, meanwhile, had been a big part of the Indian revival as a power-hitting second baseman, but the Tribe decided they could do without him. Perhaps he could turn it around at Shea, though once Carlos came to New York, he struggled, ached, and mostly sat in September.

Loudly departing the muted Flushing scene was Dallas Green. He was enlisted in May 1993 to clean up a horrible mess. He left a different one behind in August 1996, not necessarily his own doing. Green didn't have the full complement of pitchers he thought he'd have when what became his final season began. Then again, just before he was fired, he said of Wilson and Isringhausen, "These guys don't belong in the big leagues. That might sound harsh and negative. But what have they done to get here?"

Replacing Green (who was a former Yankee manager, indicating perhaps that the Triborough karma lane operated one-way only in 1996) was Norfolk Tides manager Bobby Valentine, who finished out the season and was entrusted with the reins for 1997. Valentine, who led the Texas Rangers from 1985 until 1992, was a familiar figure to Mets fans from his time as a player—he was acquired for Dave Kingman on the same night Grant traded Seaver—and later coached for Davey Johnson before receiving his shot at managing with the Rangers in the mid-'80s. His initial exposure to the big leagues came as a Dodger, in whose farm system he was tutored by Tommy Lasorda.

Lasorda was done mentoring Dodgers in July when he announced his retirement a month after suffering a heart attack. Lasorda had been managing the Dodgers since before Torre was hired to manage the Mets. His predecessor, Walter Alston, began managing the Dodgers in Brooklyn when Campanella was catching. It wasn't an easy bond to break, particularly for the Dodger who, more than any other, owed his opportunity to Lasorda.

Piazza persevered under new manager Bill Russell, but it wasn't the same, as the Dodgers felt less like family to Mike than ever. In the business of baseball, he continued to catch and hit and push L.A. into the postseason. They arrived there as a wild card, having come in second in the West, one game behind the Padres. Mike did all he could, batting .336 and driving in 105 runs, good enough for second in NL MVP balloting; it was his fourth full season in the majors and the fourth in which he placed among the top ten Most Valuable candidates. His 3-for-10, all-singles performance in the NLDS, however, couldn't help stave off a three-game sweep at the hands of the yet-again NL East champion Braves.

The defending world champs were a juggernaut. After taking out the Dodgers, they spotted their next opponent, the Cardinals, a 3–1 lead and then took the final three to earn another pennant. Atlanta was rightly considered a heavy favorite to win the 1996 World Series. The Met-blooded Yankees had other ideas, and after falling behind two games to none, the AL champs undid Atlanta's reign, winning four straight. The Yankees were world champions for the first time since 1978, the uncontested apple of New York's eye and showered with ticker tape, confetti, and plaudits.

The Mets went quietly as could be into winter. Anything they did was incapable of making a sound. Ten years removed from their last World Series, they could have been in hibernation for all the city that once adored them noticed or cared.

SENSE BE DAMNED
April 1, 1997–September 28, 1997

At the rate it was going, Generation K would never learn its ABCs. The trio of young pitchers who were going to lift the forever earthbound Mets on their collective wings and deliver them to the promised land were not going to get another chance to take off for real in 1997. Instead of Bill Pulsipher recovering from injury and rejoining Jason Isringhausen and Paul Wilson, Izzy and Paul required surgery and joined Pulse, who still wasn't ready to resume pitching in the majors, on the sidelines. Pete Harnisch wound up the opening day starter, and then he didn't throw again for another four months.

Well, if the Mets couldn't plan on their three promising pitchers composing the heart of their rotation, at least they had those three accomplished hitters to lean on. The Mets still had Lance Johnson under contract and retained the services of Bernard Gilkey (four years, $20.4 million) and Todd Hundley (four years, $21 million). If they couldn't count on much else, they could count on this triumvirate.

No, they couldn't. Johnson battled shin splints and was deemed dispensable enough to deal to the Cubs in August. Gilkey slumped from 30 homers, 117 ribbies, and a .317 average to 18–78–.249. Hundley's dropoff wasn't as resounding, but his 1997 power totals were nowhere near as impressive as what he achieved in the year that had just made him a star, though an aching elbow certainly gave him an alibi if he wanted one. Carlos Baerga played plenty, but didn't post statistics on the order of what he put up for Cleveland in his American League prime.

With all that the Mets projected to go right going wrong, how much worse would they be in 1997 than they'd been in 1996?

No worse. In fact, they were better—far better. The Mets turned in as good a season as any in Flushing since Darryl Strawberry was launching home runs and Dwight Gooden and David Cone were striking out batters . . . for them. These Mets were the second winning Mets of the '90s, compiling their best record since the dawn of the decade. They even contended for the playoffs for a while.

It made little sense. Not that any Mets fan minded, but it truly made almost no sense. Generation K didn't show up for class. The hitters who were supposed to provide punch didn't make much of a fist. And yet, the 1997 Mets went 88–74, finished four games from the National League wild-card slot and sprinkled their season with moments that warmed the Mets fan heart and soothed the Mets fan soul.

* * *

To a certain degree, Bobby Valentine was responsible. "The worst thing you can do as a player or manager," he said as spring training commenced, "is take anything for granted." And he didn't, particularly reputations. Having managed the Tides for two of the three previous seasons (with the one in between spent in Japan), he understood the personnel available to him, particularly the players who lacked the big names. None could have been less in lights than a journeyman right-hander named Rick Reed. The former Pirate, Royal, and Ranger found himself, at age thirty and after seven partial big-league seasons, in camp with the Reds in 1995—the camp on the wrong end of the Sotomayor settlement. Reed was picked up by Cincinnati and assigned to Indianapolis after being waived by Texas during the 1994 season. He wasn't on a 40-man roster in August of '94, so he wasn't technically on strike. When replacement spring rolled around, both the Reds and circumstances played hardball with him. Management demanded he show up and the need to take care of his diabetic mother compelled him. Rick impressed enough to be retained in Triple-A during the season and recalled by the Reds later in the year, where the major leaguers who struck did not form a hospitality committee to greet him.

It was not an uncommon phenomenon as the occasional former replacement player began to trickle into major-league clubhouses. Piazza saw it up close when the first of the rock-and-a-hard-place players, Mike Busch, was called up to the Dodgers in 1995. Cold shoulders were everywhere. Busch delivered a key blow in L.A.'s race against the Rockies, but his grudging teammates voted him no postseason share whatsoever.

In 1996, Reed pitched for Valentine at Norfolk and walked hardly anybody. In the spring of 1997, he pitched for him in St. Lucie and continued to look good. The manager needed pitchers and he had one whose only drawback was a lack of blessing from the Players Association. Bobby gauged his veterans' reaction, didn't sense any over-the-top animosity ("I never heard, 'I'm the first to burn his uniform, it's not going to happen on my team'") and added him to the rotation. A few weeks into the season, Rick was showing command, retiring batters, and being called "Reeder" by teammates who didn't much sweat what he did in the labor war two years before.

Valentine trusted several of his Tide alumni, and they repaid him in kind. Matt Franco emerged as a top pinch-hitter. Jason Hardtke won a game after coming off the bench. Steve Bieser tied another as a baserunner, distracting David Cone into balking him home from third. That was in the Subway Series, part of MLB's foray into interleague baseball, which answered the question that fans in New York had wondered for thirty-five years.

What would happen if the Mets played the Yankees for real?

This was no Mayor's Trophy Game, no exhibition excursion between St. Petersburg and Fort Lauderdale. These were three games in the middle of June that counted in the standings. It pitted the defending world champions versus the upstart underdogs at Yankee Stadium. The Metsian among the city's populace must have wondered where this matchup was in 1986. Nevertheless, when the very first game between the Mets and Yankees was complete, no Mets fan complained about the timing. Dave Mlicki shut out the crosstown rivals, 6–0, as a loud minority of attendees in the sellout crowd (by the ninth inning, they were the majority) chanted "Let's Go Mets!" Not only had Mlicki defended the honor of millions when he caught Derek Jeter looking for the final out, he pulled the Mets into a first-place tie in the city standings. The heretofore overlooked Mets and the almighty Yankees shared not just the same town, but the same record of 37–30.

In the more pressing business of the National League, the Mets were in the thick of a wild-card race with another upstart, the Florida Marlins. Their owner, Wayne Huizenga, had gone all in, investing in free agents—including the ever popular Bobby Bonilla—partly to win, like a normal owner, partly to determine just how much interest there really was in baseball in habitually rainy South Florida, where the ballpark was a football stadium and the baseball fans who moved to the area from elsewhere didn't necessarily transfer their loyalties to the new home team. Attendance had been down since the Marlins debuted in 1993. If a big-time contender couldn't draw and no municipality would do the owner the solid of throwing him additional tax breaks or a baseball-only facility, then maybe it wasn't worth the trouble.

The win-now approach worked pretty well on the field. The Fish chased the Braves for first, with the Mets staying on the Marlins' tail across the summer. Off the field, it was a different story. Huizenga decided baseball was a bad business and announced in late June that he intended to sell his team. Whereas Florida had invested in outside talent, the Mets had made only one acquisition of note in the offseason, and it was more of a reclamation situation. After sending Rico Brogna and his balky back to Philadelphia for bullpen help (that didn't help), GM Joe McIlvaine replaced him at first base with John Olerud, obtained from Toronto for pitcher Robert Person. Had this been the winter of 1993–94, it would have been enormous news. Olerud was then coming off his AL batting crown, won a .363 average that hung around .400 until early August.

In the years that followed, John's production was ordinary. The Blue Jays, spinning their wheels in a division that now belonged to the Yankees and Orioles, were done with one of the most recognizable heads in baseball, thanks to that flapless batting helmet he wore in the field. McIlvaine's head probably also deserved some recognition, because getting John constituted a steal. The former batting champ regained his stroke and drove in 102 runs his first year in the National League.

The pieces collected by McIlvaine and Valentine somehow fit. Former Phillie Todd Pratt, not long before a manager himself . . . of a Domino's franchise, was signed to Norfolk, promoted to New York, and proved a piping hot backup. Right field, which Alex Ochoa didn't grab and make his own, fell into the collective hands of Carl Everett and Butch Huskey, and each produced. Rey Ordoñez's fielding inspired enough raves to win him a Gold Glove at short. He formed what was dubbed the Great Wall of Flushing on the left side of the infield with the Mets' best everyday player, Edgardo Alfonzo.

Fonzie rose as predicted in the 1995 yearbook. After two years' use as a sub by Dallas Green, Valentine gave him the everyday third base job and Fonzie was the coolest, batting .315 and making just about every play. Whatever Fonzie didn't get to, Rey-Rey did, and vice-versa. Among those pitchers thankful for their defense was sudden ace Bobby Jones, flourishing in his fifth season. After a 12–3 start, Bobby Cox named him to the NL All-Star team, along with Hundley, who earned an invite behind Piazza for the second time. Hundley, however, declined the offer, opting to rest a right elbow that seemed destined for surgery. "I've got to listen to my elbow and see what it tells me," Todd said.

The first half ended with the Mets 10 games above .500 and two behind the Marlins. Jones went to the All-Star Game in Cleveland and represented well, striking out Mark McGwire and Ken Griffey—who were on their way to 114 home runs combined—back-to-back. When the break was over, the Mets traveled to the new ballpark in Atlanta, Turner Field, and took three of four, the last of them by rallying from a 6–0 deficit to win, 7–6, on ESPN's *Sunday Night Baseball*.

A team that hadn't finished with a winning record in seven years was winning with regularity. They were contending like it was 1990. It was, within the context of year that preceded it, a smashing success.

Then why, three days after they left Atlanta on a high, did the Mets fire their general manager?

* * *

It was an intriguing question asked in response to an almost Steinbrennerian action. Fred Wilpon wasn't beyond making changes midseason—McIlvaine took over for Harazin while 1993 was falling apart—but doing so when McIlvaine's Mets were doing so well came off as mystifying. Wilpon said something about who did and didn't have the proper "skill set" to be GM, indicating the club saw Joe's talent residing more in player evaluation and scouting than running an organization. For that larger task, they turned to McIlvaine's assistant, Steve Phillips. Whereas Joe Mac made small moves that were at last paying off, Valentine guessed to the press that perhaps the new general manager would be, as Buster Olney put it in the *Times*, "quicker to pull the trigger."

And he was. The thirty-four year-old executive's first move came a little more than three weeks after he was hired, bundling Johnson, Mark Clark, and Manny Alexander and shipping them to the Cubs for Brian McRae, Turk Wendell, and Mel Rojas. McRae would replace Johnson in center, while the two relievers would supplement the setup corps in front of John Franco. None of the three acquirees made an immediate positive impact, however, and the Mets' pursuit of Florida ran out of fuel. The Marlins won not only the wild card—which drew them fewer than 30,000 fans per game—but the World Series.

Not to say it wasn't a beautiful September at Shea. With two weeks to go and the Fish not quite out of sight, the Mets' most emblematic game of 1997 unfolded against Montreal. They were down 6–0 in the ninth with two outs, cut the Expos' lead to 6–2, and loaded the bases for Everett. Everett, two pitches after a near-home run went foul, performed an encore, blasting a game-tying grand slam off Uggie Urbina. In the 11th, Gilkey enjoyed his best moment of the year and delivered a three-run homer to win it for New York. These Mets won 47 games in which they once trailed, the most by any team in the majors.

It was no wonder that on the final day of the season, though the Mets were eliminated, their hardcore fans—despite improving by 17 games, the team finished tenth in NL attendance and a distant second in New York—stood and applauded throughout the ninth inning of their 162nd game and 88th win. There was nothing within the MLB-sanctioned infrastructure capable of processing the kind of success that tasted great even if it was technically less fulfilling than a playoff spot. Teams about to go home are not normally zoned for extraordinary giddiness. Yet the Mets went with the flow their fans established. The players assembled on the field when it was over to wave their caps in appreciation, showing no particular desire to rush into the offseason. Valentine, who didn't click with every Met he managed in 1997 (Harnisch, in particular, left on bad terms), hugged each of his men. Baerga was spotted with tears in his eyes. Hundley, in street clothes and a sling after ending his season a little early in deference to inevitable elbow surgery, said he didn't want to miss the annual showing of the highlight video on DiamondVision. Todd had been a Met long enough to know how closing day at Shea worked. His elbow, he hoped, would be better in 1998, but he also knew he wouldn't be back in time for opening day. As he healed, the Mets would have to think about replacing him behind the plate, at least in the short term.

* * *

The Mets' record of 88–74 would have been good enough for the play-offs had Flushing mysteriously shifted to the Midwest. The Central Division champion Astros didn't win as many games as the Mets. Only three teams in the NL won more—Florida, Atlanta, and San Francisco. Los Angeles won exactly as many, but also missed the postseason despite another monumental contribution from their catcher.

Piazza had his greatest year yet: 40 homers, 124 runs batted in, .362 batting average, .638 slugging percentage. It won him only enough votes to finish second again in the MVP tabulations and his team second place, two games behind the Giants. Behind the scenes at Dodger Stadium came a change even more overwhelming than Piazza's statistics. Peter O'Malley sold the team that had been run by his family since 1950. First Lasorda, now O'Malley. Vin Scully was still in the booth, but otherwise the active iconography of Chavez Ravine was undergoing a facelift. The new look in the owners' suite belonged to News Corp., the umbrella organization encompassing Rupert Murdoch's media empire. Though the O'Malleys were still akin to the devil in certain precincts of Brooklyn, their business was baseball. Murdoch's outfit was better known for television programming. The Dodgers could definitely fill a lot of hours on local cable in Southern California.

But who would be their prime time star and what was it worth to them? Dodgers fans and baseball fans everywhere were about to find out. Mike Piazza stood one year from free agency.

CAUGHT MET-HANDED
March 31, 1998–May 22, 1998

It was precisely the stuff of Mets fans' dreams. An unbelievably sunny afternoon. A packed Shea Stadium. The game on the line. The catcher stepping up. He swings and . . . yes! The catcher comes through with the big hit and the Mets win!

How about that Alberto Castillo?

So maybe Castillo—nicknamed Bambi, as in The Bambino, as in ironic for a hitter who wouldn't be mistaken for Babe Ruth in this or any other lifetime—wasn't who Mets fans hoped would be at bat with the bases loaded in the 14th inning of a scoreless game. Bambi had played in morsels of the three previous seasons with the Mets, yet still retained his rookie status entering 1998. He was in the majors mainly for his defense. It took 65 at-bats for Castillo to collect his first RBI. It took desperation for Bobby Valentine to send him to the plate as a pinch-hitter on opening day. Bobby had used every other position player. Bambi worked the count against the Phillies' Ricky Bottalico to 3-and-2 and drove a single through a drawn-in infield, scoring Brian McRae with the first run of the season and giving the Mets their first win in the first year in a half-decade in which they carried expectations forward from the last one.

Good expectations, that is. The Mets and their fans expected to prevail, maybe all the way to October. Why not? They had finished 1997 close to the Marlins, and the Marlins went all the way. Now the Marlins were going all the way in the other direction. Their world championship thrilled South Florida for about ten minutes, or just long enough for Wayne Huizenga to start selling off his champions. If he couldn't do it en masse yet, he'd do it piecemeal. The fire sale was on. Moises Alou to the Astros. Jeff Conine to the Royals. Kevin Brown to the Padres. The Mets got in on the action, grabbing lefty reliever Dennis Cook in December and Al Leiter, who started the seventh game of the World Series, in February. Leiter was a New Jersey native who came up with the Yankees and earned his first ring with the Blue Jays, but swore allegiance to the orange and blue, recalling for anyone who asked how much he loved the Mets of Seaver and Koosman as a kid.

It was nice to know somebody did. Al and the 49,142 optimists who filled Shea on opening day were certainly enthusiastic, but you had to wonder about those who ran the Mets. They'd brought Mr. Met out of the attic when they needed a smiling face in 1994, yet otherwise hadn't been much on stoking Met tradition. They let Old Timers' Day lapse after 1994 and folded Banner Day following 1996. After a two-year hiatus, they inducted Mookie Wilson and Keith Hernandez into their team Hall of Fame in '96 and '97, the first '86ers so recognized, but scheduled no similar ceremonies for '98. The only number they'd retired since Seaver's 41 in 1988 was Jackie Robinson's 42, and you didn't have to be Ken Burns to know the honor for Robinson was baseball-wide. There was a special ceremony at Shea in 1997, attended by President Clinton, Acting Commissioner Selig, and Rachel Robinson, and it drew the biggest crowd of the year (on a cold night before the Mets started playing well), but its relevance to the Mets was more about geography than proprietary history. Robinson, whose playing career finished in 1956, had everything to do with baseball, but nothing specific to do with the Mets, who weren't born until 1962.

On Opening Day 1998, the Mets stepped just a little further away from whatever identity they maintained and took the field in black caps. The brims were blue and the NY was two-toned, but the trimmings of their warmup jackets and other accoutrement registered in Shea's mezzanine as Oriolesque. To confuse aesthetic matters further, the Mets added a black uniform top to their wardrobe, which they wore for the first time in their second series of the season. As every schoolchild knew, the Mets adopted blue from Jackie Robinson's Brooklyn Dodgers, orange from Willie Mays's New York Giants. The National League tradition lived on through the Mets. Black mostly looked right on a marketer's spreadsheet.

But the caps sold and so did the seats for opening day. BELIEVE, the (presumably) history-minded mass transit ads implored as part of a message that encouraged commuters to SHOW UP AT SHEA. Neither was a tough sell for the first day of a season after such good vibes emanated from the previous year, especially with the Marlins dissolving and the idea the Braves might be in reach in the air. That, though, was only enough to get people excited for a day.

For the rest of the season, some more convincing might be in order. The Mets got off to a good start, primarily via dependable pitching—Leiter proved a splendid addition to a rotation anchored by Bobby Jones and Rick Reed—and timely hitting, which is to say they weren't exactly knocking those home runs over the wall. Their primary slugger, Todd Hundley, was projected as being on the shelf for at least half a season, and the sum total of his replacements couldn't approach him for power.

Castillo, despite his opening day walk-off pinch hit, was neither Ruthian nor Hundleyan at the plate. The backstop tabbed to take Todd's place in the starting lineup most often, Tim Spehr, came to the Mets with nine homers in parts of six seasons. Todd Pratt, one of the small surprises of 1997, was just as surprisingly deemed to have backslid during spring training, and was assigned to Norfolk. He came back after a fashion, as the Mets groped about for further alternatives. Jim Tatum, a journeyman pinch-hitter who played mostly other positions when he played at all, was told to grab his catcher's mitt and give it a whirl behind the plate. Rick Wilkins, who'd hit 30 home runs as the Cubs' catcher in 1993, hit none for the Mets in four starts as their catcher in 1998.

Showing up at Shea was purely optional, and nobody catching or doing anything else made it a compelling choice. Perhaps the most embarrassing turnout occurred for a matinee on April 15, when more than 40,000 passed through the turnstiles for a New York victory. The problem, from a Met perspective, was that crowd materialized to see the Yankees, who borrowed Shea while their Stadium (or at least a piece of it) was literally falling apart. Joe Torre's Yankees beat Terry Collins's Angels, 6–3. Darryl Strawberry homered for the "home" team, raising the home run Apple about halfway before its operator realized that was a salute reserved for current Mets. The Yankees cleared out and gave Shea back to the Mets for their night game

against Chicago. Paid attendance for the regularly scheduled affair was a
hair over 16,000.

* * *

It was a bad look, but it wasn't the only one in baseball. The Mets
couldn't draw with a decent team. The Marlins, under reluctant ownership,
refused to attempt to field a decent team. And the Dodgers, under new ownership, were antagonizing their best player. Mike Piazza was the least happy
camper in Los Angeles as negotiations toward a contract that would keep
him in Dodger blue for the balance of his career turned everybody involved
red in the face. If you listened closely, you could hear echoes of the ire that
catapulted Tom Seaver to Cincinnati more than two decades before.

Piazza was being offered an enormous wheelbarrow of money—*Billionaires vs. Millionaires, Part Infinity*—but not an amount he and his agent
judged commensurate to his talent and impact. Mike, now twenty-nine, had
been far and away the best-hitting catcher in baseball for five seasons. He'd
been as popular an athlete as Southern California had seen since the prime
of Magic Johnson. The Dodgers were a mess when Mike arrived and had
been at or near the top of their division ever since he settled in. By industry
standards, he deserved pretty much whatever he wanted.

The Fox broadcasting executives who were running the Dodgers for
Rupert Murdoch's News Corp. weren't interested in wheeling out multiple wheelbarrows. They offered a substantial sum: close to $80 mil-
lion over six years. Piazza's side countered with a desire for a larger sum:
$100 million over seven years. It would be the most any player in base-
ball would make, which, in context, fit with how good Piazza was. The
Dodgers certainly weren't hurting at the gate (they'd drawn more than
3.3 million the year before, better than every National League club that
didn't have a new ballpark) and they played in the nation's second-largest
television market. They were *the Dodgers*, for Campanella's sake. And this
was *Piazza*.

None of this necessarily impressed the Murdoch operation, which preferred to set the terms of engagement with its employees, no matter how
famous or capable. They were not baseball people. The man who was osten-
sibly running the show, GM Fred Claire, was not a factor in the negotiations.

This was a Murdoch production as much as anything that aired on the burgeoning Fox News Channel.

Piazza publicly expressed his displeasure with the process despite pulling down $8 million for the last year of his old deal. Suddenly, he wasn't so popular in L.A. Mike Piazza was getting booed at Dodger Stadium. Negotiations broke off.

Except for those between the Dodgers and the Marlins, of all teams. If Los Angeles couldn't sign Piazza long-term, it made sense that they'd rather trade him than watch him walk with nothing but draft picks as compensation, but what would Florida, getting rid of every star in its stable, want with one of the biggest stars in the game? For one thing, in the bizarro Huizenga world, you had to take something to give something, and the Marlins could unload several of their salaries on Los Angeles. For another, there was some business to be done concerning the regional sports channel Huizenga owned in the Sunshine State, the one that aired Marlins games. That's the industry that most concerned News Corp. Wires crossed between baseball talk and cable talk and a trade was programmed.

On May 14, 1998, the Marlins sent four major leaguers—Gary Sheffield, Charles Johnson, Jim Eisenreich, and good old Bobby Bonilla—to the Dodgers and accepted in return Todd Zeile and Piazza.

Mike Piazza, maybe the most sensational Dodger since Fernando Valenzuela; probably the most accomplished since Sandy Koufax; inarguably their catcher of catchers since Roy Campanella; and no doubt the biggest thing they'd had going for them from the moment he broke in on September 1, 1992, was exiled from L.A. He was a Florida Marlin.

This would not stand. No, the swap—"The Trade of the Century," according to the cover of *Sports Illustrated*—wouldn't be reversed by Bud Selig in the best interests of the sport or the fan base that revered him unconditionally until very recently, but the immediate aftermath it wrought was not intended to be a permanent condition. The Marlins were a way station, a spot to rest a superstar who, like the Dodgers, they didn't plan on paying for the next four-and-a-half months just to have him leave them as a free agent, either. They cast themselves as no more than a player in a retelling of Glenn Frey's "Smuggler's Blues": the Marlins would move Mike through Miami after shipment from L.A.

A big-league baseball team was, for the next week, a money-laundering operation. The Marlins would exchange Piazza's contract pronto for minor league talent that would cost little now so Huizenga wouldn't have much on the books when he found a buyer for his franchise. Maybe down the road whichever prospects he collected would become legitimate players and attract eyeballs to SportsChannel Florida . . . which, incidentally, was on its way to becoming rebranded as Fox Sports Net Florida.

* * *

The Marlins had the best-hitting catcher in the universe on their roster. What team needed both hitting and catching and could use a dash of glamour?

Hmmm . . .

Probably not a team that was already paying an All-Star receiver who'd belted 71 home runs over the previous two seasons close to $5 million this season. Except that All-Star receiver, Hundley, was still not at Shea, still overcoming his elbow surgery, still leaving a void behind the plate. The Mets were doing respectably without him, but they weren't much slugging in a season when home runs couldn't have been a bigger draw—Mark McGwire, now in St. Louis, and Ken Griffey, still with Seattle, were eliciting amazement and sticking fannies in seats amid speculation that Roger Maris's record of 61 home runs was ripe to be had—and they weren't drawing too many fannies or other body parts no matter what they did. On May 19, the Mets hosted a makeup doubleheader against the Reds. The prospect of showing up for two games at Shea apparently struck New Yorkers like the old joke about first prize being a week's vacation in Philadelphia and second prize being two weeks' vacation in Philadelphia. The Mets swept Cincinnati in front of 15,558 who went to the ballpark only to hear a library break out.

It was quiet at Shea. Too quiet. Conversely, it was loud over their flagship radio station, WFAN, which took calls around the clock from Mets fans filling the time they were spending not buying tickets to games to advise one host after another that the Mets should go out and get the best-hitting catcher in the universe. It was hard to ignore the 50,000-watt transmission tower of babble, but the voice of the people had a point. Mike

Piazza was on the market. He could be picked up for the rest of the year, a year in which the Mets were still in contention for a wild-card spot. After sweeping the Cincinnati doubleheader, they sat 2 1/2 behind Chicago in this season's scramble. The Cubs were rumored as suitors for Piazza. If Mike went to Wrigley and joined Sammy Sosa, it would change the Mets' playoff hopes for the worse.

Fans who'd waited ten years to return to October sought better. They sought good news, hope for 1998 on top of hope from 1997 on top of the malaise that had defined the '90s in Queens since the last whiff of happiness from the '80s evaporated. Things had improved, but not enough. The Braves weren't going away from the top of the division. The Yankees, off to a hellacious start of their own, weren't exiting the back page without a mighty shove. The Mets had a sharp manager. They had Olerud and Alfonzo, Reed and Jones, Leiter and Cook, and, since the dawn of time or at least the decade, No. 31 John Franco. But after nearly 40 games, they didn't have Hundley and they had no idea when exactly they would have him back.

The Mets needed more. The Mets fans needed more. No offense to Johnny from Bensonhurst, they needed another No. 31.

They needed Mike Piazza of the Florida Marlins.

While Piazza dutifully reported to his new team and set about hitting in teal (not homering, yet recording the fourth triple of his career), the Mets mulled acting. One Mets owner, Nelson Doubleday, didn't need much convincing. He generally came down on the side of action, little of which was transpiring on the field or in the stands at Shea thus far in 1998. The other Mets owner, Fred Wilpon, had to give it some thought. WFAN told him to act, though sports talk radio didn't make its reputation on callers and hosts who demanded local teams stand pat. Fred was quite fond of Hundley, who was coming back eventually, and neither Todd nor Mike had an obvious other position to play. Steve Phillips, the Mets' GM installed in his position because he was supposed to have the right skill set for the job, was prepared to act. Wilpon thought about it some more and added his approval to Doubleday's.

Phillips acted as skillfully as he could. These were the Marlins. He'd dealt with them twice over the winter. The familiarity certainly didn't hurt. But there was competition. The Cubs called Florida. The Red Sox, Orioles, and Rockies were interested. Who wouldn't be? (Not the Yankees—they had Jorge Posada, Joe Girardi, and a record that had soared 20 games above .500.) But the Marlins had a working knowledge of the Mets' farm system and Phillips could claim insight into who his counterpart, Dave Dombrowski, might like from it.

The package he put together consisted of lefty pitcher Ed Yarnall, the Mets' third-round pick in 1996; Geoff Goetz, another southpaw arm and the club's top pick in 1997; and a first-rounder who'd been in the Mets chain a long time by 1998, Preston Wilson.

It was the same Preston Wilson the Mets drafted ahead of all others in 1992, the same Preston Wilson the 1995 Mets yearbook promised would be playing left at Shea in 2000, the same Preston Wilson whose last name evoked a man unsurpassed for affection in Flushing, his stepdad Mookie Wilson. Preston had finally reached the majors in May, going 6-for-8 in his first two games for the home team. It was a beautiful story after those six years climbing the minor league ladder from Kingsport to Pittsfield to Capital City to St. Lucie to Binghamton to Norfolk to New York.

Two years earlier, when the Mets inducted Mookie into their Hall of Fame, Lance Johnson, who wore Mookie's No. 1 as he stole and tripled like its previous bearer, took it off for the day in homage to the man of the hour. One Dog wore No. 51 for the afternoon. A year later, upon his trade to Chicago, he said he had wished he'd had the chance to "have kept No. 1" a while longer "and then given it to Mookie's son. That would have been the ultimate."

Preston wound up being assigned No. 11 when he reached the Mets (for whom Mookie was coaching first base). He was the first No. 1 pick to make it to the Mets since 1994 first choice Paul Wilson, who was now in his second year of attempting to overcome arm trouble. Top 1993 pick Kirk Presley—Elvis's young cousin—never made it to the Mets. Nor did 1995's Ryan Jaroncyk, a shortstop who retired from baseball rather than take on the challenge of turning Shea Stadium into Jaroncyk Park. Bobby Jones had done fine for himself as a supplemental first-rounder, but you had to go back to Jeromy Burnitz, the Mets' first pick in 1990, to find one of their top selections having an impact in the majors in the late '90s . . . and Burnitz was doing his hitting for Milwaukee.

The Mets finally successfully nurtured a No. 1 pick, their legacy guy, the same young man who spent a chunk of his childhood at Shea. Would they really trade him to get a 62nd-round draft pick?

You bet your Bambi they would. And the Marlins would take him, which was not known to Mike while he awaited word of his next destination. Holed up temporarily at his family's South Florida house, he decided to interrupt the tension on Friday afternoon, May 22, by taking a shower. Just before he did, his agent, Dan Lozano, told him it looked like a trade was about to come down, and that it appeared Mike was headed for the Cubs.

Mike went into the shower. When he came out, he wasn't a Marlin anymore. But he wasn't a Cub, either. The last time anybody expressed as much shower-related surprise as Piazza did was on *Dallas* when Pamela Ewing heard the water running and discovered her presumed-dead husband Bobby was alive, well, and soaping up.

That was a dream—though to Mets fans, so was this. It was also a much better dramatic device than any nighttime soap could script.

* * *

Mike Piazza was a Met. He was Mike Piazza of the New York Mets, traded for Yarnall, Goetz, and Wilson. He was Mike Piazza of the New York Mets, all 177 home runs, 568 runs batted in, and .331 batting average of him. Mets fans were used to seeing Piazza pad his totals against their team. He'd batted .367 versus the Mets from 1993 through 1996. His first home run against them came off Dwight Gooden, his most recent, on August 21, 1997, with Joe Crawford pitching. Piazza did damage against Cy Youngs and regular Joes.

But he wouldn't be doing any to the Mets anymore. It would all be for the Mets, at least for the rest of 1998, maybe deep into the autumn of 1998, maybe for the years after 1998, to 2000 and beyond.

It was as futile to project from a distance of two years the baseball details that awaited on the other side of the millennial divide as it was in that Mets yearbook from three years before. Just the same, this little revision of the roster was Amazin' to contemplate and something to celebrate. That's what every Mets fan who wasn't wondering what would become of Todd Hundley started doing when the news broke over WFAN late in the afternoon of the twenty-second day of this suddenly very merry month of May. Mike Piazza was a Met . . . No. 31 of the New York Mets, courtesy of John Franco. The closer statesman of the ballclub gracefully gave up the digits he'd worn prominently since 1984 and slipped his left arm into a jersey bearing No. 45, same as that worn by Tug McGraw when Franco, like Leiter, was growing up a Mets fan.

What a Mets fan thing to do.

There was tradition to the Mets, no matter how little mind management paid it. It resided first and foremost in the hands and hearts of those who rooted for the team. Franco knew it. The fans Franco drove crazy with his bases-loaded saves knew it, too. And now kids growing up as Mets fans—including some who wouldn't otherwise be growing as up Mets fans if not for the trade of May 22, 1998—would have Mike Piazza to root for; to reflect on; and to pay tribute to thirty-one different ways when they got older.

Or they would as soon as their new favorite player arrived to play in the first game of the rest of their lives.

PART IV
AS GOOD AS IT GETS

THE COMMITMENTS
May 23, 1998–October 26, 1998

Because nothing so epic could possibly come so easy, Mike Piazza left his Florida home after his five-game Marlin career on Saturday morning, May 23, and went to the wrong airport. It was Fort Lauderdale, not West Palm Beach, where his flight to LaGuardia and into the unknown awaited. Somehow, he got to Shea in time for the Mets' 4:10 engagement with the Milwaukee Brewers, batting third and catching Al Leiter, the latter notwithstanding the small detail that they had never worked together professionally before. Mike entered the stadium; then talked to reporters; then talked to his pitcher; then flung a Mets-logoed equipment bag over his right shoulder and toted it through the tunnel on the first base side; then emerged into the home dugout; then accepted a ceremonial first pitch from a little girl as part of a previously scheduled promotion; then got behind the plate for real; and then added his presence to a lineup that otherwise consisted of Brian McRae in center, Matt Franco at third, John Olerud at first, Carlos Baerga at second, Butch Huskey in right, Bernard Gilkey in left, and Rey Ordoñez at short.

This was his new team, his new park, his new life, all of it arranged barely twenty-four hours before. Dazing and confusing culture shock, you'd think, for a Pennsylvanian who'd just spent five years exuding California cool. But Mike Piazza was Mike Piazza, whether of the Los Angeles Dodgers, the Florida Marlins, or the New York Mets. By the fifth inning, he was doubling to right-center off Jeff Juden, driving Franco home from first, taking third on the throw home, and extending the Mets' lead to 2–0. By the ninth, he was up on his feet to congratulate Leiter, with whom he had collaborated on a four-hit shutout. All around, he was the center of attention of a 3–0 victory, luring to Shea 13,000 walkup ticket-buyers and making John Franco sit in pregame traffic "for the first time in a long time." One of those in the crowd of 33,000 repeatedly zoomed in upon by the Fox Sports Net New York cameras was Jerry Seinfeld, whose eponymous sitcom "about nothing" had just ended its nine-year NBC run. Jerry played a Mets fan and was a Mets fan. Real-life Seinfeld appeared as excited as anyone that the Mets were now about something.

The next day, the Mets drew 47,000, Piazza got another hit, and the Mets won again, with Mike successfully catching Bobby Jones for seven innings. They swept the Brewers and were swept up in the first hype to surround them in ages. "There's a marquee player, in a Met uniform, behind the plate," marveled Fred Wilpon. "The fans have reacted. The media has reacted. I think New York is going to love this player." The team Piazza joined was reacting well, too. After a spring of sporadic hitting and personnel shortfalls (Edgardo Alfonzo missed a couple of weeks with a strained rotator cuff), the Mets were rounding into form, finishing May on a nine-game winning streak and in possession, however tentative, of the National League wild card. Piazza's first road trip as a Met was practically old home week, taking him to Miami, then Philadelphia. The comfort zone did him good while adjusting to his new surroundings. In his first seven games as a Met, Mike batted .419.

Piazza's Mets finally lost a game on June 1, in Pittsburgh, but Mike posted his first home run for his new club at Three Rivers, a solo shot off Jason Schmidt. A week later, he entertained the home folks with his first Shea home run, versus the expansion Tampa Bay Devil Rays. The victim this time was Dennis Springer, though for a change Piazza wasn't the object of all eyes. Rick Reed carried a perfect game into the seventh inning, an effort not broken up until there were two out and Wade Boggs doubled. Piazza handled all 121 pitches of Reed's eventual three-hit shutout just three nights after having to leave a game in Boston when his former Los Angeles batterymate, Pedro Martinez, committed a bit of battery himself, hitting Mike on the hand in what was taken as a less-than-coincidental hit-by-pitch between ex-Dodgers who weren't crazy about each other. Karma awaited Pedro in what would have been Piazza's next at-bat when Mike's replacement, Alberto Castillo, went full Bambino on him at Fenway Park, homering off the Red Sox ace and opening a barrage of what totaled four long balls in a 9–2 Mets win.

Mike wasn't done with old Dodger pitchers. The Mets made another trade in June, this one to bring in another former Rookie of the Year from L.A., Hideo Nomo. The Tornado who blew through the National League in 1995 was reduced to a wayward wind of late, but the Mets were willing to take a chance on Hideo, trading Subway Series hero Dave Mlicki and reliever Greg McMichael to get him and throw-in Brad Clontz. The name addition didn't really enhance the Mets' pitching staff, as Nomo struggled to find consistency. After a while, not even Piazza could keep the team hovering above the playoff chase. The wild-card stakes were developing into a three-team tussle, with the Mets battling Barry Bonds's Giants and Sammy Sosa's Cubs. Bonds was having a typically excellent if relatively quiet 1998, while Sosa crashed into the public's consciousness via a scorching June.

When Sosa homered at Shea on the night of April 15—the nocturnal half of the de facto Yankees-Mets doubleheader—it was his third of the year and it wasn't even the most noteworthy home run of the evening; Reed had homered in his own cause and provided all the runs he would need for his 2–1 win. By June, Sosa was a slugging sensation, going deep twenty times to set a new monthly record. Sammy had injected himself into the race all fans were watching, the derby to top 61. He was now in the same conversation with Mark McGwire and Ken Griffey and, not incidentally, helping the Cubs charge toward the postseason for the first time in nine years.

While Sosa lit baseball on fire, New York sizzled with the second iteration of the Subway Series, this one at Shea Stadium, sold out for all three games. The Yankees carried an otherworldly record of 53–19 into the intracity squabble, the Mets a more than respectable 42–32, which would look lovely in any city that wasn't their own. The visiting American Leaguers took two of three in front of a decidedly mixed crowd. Paul O'Neill launched the signature shot of the set with a three-run bomb off Mel Rojas on Friday night, a righty reliever vs. lefty hitter matchup Bobby Valentine seemed to calculate out of frustration with not having better options at hand. Piazza collected one hit in 11 at-bats.

If playing the Yankees in Queens was an arduous challenge, taking on the Braves in Atlanta one weekend later was a horror show. With the All-Star break beckoning—Piazza and Reed would be representing the Mets in Denver—the Braves took the first two in what could be categorized as dreadful Turner Field fashion. On a steamy Sunday, the budding rivals dragged their finale into extra innings. In the bottom of the 11th, with Franco pitching, the bases loaded and one out, Braves shortstop Walt Weiss lined out to short left field. Michael Tucker took off from third. Gilkey fired from left. The ball came to Piazza on one bounce. He tagged Tucker, but not to the satisfaction of home plate umpire Angel Hernandez, who claimed Tucker's foot reached the plate first.

The Mets didn't agree. According to the *Daily News*'s tally, Mike "used the word ridiculous nine times in nine minutes" to describe his reaction to the call, and at no time did he mean ridiculous in the Sosa hitting home runs sense. Valentine characterized Tucker's landing as his having fallen "into Mike's lap with a lousy, illegal slide. He cut him up, never touched the plate, got tagged out, and they boarded the plane. I saw what everyone else saw: no marks on home plate, a lot of marks on Mike's leg where the cuts are." Valentine and Franco were angry enough to make contact with Hernandez, who rocketed to No. 1 on every Mets fan's list of least favorite umpires. Piazza intimated Angel and his fellow officials simply wanted to get the game over with and move on to their own mini-vacation.

With three straight losses to end the first half, the Mets were 13–19 since the nine-game winning streak that ushered in Piazza's tenure. The Braves were 12 1/2 games beyond their reach in first place and the Giants led them by five for the wild card. The most encouraging thing awaiting them after the All-Star break was the imminent addition to their ranks of another player with All-Star credentials. Unlike Piazza and Nomo, he wasn't coming from another organization. The Mets had this guy all along.

They just had to figure out what to do with him.

* * *

They thought they knew. With Piazza installed as their catcher (and taking the beating to prove it, not only absorbing Tucker's "lousy, illegal slide," but also a backswing to the head from the Braves' Gerald Williams the night before), Todd Hundley wasn't getting back the position he'd manned for the Mets over the previous eight seasons. Catchers sometimes shift to first, but first base was the province of Olerud, batting .326 at the break, so there was no reason to sit John. Todd's destination was designated as left field. Gilkey had made that good throw to all but nail Tucker at the plate, but he was batting .229, and—despite etching himself into the Mets' pop culture annals with an endearing coconut-conking cameo in 1997's *Men in Black*— no longer a piece of the Mets' long-term plans. Then again, the only term that really concerned the Mets in 1998 was the one slated to expire on September 27. They were trying to make the playoffs for the first time in ten years. Everything they did was in service to plowing through the regular season and seeing the postseason.

Hundley wasn't a left fielder, but once Piazza became the Mets' catcher, turning himself into a left fielder became Todd's minor league rehab assignment. He was being asked to not just regain his batting eye and swing but to cobble together a competency totally new to him and do it well enough so it could prove useful at the highest level of his profession, that's all.

Todd did as he was asked, even if he was never going to be anything but a catcher at heart. Wilpon figured the way to Hundley's better angels might be through his finger, so the owner loaned his supplanted backstop his own 1986 World Series ring. It was his way of saying *You'll win one of these on your own with us soon, but until then, will you take left field as your ad hoc wedded position?*

It was a shotgun defensive marriage, but when Hundley returned to the Mets on July 11, it seemed the stuff of bliss. The walkups came out in force again. Some 13,000 tickets were sold day-of-game for the new and improved Mets lineup that featured Olerud batting second, Piazza third, and Hundley cleanup. Todd received a standing ovation in his first at-bat since the previous September and showed his appreciation with a single to center off the Expos' Carl Pavano. "I was floating," Hundley said later. Everything was beautiful. Olerud homered twice and the Mets won, 8–4. This new arrangement was going to be great, particularly if no opponent ever hit a ball to left field.

Unfortunately, balls did get hit to left and the repurposed catcher was exposed. Hundley handled 49 chances out there and made five errors. That amounted to a fielding percentage of .898, a splendid result for, say, an algebra final, an embarrassment for a major-league outfielder. Also, he didn't hit, which made the experiment pointless to the point of reckless. Todd Hundley was not going to help himself or his team win any rings as an everyday left fielder.

The catcher who took his job, meanwhile, was pressing. Piazza's ovations receded. Soon, Mike inspired a monosyllabic expression of impatient frustration—boo—whenever he struck out (sixteen times in July) or grounded into double plays (twice in an aggravating loss in his first game against the Dodgers on July 31). The great Mike Piazza, he whose arrival was welcomed as if it was the second coming, was being jeered by Mets fans not too many weeks after they cheered him as their savior. It was by no means a universal reaction, but it was loud enough to be heard by the object of the Shea throng's conflicted emotions every time he batted and didn't come through for them.

Tough room. Again, not all of it, but a vocal portion, and those who make noise tend to obscure those who are offering ordinary encouragement. Applause for a star player in a slump is never as loud a collective fit of dissatisfaction. Piazza could tell his stay at Shea's honeymoon suite had been a short one, which couldn't help but enter his thinking as he decided what to do with himself when the season was over. He still had free agency waiting for him if he wanted it. It wasn't like he wasn't going to be paid a kajillion dollars somewhere. A ballpark where they weren't so quickly moved to boo his rough patches surely existed somewhere outside New York.

New York, though, was where he was for the balance of 1998, and the ever fluid wild-card race was still where the Mets hung in by the second week of August, 2 1/2 behind Chicago, a half-game behind San Francisco. The club had split four with the Cubs at Wrigley (Hundley looking particularly maladroit in left in the ballpark where his father Randy had starred behind the plate a generation before) and took two of three from the Giants at Shea, with the one loss featuring the Mets turning their first triple play in nine years for solace. Amid the pursuit of playoffs, Steve Phillips continued to attempt to fine-tune, his trigger finger dialing for more deals.

Gilkey and minor leaguer Nelson Figueroa went to the expansion Arizona Diamondbacks and brought back a spare starting pitcher, Willie Blair, and another backup catcher, Jorge Fabregas. Veteran utilityman Tony Phillips was obtained from Toronto for a minor leaguer; Tony, not Hundley, would serve as the more-or-less everyday left fielder down the stretch. Outfielder Jermaine Allensworth came from Kansas City to play a little outfield as well. Greg McMichael was refetched from the Dodgers for Brian Bohanon almost as swiftly as he'd been sent to get Nomo. Bill Pulsipher, who finally worked his way back to the majors after three years, pitched his way out of Flushing after 15 appearances. Pulse was shipped to Milwaukee in a small deal that ended the illusion of Generation K. Paul Wilson still hadn't returned and Jason Isringhausen, after a late-1997 recall, was again set back by injuries throughout 1998.

The Mets were proceeding, just not as planned. Who among those that followed this team loyally through the mid-1990s saw a contender coalescing with nary a contribution from its three most vital pitching prospects? Who saw Bernard Gilkey as utterly disposable, Todd Hundley as a starter in left field thirty-four times, and Mike Piazza as a Met at all? Yet here they were, in the thick of it, led by Leiter, Olerud (challenging Cleon Jones's franchise record .340 batting average), and, all of a sudden, Turk Wendell, who was pitching and getting outs almost every day from the bullpen. Valentine would call on Wendell; Wendell—always wearing a necklace decorated with animal teeth and claws he gathered from hunting—would grab and slam the rosin bag the mound; the crowd would swoon; and the Mets, more often than not, would hang on to a lead or at least a tie. Turk was turning into a latter-day Tug, while 1998 awaited the spirit of 1973 to imbue it.

And fans wanted to believe that Mike would hit in New York like he'd hit in Los Angeles.

It wasn't as if he wasn't hitting at all. In his first three months as a Met, Mike belted 14 homers, drove in 46 runs, and batted .320. He also grounded into 10 double plays, which will happen when you're an everyday catcher in the heat of summer who stomps down the line at speeds that would never challenge Lance Johnson or, for that matter, Lyndon Johnson. DPs notwithstanding, these were excellent numbers in the standard Mets universe. Gilkey dined out on such numbers two years earlier. But this wasn't the Piazza of legend; the Piazza of L.A.; the perennial MVP candidate who didn't have a trophy to show for it only because Ken Caminiti and Larry Walker picked 1996 and 1997 to be veritable flukes of nature; the catcher who outhit everybody who'd preceded him, including Campanella, Berra, and Bench. It wasn't enough to singlehandedly make the Mets a playoff team, and it certainly wasn't enough to maintain the spotlight at Shea when 1998's gaudiest road show came to town.

Because of heavy spring rains in New York, the Mets found themselves with a backlog of home doubleheaders in August, including twin bills on consecutive nights against the Cardinals. The Cardinals meant McGwire, with batting practice a bonus attraction to the massive crowds who came out to see the massive slugger on the verge of breaking massive records. With 38 games remaining, McGwire had 49 home runs already, just a dozen fewer than Maris did for all of 1961 as a Yankee. No asterisks about it, Mark was coming for Roger, and he was doing so, at least for a couple of days, in the town that didn't necessarily make Maris feel at home.

Sort of like Piazza lately, come to think of it.

In the first game of the Mets-Cardinals doubleheader of Thursday, August 20, McGwire took Blair deep for No. 50, helping St. Louis to a 2–0 win. After smacking 52 in 1996 and 58 in 1997, the Redbird established himself as the only player in baseball history with three consecutive 50-plus seasons in the home run department. The Shea fans, whether they were on hand to see him or the Mets, rewarded him with a significant ovation. Then he kept going. In the nightcap, the most famous baseball player in America did the same to Reed that he had to Blair in what became a 5–4 Mets win (Piazza hit his 22nd overall, his 13th since coming to the Mets). Mark now had 51 home runs on the season and dropped his characteristic reticence to comment on his powerful progress.

"I'd have to say I do have a shot," McGwire said. "But I know it's going to be tough." He also added that despite his enhanced fame and the support he was receiving from fans nationwide, "I don't want people to know me. It's not for the public to know. There are some things I have to keep private. I have a private life. I'm entitled to a private life."

Where his clubhouse stall fell in that appraisal was probably a gray area, but because McGwire attracted reporters before the second doubleheader on Friday, whatever sat on his shelf was there for the noticing, and Associated Press reporter Steve Wilstein couldn't help but notice a bottle of something called Androstenedione. It was an over-the-counter steroid that, when Wilstein asked about it, McGwire dismissed as nothing out of the ordinary. "Everybody in the game of baseball uses the same stuff I use," the man nicknamed Big Mac said. With that explanation, he went out to play some more ball. McGwire hit no home runs that night and his team split another two with the Mets. St. Louis moved on, out of playoff contention. The Mets were tied for the wild card with the Cubs, whose own Maris-chaser, Sosa, was up to 49 home runs with 34 games to go.

* * *

Piazza wasn't on the heels of any ghosts, but he did have one specter to beat back as August ended. The Mets were heading to Los Angeles, Mike's first trip to the city he'd called his professional home. He'd left less than popular, but was welcomed back as a prodigal son. Dodger Stadium's parishioners cheered the slugger in the road uniform as those at Shea had done for McGwire the week before. In this case, it was personal, the Dodgers fans letting it be known they remembered all that was accomplished in their name between 1992 and 1998. If Piazza was going to be a free agent, maybe an L.A. reconciliation wasn't beyond the pale. It wasn't like the Dodgers (who had elevated Tommy Lasorda to interim GM after they traded Mike) had sprung back into contention without him. If absence made the heart grow fonder, Piazza's home run off Carlos Perez stuck the needle of recriminations a little deeper into News Corp. management. The Mets won three of four in Los Angeles. Mike went 8-for-13.

August morphed into September. Piazza stayed hot. He homered in three consecutive games, two in San Diego, once upon the Mets' return home to face Atlanta on Mike's thirtieth birthday. Blowing out candles was passé; Piazza celebrated by walloping a Tom Glavine pitch over the left-field Picnic Area bleachers. At the end of a summer when measuring home runs was baseball's latest craze, Piazza's was estimated to have traveled 485 feet. Most importantly, it gave Leiter the extra run necessary to outpoint Glavine, 2–1, and it seemed to touch off a case of dinger fever in Flushing. The next afternoon, Tony Phillips poked a two-run homer in the eighth inning to key a 5–4 win. Two days later, the Mets won the four-game series from the Braves when Alfonzo took rookie reliever John Rocker over the left-field wall in the eighth for a come-from-behind 8–7 Labor Day victory. With 28 games to go, the Mets and Cubs were tied, and the Giants were two back.

While the Mets went on a 10-game road trip, the record books went in for revision. On September 8, batting against the Cubs' Steve Trachsel, Mark McGwire hit his 62nd home run of the season. Roger Maris was now history. On September 13, Sosa hit his 61st and 62nd amid a Cubs victory over Milwaukee. Sammy and Mark sat as single-season co-home run champions of all time . . . until the next of their swings produced another wall-clearing bulletin.

As the sluggers slugged, the Mets attempted to ward off sluggishness. They took two of three in Philadelphia after Nomo imploded in the Veterans Stadium opener and appeared to lose his spot in the rotation. They lost two of three in Montreal, salvaging the finale with that rarest of birds, a start behind the plate by Hundley. The erstwhile All-Star catcher even threw out Shane Andrews attempting to steal in the fourth and blocked the same runner from scoring in the ninth with two out, preserving a 1–0 win for Blair, who bumped Nomo following Hideo's abysmal 16–4 defeat in Philly. It had been almost exactly a year since Hundley last caught. "I'm back to my world," Todd said, even if it was only as Piazza's backup.

The Mets departed Quebec one game behind the Cubs, 2 1/2 ahead of the Giants, with four to play in Houston. The Astros were enjoying their best season ever, having fortified their World Series aspirations by picking up Randy Johnson from Seattle at the trade deadline. The Big Unit was practically unbeatable for his new team. That the Mets wouldn't have to face him was a de facto victory in advance.

This series didn't need Johnson. It contained everything else, including echoes of Game Six of the 1986 NLCS, the last time the Mets and Astros combined to nearly blow the roof off the Astrodome. At stake a dozen years earlier was the pennant. The impenetrable Astro ace then was Mike Scott. Not facing him represented a Mets victory in its time. Scott was to pitch Game Seven. The Mets, leading three games to two, were determined to win Game Six and avoid Scott altogether. It took 16 smoking innings, but the Mets did it, winning, 7–6. These were different Mets and different Astros playing under different circumstances in 1998, but the angst they manufactured across four games was recognizable to any fan who remembered the '86 proceedings. Of the first three, the Mets won two. In the first, Piazza blasted a 480-foot homer, the longest in Dome history. But the explosive game of Wednesday night, September 16, outdid them all.

Mike Hampton toed the rubber for the Astros. Carl Everett, traded to Houston in the previous offseason, reminded his old club of what he could do, homering in the third inning with a man on. Jones and Hampton dueled otherwise untouched through eight. The Astros didn't badly need this game, but would be happy to take it. The Mets were desperate to not let them have it.

The ninth was the responsibility of Billy Wagner, Houston's fireballing closer. Triple-digit MPH readouts were not uncommon for the smallish lefty with the gargantuan strikeout totals. Wagner was fanning more than 14 batters per nine innings, one inning at a time. He wasn't necessarily infallible—McRae solved him for a game-tying home run a couple of nights earlier—but his arsenal was intimidating. With the Cubs a half-game ahead for the wild card, the Mets could afford no fear. So bring on Billy Wagner.

Todd Pratt pinch-hit and singled. Phillips struck out swinging. Alfonzo flied out. Olerud, whose bat was hotter than his feet were slow, managed an infield hit and was pinch-run for. The Mets had Pratt on second, Ralph Milliard on first, two out, and coming up the guy they got for a situation like this. Conversely, the guy coming up was as good an explanation as any that the Mets had a situation like this at all. It was Piazza as the Mets' last, best hope, September baseball with everything on the line for the first time in a long time for this franchise. This was, to borrow a phrase from 1986, baseball like it oughta be.

This was Piazza like he was supposed to be. He had 199 home runs in a career that had taken root elsewhere. He had an undetermined number of home runs ahead of him somewhere. On September 16, 1998, there was no telling where or for whom those home runs would be hit. Eight games remained after this one, and however they turned out, there was still the matter of a contract to be settled. Maybe Mike and the Mets would reach an accord. Maybe it would go down as a summer rental that was fun while it lasted. On September 16 in the top of the ninth at the Astrodome, though, the lease was still in effect.

Wagner worked the count to 2-and-2. One more strike would end it. That was also a familiar refrain from 1986. The Mets had been down to one swing and kept swinging it until they won the World Series. They weren't yet that close to going so far in 1998.

But it wasn't because the next swing Piazza took didn't saddle Houston with a problem. Mike lined a ball over the right-center field fence, exemplary of the kind of opposite-field power that separated him from most of the rest of baseball. It put the Mets ahead, 3–2, and it gave No. 31 No. 200 in the bargain.

And if that was how the Mets won the final game of their four-game September series in Houston, that would have been smashing. But like getting Mike to the Mets in the first place in May, nothing so epic was about to come so easy. Dennis Cook was entrusted with the ninth inning, what with Franco's left arm pretty much falling off. Not that Cook's wasn't, either. Brad Ausmus, the Astros' backstop, showed Piazza he wasn't the only catcher under the Dome who could go deep, homering to knot the affair at three.

The top of the 10th yielded no runs for the Mets off Wagner. The bottom of the inning was no picnic for McMichael, who loaded the bases but escaped damage. The top of the 11th saw Sean Bergman come on to pitch. After he got two quick outs, he came to the three-hole in the order, which, when the game began, was Olerud's. That little pinch-running maneuver in the ninth, however, took John out of action, and now it was the pitcher's slot. McMichael certainly wasn't going to hit, so Valentine went with the man he once saw pass Roy Campanella.

Todd Hundley came up to pinch-hit. His work over the weekend in Montreal notwithstanding, Todd was hardly the same threat he'd been in 1996. This Hundley carried a .161 batting average and a .246 slugging percentage to the plate. It was hard to envision him keeping this inning going, except to its bottom.

But sometimes you have to keep watching, just as Mets fans did through all 16 innings in 1986, just as they did here, following the flight of the ball Hundley connected on until it, like Piazza's two frames before, cleared the wall. The Mets led and would go on to win, 4–3. Hundley just had his 1998 highlight film unspool in real time. Piazza, the on-deck batter, congratulated him as he scored. Mike and Todd, together at last.

It wound up essentially for naught. The Mets lost a heartbreaker to the Marlins when they returned home, took the next two to grab a one-game wild-card lead, then lost their last five—three at Turner Field—to finish behind the Cubs and Giants, who played a decidedly Metless one-game playoff taken by Chicago.

The Cubs would then lose to Atlanta, who would go on to lose the NLCS to San Diego. The Padres had knocked out Randy Johnson and the Astros, but in the World Series went up against—who else?—the mighty Yankees. New York's American League entry went 114–48 during the regular season, clinching their playoff berth sometime in May, or so it seemed.

Mets fans who watched their own team fizzle at the end of September could either avert their eyes through most of October or bear witness to a predictable World Series sweep in which the Padres were incidental guests. When the latest round of ticker tape settled over Lower Manhattan, Yankee propagandists grafted their postseason triumphs onto the six preceding months worth of romps and boasted of a 125-win season, which was bookkeeping unlike it had ever been.

Somehow with these Yankees, it was never enough to say they won the World Series and leave it at that.

* * *

The end of the Mets' story in 1998 was bitter beyond belief, a collapse you were sure could not be matched for sheer devastation. They won the same 88 games they won in 1997, but it couldn't have been more different. The '97 Mets were a pat on the back. The '98 Mets were a kick to the groin. "I guess we just ran out of gas," reasoned part-timer Lenny Harris, "and there were no gas stations open." There were no expectations in 1997. There were a ton of them to start 1998, and then a ton more as of May 23.

Though the Mets as a whole did not meet those expectations, the player they added when they decided to get serious wound up transcending them. The unreality of Mike Piazza being a Met took a little while to melt. The tendency early on was to view him the way the underclassman trying to buy Blue Oyster Cult tickets looked at all-world football player Charles Jefferson (Forest Whitaker) in *Fast Times at Ridgemont High*: "Wow, does he really live here? I thought he just flew in for games."

Eventually, Mike's presence and affiliation clicked for all concerned. In his final 30 games of 1998, Mike Piazza showed Mets fans and Mets management what all the fuss was about: nine home runs, 30 runs batted in, a .427 batting average, a .508 on-base percentage and an .806 slugging percentage. Not only did he not make an out half the time he came to the plate, he erased existing baserunners via double play only twice in that period. Mike's phenomenal finish gave him Met totals that read 23 HR, 76 RBIs, and .348 BA in traditional statistical parlance. The 32–111-.328 he posted for all three of his 1998 teams combined was good enough to rate only fourteenth in NL MVP voting in this home run-happy year (Sosa's 66 for a playoff team won him the award, dulling the impact of McGwire's 70 where voters were concerned), but in Queens—where paid attendance rose nearly 29 percent over 1997—there was no disputing Piazza's value.

Mike couldn't put the Mets in the playoffs all by himself, but the Mets couldn't hope to approach the playoffs without him. They were a wonderful story the year before he arrived, but a barely adequate one in the weeks before they acquired him. To theorize the Mets' immediate future sans Piazza was about as appetizing as taking in a replay of the just-completed World Series. In *Fast Times* parlance, nobody wanted to picture Steve Phillips channeling Jeff Spicoli and saying, "Aloha, Mr. Piazza" at the end of the year.

The worst a Mets fan could imagine in late October of 1998 never came to pass. The Mets committed themselves to signing Piazza and Piazza committed himself to remaining a Met. Two-thirds of a season playing for fans who cut him only so much slack when he struggled did not turn him off from the city. When he hit enough, they responded enough. They wanted to see more of what he could do and he did as much as he could. There was synergy, there was energy and, let us not discount, there was money. The Mets made an offer Piazza was not of a mind to refuse, proposing seven years for $91 million. It would make him the highest-paid player in baseball on an annual basis, surpassing Pedro Martinez's arrangement with the Red Sox, at least until the next mega-contract was signed by somebody else. It was like McGwire and Sosa knocking down home run barriers; there was always going to be another to fall. Sure enough, by the time the next spring training rolled around, Mo Vaughn of the Angels and Kevin Brown of the previously unbending Dodgers had bigger deals from their new teams.

That was fine by Piazza, who accepted what the Mets put on the table. The rental was over. On October 26, 1998, his decision to become a permanent fixture in Flushing was made official. Mets fans, with nothing to cheer since the season ended on September 27, now had 1999 through 2005 to anticipate. They couldn't tell what those next seven years would entail, but facing them with Piazza figured to make the turning of the century a baseball joy. For his part, Mike understood the cheers would be neither endless nor unconditional, but rationalized perfectly the so-called pressure of playing in New York: "I might as well get booed by the best if I was going to get booed by anyone."

Elias didn't track it, but Mike appeared to lead the majors in self-awareness. He knew who he'd be playing in front of and he knew what he was capable of giving them. He hadn't been a Met that long, but he'd been as elite as a player could be for six full big-league seasons. Barring the unforeseen, he sensed where his career was taking him over the length of his new contract.

"The Mets showed incredible commitment to me," Piazza said at the press conference that announced his and the club's intentions. "If I'm so fortunate as to go into the Hall of Fame someday, it definitely will be in a Mets uniform."

Now to go and make that happen.

DRAMA QUEENS
October 27, 1998–July 10, 1999

Once the services of Mike Piazza were secured, Steve Phillips went about revamping the team around him. The frustrations of 1998 were peeled away, name by name. They had belonged to players assigned to help boost a franchise past 162 games for the first time in a decade, and when they missed their target by a Met-aphorical eyelash, they proceeded to vanish from collective memory without ceremony, no matter how slight of a fraction of the near-miss could be attributed to any one of them. Win as a team, lose as a readily disassemblable collection of individuals. Carlos Baerga left as a free agent. So did Armando Reynoso, who started and lost the last game of the five-game losing streak that ended the previous season. Hideo Nomo, who declined the opportunity to take that start after nearly three weeks of inactivity, was released. Butch Huskey went to Seattle. It was less than a purge, but it was more than your average offseason churn. Tony Phillips. Willie Blair. Jorge Fabregas. On and out they went, essentially to be never spoken of again in Met circles. That was the business of baseball. That was the way contenders were honed hopefully into champions. You can only save so many souvenirs of so many seasons that don't extend beyond their naturally allotted lives.

Mel Rojas was never the same pitcher after he gave up that home run to Paul O'Neill during the Subway Series; he was used nineteen mostly low-leverage times from July to September and gave up 25 earned runs. To be fair, he was never the same pitcher after he left Montreal and signed with the Cubs. As an Expo, he'd put together consecutive seasons of 30 and 36 saves. The market rewarded him with a three-year, $13.75 million contract. The

Cubs pawned his paper off on the Mets two-thirds of the way through 1997. They were stuck with him for one more year of it—more than four-and-a-half million dollars' worth—and wanted to shift the burden onto some other sucker.

Enter the Dodgers, who had a player they and their new manager Davey Johnson wished moved: Bobby Bonilla. Johnson and Bonilla weren't the best of Birds in Baltimore, and Davey retained the right to clean a little house at Chavez Ravine. In a classic Excedrin deal, the Mets and Dodgers swapped headaches. Rojas and his remaining year went to L.A., Bonilla flew home to New York packing a two-year commitment worth $11.8 million.

It would have seemed surreal had it not made a modicum of sense on the surface. The Mets needed a right fielder, and though Bobby Bo hadn't won any Gold Gloves, he was barely a year removed from 96 Marlin RBIs and a World Series ring. Besides, who doesn't like a good homecoming story?

A warmer tale would have been the happily-ever-after that might have awaited Todd Hundley once he healed from elbow surgery, but Todd wasn't going to find it in Mike Piazza's New York. What was left of Hundley's contract had to go, too, and it wound up, like Rojas, in the hands of the Dodgers, though this maneuver required a three-corner trade. Todd wound up in L.A., where he'd take the place of catcher Charles Johnson, who was sent to Baltimore. From all this moving and shaking, the Mets received speedy Dodgers outfielder Roger Cedeño and hard-throwing Orioles reliever Armando Benitez.

Other Mets additions for 1999 came via free agency. Robin Ventura, who'd survived the infamy surrounding the pounding he took from cranky Nolan Ryan in 1993, was signed to play third. The former White Sox star was certainly qualified, having earned five Gold Gloves in the American League, which made him a match for his new left-side partner, Rey Ordoñez. Rey now had two Gold Gloves in his portfolio, not to mention a VHS tape given to fans early in 1998 to celebrate his defensive prowess. *Rey O!* was primarily an extended highlight montage, interspersed with fielding lessons narrated by coach Cookie Rojas (Rey didn't speak much English). If ever a Met could get by on his glove, it was the dazzling shortstop with the lifetime .276 on-base percentage.

Robin's arrival in time for spring meant Edgardo Alfonzo, who was less of an offensive threat in 1998 than he'd been in '97, would move over to second, playing between Ordoñez and John Olerud. Assuming Fonzie was cool with his new position, the foursome shaped up as a formidable infield. And topping the lineup they, Piazza, Bonilla, and holdover Brian McRae would be part of was going to be perhaps the greatest leadoff hitter of all time, Rickey Henderson. Since setting the stage for Joe Carter's walk-off World Series home run in 1993, Rickey had bounced around a bit, and at forty, was a free agent once more. In his age thirty-nine season, he'd stolen 66 bases for Oakland, so his tank was judged reasonably full, and the Mets grabbed him for two years. They stayed in the experienced range to round out their starting rotation when they signed Orel Hershiser, also forty. It had been just over ten years since Hershiser put the Mets away in the seventh game of the 1988 NLCS. Perhaps his presence at Shea wouldn't trigger flashbacks.

"Are You Ready?" was the marketing slogan applied to the 1999 club, and anybody who cared about the Mets was prepared to step up in class. The playoffs, maybe the division, maybe even the World Series were in view. Nothing was out of the question after coming so close in '98 and adding so tactically for '99. These were the new Mets, resplendent in orange, blue, and a little more black (another alternate cap and jersey were added to their uniform mix) and featuring Piazza as their rock, their star, and their cleanup hitter. Mike was clearly their indispensable man.

Less than a week into the season, they were without him. He sprained a ligament in his right knee in Montreal during a game in which he drove in five runs and, to be as cautious as possible with their investment, the Mets put him on the DL. The home opener on April 12 would have to proceed without him, but the Mets were doing all right for star power in his absence. They had a Met legend on the field, albeit just for one pitch. Tom Seaver, who'd remained estranged from the Mets for most of the '90s, was back in the fold. He'd instructed pitchers informally in St. Lucie and was going to do color commentary on games broadcast over Channel 11 (the Mets had left Channel 9 after thirty-seven seasons). Tom replacing Tim McCarver in the booth sparked a little controversy—Bobby Valentine was said to be fed up with McCarver's criticisms—but The Franchise taking first pitch duties amid the pomp and circumstance of a Shea curtain-raiser was something no Mets maven could argue against.

Though disabled, Piazza was deemed healthy enough to show up at Shea, accept the good wishes of a sellout crowd, and catch one pitch of the ritualistic kind from Seaver, 41 to 31; good thing they were both so recognizable, since the Mets decided to tear the names off the backs of their jerseys this year. Fresno's own Bobby Jones did most of the rest of the throwing and even homered. The Mets beat the Marlins, 8–1, as Todd Pratt caddied ably for Piazza. Two nights later, it was Pratt who caught Franco in more ways than one, receiving his final strike of another Mets win and then letting the excitable lefty jump into his arms to celebrate the nailing down of Johnny's 400th career save. The Mets held the fort admirably during Piazza's absence, waiting for him with an 11–7 record and tied for first place when he returned to action at Wrigley Field in late April. But the difference Piazza made to a pretty good team became apparent soon.

On Wednesday night, April 28, the Mets trailed the Padres at Shea, 3–2, going to the bottom of the ninth. Trevor Hoffman was on for San Diego, which usually meant the lights were soon to go off for whomever he was about to face. Hoffman had blown a save the previous July and had absorbed a loss apiece in August and September. Otherwise (not counting the World Series), he was essentially perfect in 1998, recording 53 saves for the eventual National League champs. If the Padres led a game after eight—as they had on 181 regular-season occasions since the summer of 1996—they won that game. Most of it was Hoffman's doing. His reputation preceded and rarely exceeded him.

Yet against the Mets, Trevor was trumped. Olerud led off the home ninth with a line single and then Piazza's opposite-field power struck. Mike drove the first pitch he saw over the right-field wall, lifting both his arms in triumph before rounding the bases. The Mets were 4–3 winners and Mike had his first walk-off hit in a New York uniform.

Drama would be a constant Met companion as 1999 unfurled. When it was played to the hilt, it told you a season like few before it was happening in Flushing. On May 20, there was an 11–10 victory in a doubleheader opener over the Brewers at Shea and all the dizzying action that implies. Mike homered. Call-up Benny Agbayani, whose résumé included a stint in ReplaceMet camp as a minor leaguer in 1995 and year with Valentine at Norfolk in 1996, hit two. Ventura launched a grand slam as part of the onslaught, noteworthy enough on its own. But then, in the nightcap, Ventura hit another. Nobody had ever hit a grand slam in each end of a twin bill until a 1999 Met did it.

Three days later at home, a rather ordinary loss to the Phillies was concluding when the Mets jumped up and bit Curt Schilling for five runs in the ninth. The Philadelphia ace had a shutout going, and his manager Terry Francona stuck with him to the inconceivable end. No starter had been left in to take exactly that kind of loss—turning a four-run lead into an immediate loss in the ninth without relief help—since Herm Wehmeier, also of the Phillies, suffered the same fate in 1955. Things that happened every forty-four years happened to the '99 Mets.

Through their first two months, these Mets could be and often were remarkable. What bases Henderson wasn't stealing, his protégé Cedeño was. Agbayani was a revelation, hitting .500 after his first 30 at-bats, on his way to totaling 10 homers in his first 73 ABs of the year and gaining the kind of instant cult-hero status Shea once bestowed on the likes of Ron Swoboda. Benitez proved an ideal addition to the bullpen-laden late innings, bridging the gap between Wendell/Cook and Franco. Hershiser wasn't his old Cy self, but he could still toss a representative start more outings than not. Ventura, when not making home run history, anchored an infield transformed. Robin was elite at third, Rey was as spectacular as ever as short, Fonzie appeared to have been born to play second, and Olerud was his usual quiet excellent self at first. Piazza was Piazza, having recently homered in four consecutive games. After touching off the rally that snuffed out Schilling, he was a .313 hitter in a lineup where he didn't have to carry the entire load.

So much was going so well for the 1999 Mets as May neared its end that it was hard to believe how close they were to completely falling apart.

* * *

Drama gave way to melodrama as May gave way to June and a losing streak wouldn't cease. The Mets lost three in a row at home to Arizona. *Ah, whaddaya gonna do?* They lost three more in a row at Shea to Cincinnati. *Well, them's the breaks.* Then they traveled to the Bronx and lost the first two games of the first Subway Series of the year to the Yankees.

Oh, you can't do that.

The Yankees at Yankee Stadium simply might have been the wrong opponent in the wrong place for the Mets to keep losing to and at, for the rift between GM Phillips and manager Valentine was a fact of Met life before the team arrived in the Bronx on June 4. Despite his success lifting the Mets up in '97 and driving them as far as they could be driven in '98, Bobby V didn't make friends as much as he influenced ballgames. Not every player was his acolyte, not every reporter was his advocate and if this Mets team built to win was going to lose eight straight and slip one below .500 after 55 games, the front office (with ownership's support) was prepared to send him a message. In *The Godfather*, they used a horse's head. In baseball, they lower the guillotine on the manager's coaching staff.

Gone between Saturday afternoon and Sunday night at Yankee Stadium were pitching coach Bob Apodaca, hitting coach Tom Robson, and bull-pen coach Randy Niemann. They were Valentine guys, past tense. The field manager could stay, but the general manager was hovering. "Get the ship righted" was Phillips's command. The players, whatever their feelings about their skipper, needed to coalesce to save their season, never mind his job. Valentine, at least publicly, refused to be fazed, insisting, "I believe within the next fifty-five games if we're not better, I shouldn't be the manager."

Game one of the Bobby Valentine Employment Endangerment Act came on June 6, an ESPN telecast, a showcase for rebirth or *schadenfreude*, depending on which side of the Met fence you stood. The Yankees couldn't have presented more of an impediment had George Steinbrenner ordered it. Pitching for the Bombers was Roger Clemens, a figure who was imposing as he was mercenary in an era when baseball had plenty of personalities fitting both descriptions. Clemens, thirty-six, was on what amounted to his second Hall of Fame career. In the first one, for the Red Sox, the Rocket was the best pitcher in the American League, leading them to a World Series against the Mets in 1986. Then, after a dip, he reemerged several years later as yet somehow better, dominating the junior circuit for the Blue Jays in 1997 and '98. Roger had wanted out of Boston, took his leave, earned two Cy Youngs and then wished to be gone from Toronto. The Blue Jays, he noticed after two seasons, never went to the postseason anymore.

The Yankees did all the time, so that's who he wanted to pitch for in 1999. A trade about as big as the Piazza-for-everybody deal was engineered, sending another outsize character, David Wells, to Canada and bringing Clemens to the Bronx. Roger wasn't off to a blazing start in his new sur-roundings, but he was a Yankee, and that allowed a pitcher some leeway.

Entering his matchup with the Mets, the Rocket's ERA was 4.11, but his record was 5–0, meaning he hadn't been defeated in his previous 20 decisions dating back just over a year. Meanwhile, the Mets had been nothing but defeated since May 28.

In a trade that rivaled Wells-for-Clemens for headlines, the Mets and Yankees swapped roles on *Sunday Night Baseball*. The Rocket fizzled and the Bombers went silent. Derek Jeter, who carried his own streak of note—on base every one of the 53 games his team had played to date during this season—never saw first base. Clemens didn't see the fourth inning. After the Mets tagged him for four runs in the second (Bonilla and Agbayani each driving in a pair), Piazza took him over the Yankee Stadium wall for a two-run homer and a 6–0 lead two batters into the next inning. Joe Torre, like Francona for Philadelphia, gave his ace the benefit of the doubt, but it was wasted. Clemens gave up another run and had to be pulled with two out in the third, behind 7–0. Leiter, who hadn't been pitching all that well before this game (2–5, 6.39 ERA), found his form under new pitching coach Dave Wallace and cruised to a 7–2 win. Jeter's streak was over. Clemens's streak was over. The Mets' streak was over.

The Mets were a .500 club again. Valentine's self-imposed lease on life had 54 games to go.

* * *

After it had seemed the Mets were never going to win again, they got themselves into a groove in which they lost infrequently. Their streaks weren't endless, but their spurts were effective. Win a bunch, lose one, get back on the horse, keep their heads, and win a bunch more. Drama was still capable of becoming them, as evidenced by the evening of June 9 at Shea, when they were down, 3–0, to Wells and the Jays entering the ninth and appearing ready to go quietly into not such a good night. Wells couldn't untangle from the ninth, however, allowing two runners on bases, one of them—*Piazza!*—to steal and Ventura to drive them both in before McRae doubled Robin home. A whole new ballgame ensued for five more innings, but not without pausing to encompass something baseball was pretty sure it had never seen before . . . a manager in disguise.

Piazza inadvertently caused this sojourn into heretofore untrod territory by having catcher's interference called on him by Randy Marsh in the

12th. Valentine came out to argue and was ejected. Nothing unusual there; managers getting thrown out for contesting umpires' judgment is a grand baseball tradition. Everybody understands what happens next: the manager turns the lineup card over to a trusted lieutenant, heads down the tunnel, and disappears from view.

That didn't happen next, not with Bobby V. He went through the theater of vamoosing, but decided, in order "to loosen up the team for just a minute," to remove his uniform top, don a non-Mets cap, slip on a pair of shades and adorn his upper lip with a couple of strips of eyeblack mustache-style. That he did this while poking his incognito head into the dugout and getting picked up by television cameras is what made it something nobody had ever seen before. This was seen and it got the manager suspended for two games by the National League. Had the Mets not been in the midst of their new winning ways—they beat the Jays, 4–3 in 14—one imagines it could have gotten Valentine fired.

But first you'd have to imagine a manager doing what Valentine did to begin with, and nobody had nearly that much imagination.

What the Mets did have as they righted their ship was, as if it could be forgotten, the greatest-hitting catcher in captivity on board. Even while the Mets were losing, Piazza hit. As the Mets started winning, he hit. As they continued winning, he hit. On June 22, at Shea against the Marlins, he hit a home run off Vic Darensbourg in the bottom of the eighth, extending his hitting streak to 24 consecutive games, tying the team record set by Hubie Brooks in 1984. Mike was a .353 hitter over that span, a .326 batter overall, and well on his way to election as the NL's starting catcher for the sixth straight All-Star Game, his seventh celestial appearance in a row.

And while Piazza hit, the Mets continued to win. From the night they strafed Clemens at Yankee Stadium to the night they went down to Georgia for their first clash of the year with the Braves on June 25, they won fifteen of eighteen and pulled to within two games of eternally first-place Atlanta. Capturing their first game at Turner Field since July 13, 1997, felt awfully good, but apparently too unfamiliar to take, for the Mets dropped their next two and drifted four games from the top spot in their division.

The Braves visited Shea the first weekend of July and the width of the Mets' dramatic spectrum went on full display again. On Friday night, July

2, the Mets pitched both of their Francos, and since only John pitched for a living, you knew something was up . . . namely the visitors' side of the scoreboard. Atlanta pounded the Mets, 16–0, the worst shutout ever suffered by a franchise that had experienced its share of embarrassments since 1962. Matt Franco was a bullpen-saving contrivance (he'd pitched twice in the minors) in a game already blown out. John was getting some work in when he strained a tendon in left middle finger, one he'd be flipping toward fate soon enough, as he and his 19 saves were bound for a two-month stay on the DL.

Saturday afternoon brought more zeroes, the last of them perhaps the most vexing. Trailing Kevin Millwood all day, the ninth opened with a hint of a rally when McRae walked to lead off. Bobby Cox pulled Millwood with a 3–0 lead and sent in John Rocker, the closer the Braves had been looking for ever since they became perennial divisional titlists. Throwing harder than both Francos combined, the hulking lefty racked up 16 saves over the first three months of the season. He gave the Mets a little daylight, wild-pitching McRae to third and allowing a single to pinch-hitter Pratt. Alfonzo, Olerud, and Piazza were up next, as good a setup as the Mets could have asked for. Except Fonzie flied to center, Oly flied to left, and Mike struck out on three pitches.

The Fourth of July was about to blow up in the Mets' faces, too, with Hershiser getting knocked out in the third and the Braves building a 6–4 lead for John Smoltz. But in the seventh on this Sunday night, the Mets got their version of even, which is to say they took one of three from their archrivals. Still, it was a pretty sweet comeback, capped when Alfonzo smacked a three-run homer off Smoltz to put the Mets up, 7–6. Their temporary closer, Benitez, made the ninth look easier than any Franco ever did, striking out the side.

Maybe Armando wasn't so temporary after all. But maybe the second dalliance with Bonilla wasn't such a hot idea. After the Braves series, the club stuck Bobby Bo on the DL with a bad knee, though the most recurring pain was the one he was inflicting into the manager's rear end. With Cedeño and Agbayani emerging as a de facto platoon in right, Bonilla was now a pinch-hitter, which he didn't care to be. Valentine didn't much care for Bonilla. The feeling was mutual. There'd already been one shouting match between manager and player and there'd soon be another. "It hasn't worked out the way would've liked," was Phillips's characterization of the reacquisition of Bonilla, but at least Rojas was still gone.

* * *

On Friday night, July 9, the Yankees came calling. Another weekend, another heightened atmosphere at Shea. The Subway Series was in its third year, though for the first time it was a home-and-home affair. It was great box office, it generated immense passion, and it was a bigger pain to the world champs than Bonilla was to Valentine. The Yankees' attitude was they had bigger fish to fry than intracity bragging rights, and maybe they had a point. They had become the baseball embodiment of Jonathan Winters's character from that *Twilight Zone* episode in which the greatest pool player on Earth, since deceased, is constantly beckoned from the great beyond to take on every challenger who wants to wear his crown. In Rod Serling's world, Winters is relieved when a feisty Jack Klugman finally dethrones him.

In George Steinbrenner's world, such an attitude was anathema. Nevertheless, Joe Torre and his dynasty-defenders pretty much rolled their eyes and gritted their teeth at the thought that playing the Mets was any different from making a pitch against the Angels, the Royals, or anybody else who wandered across their field of vision. For the Mets, these were vital dates on the calendar, in that every game was a must-win a year after missing the postseason by one game.

For Mets fans, especially on their own turf, it would have been inaccurate to call the Subway Series life and death, because that would have understated the importance they placed on beating the Yankees. And if any extra incentive was needed in the stands, it could be found on the mound, where the man throwing for the team from across town was someone whose mere presence had been rubbing them the wrong way for thirteen years.

Roger Clemens was back at Shea. It wasn't the first time since the 1986 World Series. He'd returned in September of 1997 as a Blue Jay and got lit up. The crowd wasn't half what it would be for the Yankees, but the venom left over from his pair of Series starts was surprisingly durable. Fitting Clemens for pinstripes hadn't made him any more lovable in the interim. Amid a 2–2 game in the sixth, all Mets apparel would be sized XS, as in Extra Satisfying. Clemens was still pitching. The same crew that fizzled versus Rocker was up. They did better this time around. Fonzie singled. Oly walked. Mike . . . well, Mike ripped a 2–1 pitch over the left-center field wall and into the Picnic Area seats for a 5–2 Mets lead that eventually became a 5–2 Mets win.

For the slightest instant, Piazza—his face still in full grunt from the swing—paused to watch its lining arc, the knob of his bat frozen belt-high as if it was a sword ready for its scabbard. The man in the mask behind him, Jorge Posada, was up on his feet, staring in awe through his equipment, appearing to wonder how somebody who crouched as much as he did had enough strength left over to hit a ball that hard.

Posada and his fellow Bombers would do all right for themselves in power department the next afternoon. The Yankees spent Saturday in the Mets' park dropping homer after homer behind the fence. Through six and a half innings, they'd drilled five of them, positioning Andy Pettitte for a win. It was 6–4 for the visitors and their relievers were lining up to do what they usually did, get the ball to Mariano Rivera. The first man in Torre's bucket brigade was Ramiro Mendoza, who sandwiched two outs around a Henderson double and then walked Olerud, which brought Piazza to the plate as the potential go-ahead run.

Nobody had a greater knack for fulfilling his potential than No. 31 in home whites. What he hit was so prodigious that it required both Mets radio men to call it completely.

> BOB MURPHY: *The two-one pitch . . . HIGH FLY ball hit deep to left field . . . way, way back, it's going . . . yah, there it goes! Mike Piazza, three-run homer!*
> GARY COHEN: *Oh my goodness!*
> MURPHY: *Where did that land?*
> COHEN: *It hit the picnic tent, beyond the left-field bullpen, about halfway up on the picnic tent roof!*

The tape measures said it flew 482 feet. The emotional sensors of July 10 indicated it landed on the moon. The Mets were leading, 7–6, and there was no way they couldn't win after a lunar shot like that.

Except two more innings remained, and nobody told the Yankees home run derby was over. Posada, who'd gone deep in the fifth, had another dinger in him in the eighth, this one with a man on. The Yankees took an 8–7 lead to the bottom of the ninth. It would take a dramatic comeback to make the day right in Flushing.

But who generated more drama in Queens than its ballclub in residence? Rivera came on and retired McRae, but then walked Henderson (Rickey was on base five times in five plate appearances). Alfonzo lofted a fly ball to deep center that Bernie Williams, mysteriously in possession of a pair of Gold Gloves, couldn't track down. It went for a double. Rickey, being careful, stopped at third. Olerud might have been walked intentionally in an alternate universe, but putting John on would have loaded the bases for Mike. Bad idea. Rivera pitched to him and grounded him out. The runners stayed frozen. Now an intentional walk was issued, to Piazza. The bases were loaded, but there were two out and the .067-hitting rookie Melvin Mora was due up. Valentine, though, had managed to hold in reserve Matt Franco for what Matt Franco did best: pinch-hit. On a 1–2 pitch from the consensus best reliever in baseball, Matt lined a single into right. Henderson scored. Alfonzo raced home. O'Neill fired in. The play at the plate . . .

Fonzie slid in safe ahead of the throw. The Mets were 9–8 winners, taking the Subway Series for anybody who was keeping track, which most definitely included the solid majority of 53,792 in attendance who did not want to walk down Shea's ramps goaded by the braying (and substantial) Yankee-supporting minority. It didn't solve the season and it didn't catch the Braves—and it's hard to say it won them back their city for more than a moment—but after two games, two Piazza blasts, and hundreds of thousands of sore throats incurred, Mets fans had everything to shout about, partying precisely because it was 1999.

LIFE IN THE CITY
AT CENTURY'S END
July 13, 1999–October 16, 1999

After the All-Star teams were announced, Bobby Valentine said he planned to use his own All-Star lineup in the Mets' next game, which was a joke, son, because the only Met named to the National League squad was Mike Piazza. A lot of Mets were having very good years, but only Piazza won enough votes to start at Fenway Park and once the NL had its Met, its quota was filled. Given the 1998 expansion and concomitant shift of the Brewers into the senior circuit, sixteen teams had to be accounted for, so even though great cases could be made all over the infield for additional Mets—especially the recently offensively competent Rey Ordoñez, someone perfectly suited to put on a fielding exhibition in an exhibition game—Piazza would represent the Mets by himself.

Major League Baseball was going all out to close out the twentieth century. With millennium fever gripping imaginations, MLB decided the 1999 All-Star Game was the perfect platform to introduce an All-Century Team . . . or introduce the players who could make the All-Century Team if you, the fans at home, voted them in. To make an awe-inspiring gathering just a little less special, the powers that be named its one hundred greatest players of the past hundred years, invited all who were living to Fenway, had them tip a cap before the All-Star Game, and then dared baseball fans to vote on which ones were extra, *extra* special. The cream of the crop would be introduced before Game Two of the 1999 World Series, which would be in the National League park, which, if the Mets stayed hot, might very well be Shea Stadium.

Even though they had only one All-Star, and even though that All-Star, who was regularly referred to as the greatest-hitting catcher ever, Piazza did not make the All-Century cut. Service time best explained Mike's omission. Nobody active among the hundred honored at Fenway had less than a decade in the books. The latest-debuting Centurion, if you will, was Ken Griffey Jr., who came up in 1989 and would be, if he announced his retirement on the spot, eligible for the Hall of Fame ballot five years hence. Griffey had ten years in, and was considered a lock. Piazza was in his eighth season. He could wait.

The focus of immortality at Fenway on the night of the All-Star Game rightly belonged to the player most identified with the hosts and their park, No. 9 for the Red Sox from 1939 through 1960, Ted Williams. Mike's connection to Teddy Ballgame was pretty strong, dating to that bit of scouting Williams did of teenaged Mike at Vince Piazza's behest. Now the car dealer's son was a perennial All-Star, one of those mingling with the Splendid Splinter at the end of the century, both of them embroidered into the fabric of this once-in-a-hundred-years celebration of the national pastime.

Pedro Martinez started and won the All-Star Game for the American League. Mike got a hit off David Cone. Nobody homered. The result didn't matter. Ted Williams rising from a golf cart with help from Tony Gwynn to throw a first pitch to Carlton Fisk while Willie Mays, Hank Aaron, Stan Musial, Tom Seaver, Ralph Kiner, Rickey Henderson, and so many others for whom "star" wasn't nearly enough of a descriptor looked on is what lingered.

That time, the feeling counted.

* * *

On August 6, the New York Mets were in first place in the Eastern Division with a mark of 67–43, reflecting a 17–4 run after the All-Star break, meaning that, yes, they had gone 40–15 when Valentine said they could go 40–15. Whether their fearless leader was confident in his players, his acumen, or just due for the scales of luck to tip his way, the word he gave to the media was gold. Bobby Valentine deserved to be hailed as genius, at least until the next time he or his team screwed up.

The club that completed the 55-game sprint as Bobby V projected it wasn't exactly the same unit that started it. Steve Phillips, as was his charge every July, stayed busy, parlaying that skill set into roster-enhancement. As well as the Mets were doing, they needed help. They were the Mets. They always needed help.

Four deals were done in an eight-day span, three of them on deadline. The first move made was aimed at deepening the starting rotation. Phillips swapped outfield prospect Terrence Long to Oakland for Kenny Rogers, the veteran lefty who hadn't flourished in New York as a Yankee, but looked like a reasonable bet to supplement Al Leiter, Rick Reed, Orel Hershiser, Masato Yoshii, and rookie Octavio Dotel. Bobby Jones was out with an injury, Dotel had been alternately brilliant and abysmal since his promotion in June, and everybody else had been too inconsistent for comfort.

Then came the July 31 barrage. With John Franco still out, the bullpen needed another lefty. The Mets got the arm they thought they needed in Chuck McElroy from Colorado. He came along with a pretty good outfielder, Darryl Hamilton. Phillips gave up a reliever and outfielder of his own—Rigo Beltran and Brian McRae—to get that one done. The GM wasn't finished fortifying the bullpen or dealing with the A's. In his second trade with Oakland, he sent Greg McMichael and Jason Isringhausen—Generation K giving up the ghost again—for Billy Taylor, who had collected 26 saves for a non-contender. If he and McElroy could take a little pressure off Benitez, Wendell, and Cook, a worry would be reduced. The final deal was for the bench: Tides outfielder Craig Paquette to the Cardinals for Brooklyn's own Shawon Dunston. Seventeen years before, Shawon was chosen first in the nation by the Cubs, four picks ahead of Dwight Gooden. It wasn't a bad pick, as Dunston's arm at shortstop became almost as legendary as Doc's was on the mound. In more recent years, Shawon had been sticking around as utilityman. As a Met, he, like Hamilton, would be looked upon to shore up the outfield.

So much fluctuation in such a short time could lead to introductions on the fly. Witness what happened at Wrigley Field when Taylor made his Mets debut in extra innings, literally meeting his catcher, Todd Pratt, on the mound. Their exchange, according to the receiver, went as follows:

"What's up, dude? What do you have?"

"Sinker, slider, changeup."

"OK, let's go."

The Mets went on to win that game in 13 when long man Pat Mahomes drove in the go-ahead run—"I always hit well in high school"—and then stayed on to protect his own lead.

That's the sort of thing that happens when your manager says you'll win forty out of fifty-five and you do.

* * *

Piazza now and then needed a day off, but the one place where the Mets didn't need to make trades or even substitutions was the infield. As a foursome, they were becoming almost as famous as Mike was by himself. You couldn't miss them, making highlight play after highlight play. Their defense landed them on the cover of *Sports Illustrated*, Ordoñez, Olerud, Alfonzo, and Ventura grouped together next to a question: "The Best Infield Ever?" While Rey-Rey wasn't on a par batwise with his compadres, all four were airtight behind their pitchers. Unearned runs were becoming as rare in Flushing as stamps with upside-down airplanes.

Infield defense wasn't the club's only calling card. The statistics Mets batters had posted through five-sixths of the season were staggering. Every regular and semi-regular but Ordoñez and Benny Agbayani was batting well over .300. Taking Henderson's tutelage to heart, Cedeño broke Mookie Wilson's stolen base record, swiping his 59th the same night Alfonzo went 6-for-6 at the plate. Piazza had already cracked the 100-RBI barrier for the fifth time in his career; the only times he didn't reach triple-digits were when strikes shortened seasons. Fonzie wasn't far behind him and Ventura was actually ahead of him.

On a team featuring several standouts, Robin was performing like its MVP: .308–29–108 as September set in and the go-to guy for the quotes Mike wasn't anxious to dispense. Despite being the superstar among stars, Piazza acknowledged a "moody" side where the media was concerned, whereas Ventura projected calm veteran leadership. His greatest clubhouse contribution, to say nothing of mark on Mets lore, may have been his injection of The Doors' "L.A. Woman" as the team's unlikely theme song. Of particular interest was the refrain, "Mr. Mojo Risin'," which somehow fit the mood of a team capable of exuding that certain something.

The erstwhile L.A. Man had quite a return to Dodger Stadium on September 9. Piazza took Kevin Brown deep, significant not just for the catcher's 34th homer of the season, but symbolically powerful in that it was Brown (in the way salary box scores are kept) who got the big money from News Corp. that Mike had asked for. You get what you don't pay for, apparently. In the background of the Piazza passion play, the Mets had Hershiser reaching back to 1988 and outdueling Brown the rest of the evening and Cedeño robbing Gary Sheffield of a home run. All the ex-Dodgers weren't getting mad, they were getting even. Even Benitez, who became a Met via the three-way trade that wound its way through L.A., got in on the action, notching his 19th save.

Armando had proven a godsend in Franco's absence, so effective as a closer that Valentine stayed with his hotter, harder-throwing hand upon John's return. The Mets needed all the bullpen depth they could get since one element suspiciously lacking from their mojo was length out of their starters. In their first 118 contests, they had thrown exactly zero complete games. Rogers put an end to that bizarre footnote on August 15 in San Francisco and made his team-leading total two when he shut the Giants out at Shea a few weeks later. It wasn't blasphemy to suggest Kenny had also been heaven-sent . . . or at least a savvy pickup from Oakland.

Despite the flashes of brilliance going off all around the diamond and up and down the batting order, the Mets could not hold on to first place. After the 40–15 stretch, they cooled off somewhat, going 25–15 over their next 40. It was just tepid enough a pace to allow Atlanta to hop back over them by a game with two weeks to go. The Braves were that stack of papers that you never fully cleared from your desk. They were just always there. Yet the Mets had not been shredded. New York sat only one game from the top of the division after defeating Philadelphia on September 19 and had the most golden opportunity they could have asked for directly in front of them: three games at Turner Field starting on the twenty-first, and three more versus their tormentors at Shea beginning the twenty-eighth. The National League East would never be more open to new management. And even if the Mets could do no more than play the Braves to a stalemate, at least they had a line on the wild card. This wasn't shaping up anything like 1998. With a dozen games remaining, the Mets led the Reds by four for that at-large playoff berth. It was hard to conceive of a worst-case scenario that would be all that bad for those whose mojo had jaggedly yet steadily risen throughout 1999.

*　*　*

Within a week and a half, the Mets had created a worst-case scenario that was all bad and left their heretofore wonderful season shaping up exactly like 1998.

They're not called Amazin' for nothin'.

Three games at Turner Field became three losses at Turner Field, a.k.a. business as usual. Chipper Jones, a leading MVP candidate, sealed his award along with the undying disdain of an entire fan base by bashing the Mets soundly and silly. Jones—actual first name Larry, but everyone persisted in calling this grown man Chipper—homered twice in the first game to literally make all the difference in a 2–1 Braves win; put Atlanta up immediately with a first-inning two-run shot in his team's ensuing 5–2 victory; and crushed the three-run game-changer in the 6–3 finale.

Four home runs. Seven runs batted in. On base seven times in 12 plate appearances. Call the man anything he wants to be called.

The Mets, who went down 1–2–3 by scoring only one, two, and three runs, had ceased to be their trademark offensive machine selves. Piazza drove in three of the Mets' six runs with home runs in the second and third games, but he was outshone by Jones and unsupported by mates. They were facing John Smoltz, Tom Glavine, and Greg Maddux, all of whom had been lowering batting averages throughout the 1990s, but slumping was becoming a team-wide epidemic, particularly among its stars. Each of the top five stalwarts who had kept the lineup aloft across a long season—Henderson, Alfonzo, Olerud, Piazza, and Ventura—saw his stats plummeting as the team moved on to Philadelphia for three against the Phillies . . . three losses.

Mojo was sinking. Mike, like everybody else in black, blue, and orange, was struggling. No hits on Friday night or Saturday afternoon, a single and double to no avail on Sunday afternoon, along with three bases stolen against thirty-one-year-old No. 31. Usually Pratt would have gotten one of the day games, but rest was for winter, a season whose arrival the Mets were desperately trying to stave off.

That task was made more difficult by what was going on elsewhere. The Braves hadn't stopped winning since polishing off the Mets in Atlanta, and they clinched their fifth straight NL East title by sweeping Montreal. There went one path to the postseason. The wild card was slipping away, too. In fact, it was out of the Mets' immediate grasp with one week remaining on their schedule. Cincinnati got Red hot and passed the Mets in the secondary standings. The Reds were now nipping at the heels of the Central-leading Astros, suddenly turning the wild-card derby into a three-team race uncomfortably reminiscent of 1998's stretch run. The difference here was at least one team between the Reds and Astros would go to the postseason. The Mets had no ticket punched.

On Tuesday, September 28, the Mets opened their final homestand of 1999 by reluctantly welcoming the Braves to Shea. A blink beforehand, this was supposed to help settle the division. The division was settled. The Braves were now an impediment to the Mets catching up to Houston and Cincinnati, each of them 1 1/2 games up on New York. The only saving grace in the opener was that the Reds and Astros were playing one another, so somebody besides the Mets had to lose.

Unfortunately, the Mets lost once more, their seventh in a row. It was ugly. Hershiser pitched one-third of an inning and was pulled amid a four-run Brave onslaught in the top of the first. Dennis Cook pitched a fit at a ball four call from home plate ump Alfonso Marquez in the eighth and was ejected. Mike brought home two runs on fielder's choice groundouts, but they amounted to two drops in an ocean of pain. The Mets lost, 9–3. Their seventh straight defeat kept them 1 1/2 behind the Astros, who had fallen to the Reds and out of first in their sector.

After doing little against Glavine, they faced Maddux. It was one dandy assignment after another for a team flailing into oblivion and, sure enough, the Mets were trailing, 2–1, after three. Finally, fate got bored torturing the home team and gave them a break. Six consecutive Mets batters—including .111-hitter Leiter—singled versus Maddux to build a 4–2 lead and load the bases for Olerud. John quadrupled the Shea crowd's pleasure by launching a grand slam to make it 8–2. Maddux was still on the mound for some reason when Piazza came up and singled. Greg said good night, the Mets said thank goodness. The losing streak without end ended at last. And with the Reds losing to the Astros, the wild card was still 1 1/2 games away.

Mike Piazza introduced himself to Shea Stadium as the kind of opponent Mets fans could only dream of one day calling their own.

Billy Wagner threw hard. Mike Piazza swung harder. The result of their September 1998 confrontation was a home run that kept the Mets aloft in their quest for the wild card.

Playing in New York agreed enough with Piazza that he consented to a lucrative seven-year deal with Met owners Nelson Doubleday and Fred Wilpon.

He wasn't known for his defense, but Mike absolutely threw himself into his catching.

Mike was used to being the center of attention during walk-off celebrations, such as when he took Trevor Hoffman deep in April 1999, yet he was a dazed bystander to the most dramatic moment of that most dramatic year as Melvin Mora scored on the wild pitch that saved the Mets' season.

Piazza time and again got the best of Roger Clemens. If Clemens couldn't get Piazza out, he thought he could sit him down. The Rocket's 2000 message pitch was not well received.

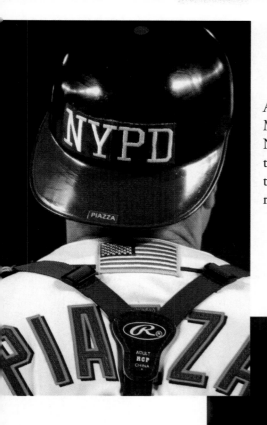

After September 11, 2001, all of the Mets found themselves standing up for New York's heroes. Piazza's home run ten days after the tragedy was destined to stand as a symbol of the city's resilience.

Above: His contract said it was time for him to go, but Mets fans didn't want to let Mike go so easily.

Left: Mets fans didn't stop embracing their main man just because he had begun dressing in strange clothing.

Piazza and Seaver, the two Met legends who came together to Shea Goodbye in 2008, reconnected upon Citi Field's opening in 2009.

Upon induction to the team's hall of fame in 2013, Mike counted Mets fans among his truest of friends.

While Ken Griffey Jr. gravitated to his first team in Cooperstown, Mike felt he belonged eternally in the cap of the franchise that traded for him.

Everything was coming up apples in 2016, as Piazza not only went into the National Baseball Hall of Fame, but saw No. 31 rise to the rafters in Flushing.

Thursday night, though, did to mojo what graters do to cheese. Alfonzo homered in the eighth to knot the game at three, which should have been a sign of wonderful things to come. Instead, in the bottom of the ninth, John Rocker, who seemed to be growing in stature and intimidation with every appearance, struck out Piazza, Ventura, and Hamilton to send the game to extra innings. The top of the 11th was where the whole affair imploded when Dunston, a helping hand since his acquisition, misplayed a Brian Jordan fly ball into a triple. Ozzie Guillen brought him home on a sac fly, then the Mets were silenced by Terry Mulholland in the bottom of the inning.

Left in the ruins of another Mets-Braves series were a 4–3 loss, a two-game wild-card deficit with three to play, and Chipper Jones shoving it in the faces of Mets loyalists by suggesting that those who taunted him could now "go home and put their Yankees stuff on." Combined with the numbers he put up at Turner Field a week earlier, those words triggered a grudge at Shea that figured to last at least as long as the building in which they were uttered.

The Mets weren't dead, but their impression of deceased was quite convincing. Only the 1962 Giants had entered the final three games of a season two games from a postseason berth (first place in the National League in those pre-division days) and made all the hay necessary to see October for real.

* * *

In the 1989 movie *Major League*, making the playoffs is portrayed as a simple matter of wanting it enough. "I guess there's only thing left to do," Cleveland catcher Jake Taylor confidently commands his teammates at a pivotal point. "Win the whole [bleeping] thing." It works because it's a movie. In 1999 major-league reality, it helped to have a catcher whose big stick did his talking.

On Friday night, October 1, Mike Piazza's bat cleared its throat effectively, speaking up in opposition to the Pirates' Jason Schmidt in the sixth inning with a home run that put the Mets up, 2–0, in their must-est win of the season. Two innings earlier, Ventura had taken Schmidt deep (only his second homer since September 4). Meanwhile, Rogers was shutting down the Bucs. Kenny kept them completely off the board through seven. In the eighth, though, the Pirates scored a pair off a combination of Rogers,

Wendell, and Franco to tie it. It inched very close to worse until John—and his catcher, who knew how to frame a pitch, steal a strike, and get a call—struck out Adrian Brown looking with the bases loaded and a full count. The deadlock endured until the 11th, when Ventura, who had played in every game this season but two despite torn cartilage in his left knee and a bruised rotator cuff in his right shoulder, batted with the bases loaded and singled in Dunston.

Baseball movies rarely mention what happens where the camera isn't pointed. For the fictional Indians to succeed in *Major League*, it is implied they did it all themselves. Of course to catch the team in front of them (the Yankees), that team had to lose. Back in real life, as great as it was that they'd secured their first necessary victory over Pittsburgh—"Somebody's doing CPR to us, baby," Rogers exuded in the provisionally jubilant clubhouse; "We're breathing! Clear! We have a pulse!"—there was still the paramount concern attached to whatever the Reds were doing in Milwaukee and the Astros were up to while hosting the Dodgers.

Had a second unit been dispatched to the Astrodome and County Stadium, it would have filmed nothing but good news from those remote locations. The Dodgers were easy winners over the Astros. The Brewers were engaged in a tenser standoff versus the Reds. The Mets, however, discovered they had a friend in beer places. With two Reds out and two Reds on in the top of the 10th, center fielder Marquis Grissom dove and robbed Eddie Taubensee of a sure go-ahead hit. Grissom's grab kept the game tied at three and set the stage for the Brewers to win it in the bottom of the inning. The Mets were now just one game out of the wild card with two to go.

Cincinnati played Saturday afternoon and lost again, 10–6, dropping them a half-game behind Houston and, of utmost consideration in Flushing, a half-game ahead of the Mets. As quickly as the Mets' demise was rumored, they found themselves capable of pushing themselves into the playoffs. If they beat the Pirates Saturday night and again Sunday afternoon, the least they'd have coming to them was a play-in game against somebody. But they had to beat the Pirates Saturday night to craft that much control of their own destiny.

For five innings, it was a pitchers' duel, Rick Reed and Francisco Cordova trading zeroes. In the bottom of the sixth, Mets hitters barged in on the duel. Olerud walked to lead off. Piazza reached on an error and Ventura doubled to score Oly. At last, a run . . . but not the last run. Piazza would come home on another error to make it 2–0. Things stayed close until the eighth when a single by Cedeño and a double from Ordoñez set up a two-run single off the bat of Reed, still in there, still pitching the game of his life. Rick would eventually be driven in from third by Olerud and, on the swing that produced his 40th home run of the season, Piazza drove John and himself in to bring the score to 7–0. Reed went out to finish what he started, ending it on his 12th strikeout of the evening. With the fourth complete game and second shutout thrown by any Mets pitcher in 1999, they found themselves tied for the wild card after 161 contests. The Astros also won, separating themselves a bit from the fray, leading the NL Central by a game over the Reds.

Therefore, Sunday, October 3, shaped up this way: The Mets had to win the whole [bleeping] thing, that thing being the only game they had left on their schedule. It dovetailed perfectly with the Bobby Valentine philosophy that the most important game the team would play all season would be the next game they played, because (give or take a doubleheader) it was the only game they were playing that night or day. It was a stock answer of the manager's, yet for once it was indisputable. The Mets had to win.

They had the ideal pitcher going for them if 1999 were 1988. Orel Hershiser had already pitched too many games of his life for anyone to expect another one to materialize out of thin air or his now forty-one year-old arm. As if to accent Orel's experience, fate—and Pirate manager Gene Lamont—matched him up with a hotshot rookie, Kris Benson, the No. 1 pick in the nation three years earlier. Benson was concluding a solid introductory season, in which he'd posted 11 wins already, including a complete game 5–1 decision over these very Mets at Shea in late July.

Well, it wasn't "these very Mets," exactly, and not just because there'd been some roster turnover during the previous two months. The night Benson beat the Mets was Mercury Mets night, part of a Major League Baseball tie-in with real estate concern Century 21. Some (but not all) teams agreed to dress up in supposedly futuristic uniforms meant to represent what baseball would look like in the far-off year of 2021. Most participating clubs incorporated some element of their current insignias. The Mets went about 21 steps further and reinvented themselves as a team from another planet. They may have appeared the most futuristic, but the game that night belonged to the pitcher who seemed to have the brightest of futures ahead of him. Benson beat not only Mercury Mets on July 27 but bested his ancient rival . . . Orel Hershiser.

Hershiser had only gotten older and thrown more innings since then. His last outing, against Atlanta five nights earlier, was a disaster. Age was going to have to find its second wind against youth. With Orel on the mound and Mike behind the plate, the Mets gave up the dinkiest of first-inning runs on a walk to Al Martin, a sacrifice bunt to move Martin to second, a groundout that held Martin at second, a steal of third by Martin and a single to center to score Martin. Never mind the Mercury Mets. The team would definitely not be hosting a *My Favorite Martin* night in 2000.

They still had matters to attend to in this century, however, and Hershiser put the first inning and any lingering concerns from the Braves game behind him. He began to retire the Pirates with ease, shutting them out through the fourth, a span during which Benson was doing the same to the Mets. New York broke through in the bottom of the fourth, though, manufacturing a Martinesque run of their own on a leadoff error that placed Olerud on second, a fly to right from Piazza that moved the glacial first baseman to third and, one out later, a double from Hamilton.

The game that would determine the Mets future here on Earth stayed tied as 50,111 craved positive resolution. Everybody pitched well—Benson through seven and Jason Christiansen in the eighth for the Bucs; Orel for five, then Cook, Mahomes, Wendell (2.2 IP), and Benitez to bring the 1–1 duel and all its attendant tension to the bottom of the ninth. Little about the wild-card race had been resolved, except that Houston probably needn't worry about it any longer. At the final regular-season game played inside the Astrodome, Mike Hampton was given four runs in the bottom of the first and cruised toward his 22nd win. The Reds were waiting out a rain delay in Milwaukee. Sunday losses by the Mets and Reds would force a one-game playoff, but the Mets couldn't count on the Brewers to do their dirty work for them a third consecutive day. The Mets needed to win the game they were playing, the only game they were playing today.

Valentine decided, or at least hoped their best chance to do it right away was via the bat of Bobby Bonilla. Bobby Bo resurfaced once the rosters were expanded in September. His 14-year career encompassed 277 home runs so far, including one season when he homered once approximately every 15 at-bats. That was in 1993, a year that felt as far removed from 1999 in a Mets context as theoretical 2021 did in the other direction. Six years before this very day, the 1993 Mets—the team whose lone, ornery All-Star was Bobby Bonilla—were finishing out a 103-loss season in the rain in Miami. The manager was Dallas Green, and when he wanted a pinch-hitter in the ninth inning, he called on Dwight Gooden.

The Mets had come a long way from the day the umpires told the Mets to never mind, just go home when the rain grew too intense over Joe Robbie Stadium. Yet here was one of their few survivors from that team (if not that day—his 1993 had ended weeks earlier) entrusted to push the Mets where they hadn't been since 1988. Bonilla had the credentials to hit a ball over a fence against the new Pirates reliever, Greg Hansell, but they were gathered in another time. In 1999, Bonilla had totaled four home runs, none since June 2. For that matter, he had only 19 base hits the whole year. It had been a miserable homecoming for Bobby Bo.

It would be a great story if he mimicked what another Bobby did on this date forty-eight years before. On October 3, 1951, Bobby Thomson won the pennant for the New York Giants, a detail a third Bobby—Valentine—knew intimately given that his father-in-law was the Brooklyn Dodgers pitcher who gave up that Shot Heard Round the World, Ralph Branca. So many forces aligning had to mean something.

Or not. Bonilla grounded out to first.

The batting order turned over, which would usually mean Rickey Henderson was up, except Henderson and his résumé were out of the game, and Melvin Mora was batting in his place. Mora's entire offensive career to date consisted of 38 plate appearances, four bases on balls, and four base hits. This was not a case of dancing with them what brung you. This tango, though, was going to be with the rookie Valentine brought in as a pinch-runner. Mora had never faced a situation exactly like this in his brief big-league career, which also meant he had never failed in a situation exactly like this.

Mora singled down the right-field line. The kid was a natural.

Now came the portion of the order that had defined the 1999 Mets season, the fellas who made the mojo rise and the guys who would be given one more opportunity to keep it airborne: Alfonzo, Olerud, Piazza, Ventura. Somewhere inside those bats had to be the one hit or walk or sacrifice fly or something to push across the run that would guarantee the season's continuation.

Alfonzo did his part, singling to right and sending the exceptionally wheeled Mora to third.

Olerud would not be permitted to do any part except stand still for four intentional balls. His run, as they say, meant nothing, and if the tactic worked, could result in a double play and a 10th inning. At the very least, there was the chance to get a force at any base. Lamont was in no hurry to get to the offseason.

Piazza would not face Hansell, his minor league roommate. Lamont took him out and brought in Brad Clontz, a Met for a few minutes in 1998 after he was acquired alongside Hideo Nomo. Mike had caught Clontz in Los Angeles. The runner on third, Mora, had played with him at Norfolk and, as Jack Curry had detailed in the *Times*, knew Brad's tendencies. With a double play in order, Melvin looked for his former teammate's slider grip. A slider meant a ball aimed in the dirt. If it tempted Piazza to swing, it could get the grounder Pittsburgh wanted. If it got too much dirt, though, that could be a problem for the Pirates.

Mora watched carefully from third and was ready to go when he saw Clontz's fingers align for a slider. Piazza, stood in the batter's box, sought a pitch he could drive and then, he . . .

He did absolutely nothing. There was nothing for the Mets' superstar to do, because that slider Mora looked for bounced in the dirt and got away from Pirates catcher Joe Oliver. Mora sprinted toward the plate. Piazza instinctively waved him in and then wandered out of the way. Melvin crossed on Clontz's wild pitch and was mobbed by teammates and cheered by fans. The Mets were 2–1 winners. They had done the improbable, if not the impossible. They rose from the dead and guaranteed themselves a 163rd game, either in Cincinnati if the Reds won or Arizona to start the NLDS if the Reds lost. They didn't know where they were going in the hours to come, which was apropos, since Piazza seemed not to know where he was going at that very moment.

The player traded for and then signed to get the Mets into the playoffs—to be at bat when the Mets were on the cusp of making the playoffs—couldn't be accused of not doing what he was supposed to do. He came to bat with the winning run on third and the winning run scored. That the Met on whom so much hope was projected succeeded in the role of innocent bystander was either ironic or just the way baseball sometimes goes.

Mike emerged from his daze and eventually joined in the jubilation that enveloped Shea, even though the fans and players were vigorously toasting something shy of a postseason, even if Piazza admitted, "It was hard to compute right then" what had happened.

It was the shock heard round the wild-card race, and it was enough to put the Mets on a plane to somewhere.

* * *

Their destination turned out to be Cincinnati. The Astros indeed clinched their third consecutive division title and guaranteed themselves a date with the Braves. The Reds and Brewers waited out one of history's longest rain delays until County Stadium was deemed dry enough for one more 162nd game. Pete Harnisch, who'd started for the Mets on Opening Day 1997 only to learn he could not co-exist with Valentine and be traded by September, easily beat Milwaukee, setting up the game that would decide whether the Mets of Mike Piazza were really and truly a playoff team.

The Mets and Reds were each 96–66, each worthy of the postseason. The wild card was supposed to solve the October omission of obviously strong teams. Whoever lost this one-game playoff would become the best team since the 103–59 Giants of 1993 to be left out of the fall fun. It would be a shame for the losers. It would be validation for the winners.

For the Mets, it would mean the seven-game losing streak of September wasn't fatal, just as the eight-game losing streak of May and June didn't torpedo their summer, just as the five-game losing streak that wound down 1998 could be forgotten. Beat the Reds, and the story of the 1999 Mets is one of resiliency, the stuff of 1969 and 1973 and October 1986.

Lose to the Reds and—nah, the Mets had come too far to think like that. The same thing was probably said on behalf of the Reds in Cincinnati, of course. Jack McKeon had led a team that had gone 77–85 in '98 to the brink of the very same golden ticket Valentine's troops were on the verge of capturing. They'd had a helluva year, and it would be all kinds of unfair that they'd get nothing for their troubles if they lost to the Mets.

Provincialism solved any and all moral dilemmas where Mets fans were concerned when Game 163 began encouragingly on Monday night, October 4. Rickey Henderson singled to lead off versus Steve Parris and Edgardo Alfonzo homered. Two batters, two runs and a two-run lead to deposit in the hands of Al Leiter.

What Leiter did with it became, in Piazza's words, "maybe the best game I ever caught." Al walked his first batter, Pokey Reese, but then teased fly balls to left out of Barry Larkin and Sean Casey before striking out Greg Vaughn. The one-out single he gave up to Jeffrey Hammonds in the second would be the only hit the Reds would record that inning, and the only hit they'd collect off him until the ninth, by which time New York led, 5–0. A minor threat was quelled and Leiter completed the shutout that boosted the Mets into their first postseason in eleven years.

This was a team effort. All teams that achieve something of substance say such things, but when you reach your heretofore unreachable goal by the skinniest skin of your teeth, you can't discount anybody's contribution. Melvin Mora was a .161 hitter, but where would the Mets be without his fifth major-league hit from Sunday? Bobby Bonilla was a .160 hitter and perhaps a net negative, but on April 20, at the very same Cinergy Field in Cincinnati where a 163rd game was played, he launched a solo home run to lead off the seventh inning against Harnisch. The Mets won that game by one run. The 97–66 Mets won this wild card by one game. Yes, a team effort.

At the center of the operation was someone whose 1999 encompassed 40 home runs and 124 runs batted in, matching his career highs. Mike Piazza shattered the Mets' record for RBIs by seven and came within one of tying Todd Hundley for the franchise mark in home runs. When Hundley—whose Dodgers totals made nobody in Southern California forget Piazza—was hitting 41 home runs in 1996, it was basically all Mets fans had to celebrate. To reiterate what infielder Tim Bogar said at the time, the way the team was playing, there wasn't much to think about except Todd hitting his 41st. With Mike and Robin and Fonzie and Oly and everybody else, Piazza's stats were almost incidental to the larger story the Mets were writing three years later.

The Mets were in the playoffs. The catcher who caught two crucial complete-game shutouts in three nights. The best infield ever. All those outfielders. Bonilla and Mora. Benitez and Franco, the latter who'd been waiting since 1984 to sniff serious October baseball. John had been a Red when the Reds weren't good enough, then a Met when the Mets weren't good at all. John arrived in Flushing when the town still belonged to Darryl, Doc, and Davey. He kept his head while everybody else's seemed filled with notions of firecrackers and bleach. The Mets tore down around him, attempted to rebuild around him, marked time around him and, finally, began to win around him. He wasn't the closer anymore, but he was a Met on a playoff roster.

There was plenty of mojo to go around, be packed for Phoenix and take to the Diamondbacks. They'd need all they could get. They were facing Randy Johnson Tuesday night.

* * *

While Franco was a stranger to postseason, Mike Piazza had had two chances to make the World Series as a Dodger. Neither went very far and neither served as much of a personal showcase: 3-for-14 against the Reds in 1995, with two extra-base hits; three singles in 10 at-bats versus the Braves in 1996. Both of those were wrong-end sweeps for L.A. Piazza had yet to shake a hand in victory in October.

A naked-eye examination of the pitching matchup for Game One against the 100–62 Diamondbacks (a second-year team that spent lavishly and invested wisely) would have indicated Mike would have to wait at least one night for satisfaction. Johnson's first full season in the National League was an artistic triumph. The Big Unit led all pitchers in ERA and strikeouts while completing more than twice as many games as the entire Mets staff. He'd soon be voted his first NL Cy Young. The Mets were countering with Masato Yoshii, whose second half was better than his first half, but together the halves didn't add up to a fraction of what Johnson had accomplished.

Yet they played the game anyway. Randy Johnson, as his birth certificate presumably confirmed, was human. Playoff neophyte Alfonzo baptized himself effectively by homering in the first and Olerud, despite being a lefty, did the same in the third. Johnson hardly ever gave up home runs to his fellow southpaws (none since 1997), but he just had here, and the Mets were ahead, 3–0.

Yoshii was serviceable until he wasn't, which got the Mets to a 4–4 tie in the sixth. By then, Johnson had shed his humanity and reverted to his usual machine-like state. Except for a walk to and a steal by Henderson, the Mets did nothing from the fifth through the eighth. The Unit was still in the game in the ninth, when he began to revert to mere personhood. Ventura led off with a single. One out later, Ordoñez singled. Mora walked to load the bases. Arizona manager Buck Showalter finally removed his ace after 138 pitches and replaced him with Bobby Chouinard. It proved a great move for one batter, when Henderson grounded to third baseman Matt Williams, who made a nifty grab and forced Ventura at the plate.

It proved a lesser move when Fonzie turned on a fastball that got too much on the plate. He sent it deep down the left-field line at Bank One Ballpark—BOB to you, pal—where it stayed fair for a grand slam. The Mets led, 8–4, on Edgardo's second lifetime postseason home run and, three defensive outs later, Piazza and Benitez were able to shake hands in victory.

The Mets had just won five games in a row, every one of them brimming with must-win urgency. Now that they had some breathing room, they let down a little. Or maybe they were just due to be beat by a pretty good club. In Game Two, the streak ended. Rogers, who thrived at Shea (the Mets won all seven of his home starts), didn't last five innings in this road assignment, giving up four runs. Todd Stottlemyre, son of Mel, the Mets' pitching coach from when the Mets last won the World Series, allowed only one run in 6 2/3 innings. The 7–1 loss was best rationalized as the Mets flying back to Queens with a split.

But there was a bigger loss coming out of Arizona than could be realized. Piazza's catching thumb was in pain. It had been bothering him for a few weeks and it kept feeling worse on the plane ride home. Rest on the off day didn't help. A cortisone shot led to swelling, which made gripping a bat impossible. The injury was diagnosed as a sprain and it did the unthinkable: it kept Mike out of action in the middle of the playoffs. Piazza had been 2-for-9 in the first two games and his average had dipped through the last month of the season (from .323 on September 1 to .303 on October 4), but there was no underestimating his presence in the lineup. He was the personification of the cleanup slot for these Mets.

Now they'd try to win a playoff series without him. Mike's thumb went into a splint. Todd Pratt, with 140 at-bats as Piazza's backup (and one strikeout in one appearance during the 1993 NLCS with the Phillies), slipped into the spotlight. "Tank," as his teammates called him, was no No. 4 hitter; he'd bat seventh. The new cleanup man in town was Benny Agbayani, whose 10 home runs in his first 73 at-bats were succeeded by four long balls in his next 203. It might have looked unorthodox, but the lineup was made out by Bobby Valentine, who fit nobody's mold.

As if the absence of Mike Piazza didn't make for enough background noise to the Mets' first home playoff game since Columbus Day 1988 (which the Dodgers won the afternoon after Mike Scioscia etched his name into Shea infamy), Valentine was getting attention for a profile in *Sports Illustrated* whose money quote, recorded in late September, was, "You're not dealing with real professionals in the clubhouse. You're not dealing with real intelligent guys for the most part . . . there's about five guys in there right now who basically are losers, who are seeing if they can recruit."

Team efforts come in all shapes and sizes. This one, led by a manager publicly expressing doubt in the middle of a pennant race and minus its biggest star, directed itself to the task at hand. The only "losers" in evidence were the Diamondbacks. The Mets prevailed in Game Three, 9–2, breaking it open with six runs in the sixth inning. Agbayani went 2-for-2, Pratt walked twice, Henderson collected three hits and stole his NLDS-record sixth base of the series, and Rick Reed notched the first postseason win of his long and winding career. Hershiser threw the ninth inning in a mop-up role, meaning Bobby V used every one of his twenty-five men, save for his Game Four starter—no matter how he judged their professionalism—inside of three games.

This was now a battle-tested October team, every one of them a recent veteran of pressurized baseball. They didn't have Piazza, but they did have the chance to advance to the National League Championship Series if they could whack the Snakes one more time. Leiter and Brian Anderson faced off on Saturday, October 9, keeping each other's batters from scoring for three and a half innings. Fonzie's third home run of the series, a solo shot, put the Mets ahead in the fourth. Greg Colbrunn got the D'Backs even in the fifth with a home run of his own (the first Arizona hit of the afternoon), but Benny from the four-hole doubled in Henderson in the sixth to make it 2–1, Mets.

Al was brilliant through 7 2/3 innings, but when he walked pinch-hitter Turner Ward and gave up a single to Tony Womack, Valentine lifted him in favor of Armando Benitez. Armando hadn't given up a base hit in his previous 5 1/3 innings and was generally overpowering in 1999. His 14.77 strikeouts per nine innings pitched set a Mets standard. Until getting tripped up in Philadelphia during the seven-game losing streak, Benitez had converted six saves in six consecutive appearances, half of them lasting more than one inning. There wasn't any reason not to bring him in to nail down the final four outs and send the Mets to the NLCS.

Except in his first postseason save situation as a Met, he let the lead get away. His first batter, Jay Bell, reached him for a double that scored both Ward and Womack. Just like that, the Mets were down a run and, if they didn't come back, would board a return flight to Phoenix, where Randy Johnson would get another crack at them. The engines might have been revving on the runway at LaGuardia had not Melvin Mora again come to the Mets' rescue. After Benitez intentionally walked Luis Gonzalez, Williams (35 HR, 142 RBIs) singled to left. Bell was heading for home with the Diamondbacks' fourth run, but he was cut down by Melvin, who had replaced Rickey for defense at the start of the inning.

Bobby Valentine may have said some weird things at some weird times, but he did know how and when to deploy his personnel.

In the bottom of the eighth, the Mets wrecked another raft of travel plans. Fonzie walked to lead off. Showalter, who seemed to enjoy making moves in the way Valentine relished giving quotes, switched out pitchers, replacing Gregg Olson with Greg Swindell. The left-hander got Olerud to fly to Womack in right . . . but Womack, who had been stationed at short for seven innings until Buck got busy, failed to catch the ball and the Mets had runners at second and third with nobody out. Roger Cedeño, who had entered for defense in the seventh and was thus the Mets' new cleanup hitter, lifted a fly ball deep enough to center to score Alfonzo. The game was tied at three. It came close to being led by the Mets in the eighth if you believed third base coach Cookie Rojas. Hamilton looped a ball down the left-field line. Had it been called fair, which Cookie asserted it should have been, the Mets would have gone ahead, but umpire Charlie Williams ruled it foul. Rojas didn't care for the official's decision or his tone. There was some shoving, an ejection, and eventually a suspension.

Bruce Benedict left his post as bench coach to take over third, but as the eighth wound down, he had no runners to send home. Arizona got out of the inning and the game went to the ninth knotted. Benitez made up for his missteps by pitching a spotless inning. The Mets got two runners on with two down in the bottom of the inning against fireballing Matt Mantei—for whom Showalter double-switched Williams out of the game—but could not cash in.

Extra innings awaited, and to pitch the first of them, Valentine called on John Franco. Franco's long wait to appear in the postseason ended in Game Two, and he had made his Shea playoff debut the night before, but this was the moment he'd been working toward for 16 seasons. Tie game, 10th inning, the playoffs, the home crowd, him in the middle of it, wearing Tug's 45.

Dreams do come true, even if they're weird dreams that include two ex-Mets—Kelly Stinnett and Lenny Harris—making the first two outs of the inning and the potential goat for the other team, Womack, making the third. However John dreamed it up, he got the Diamondbacks in order and sent the game to the bottom of the 10th still tied at three.

Mantei faced Ventura to lead off and got a fly ball to right. Womack caught this one. The next batter, Pratt, also hit a fly ball, to center. Arizona had an excellent defensive center fielder, Steve Finley. He was on his way to his third Gold Glove, an appropriate prize for someone who could get to anything in the ballpark.

Finley rushed back to the wall, a little to the right of the 410 mark in center field. The eyes of 56,177 Mets fans rushed with him. So did those belonging to the batter. Tank rolled as far as first before becoming a spectator himself. Where was his ball headed?

Just outside the confines of Shea Stadium. Maybe 411 feet from home plate, maybe 412, but just far enough of out of the grasp of Finley's gold glove to go for a home run. Mets 4, Diamondbacks 3. Tank could keep rolling all the way around the bases, accept congratulations from Benedict standing in for Rojas and get mobbed by everybody else, particularly the winning pitcher, Franco. For the second time in six days, an intense, dramatic Mets game came down to the catcher batting and ended with a celebration of the momentous. The previous Sunday, it was clinching a tie for the wild card. This Saturday, it was winning the Division Series, three games to one.

How both of those catcher-at-the-plate situations unfolded so spectacularly without a single Mike Piazza swing defied logic. The Mets got Mike so he could be the man to uncork such celebrations. Baseball found ways around obvious resolution. A wild pitch one weekend, a substitute the next. "There was so much talk about Piazza being out," Leiter said as the champagne flowed. "Obviously we miss Mike a great deal, but having Todd come up . . . it's just a great story."

* * *

The next Amazin' chapter would have to be written while dodging tomahawk chops. While the Mets were eliminating the Diamondbacks, the Braves were doing the same to the Astros, meaning one more trip to Turner Field was on the itinerary and one more opportunity was at hand to avenge the five losses Atlanta had handed New York in those six September games. The hand, by Tuesday night, October 12, would have its most important thumb restored to its usual place of prominence. Piazza would be back for the NLCS.

The swelling was down, a special brace replaced the splint, and Mike was a playoff participant again, catching Yoshii and batting fourth. What no doctor or trainer prescribed was batting against Greg Maddux, though you didn't require a special degree to realize that wouldn't be therapeutic for any ballplayer. Maddux set down the Mets in order in the top of the first and the Braves generated a run before the bottom of the first was two batters old, a steal of second by Gerald Williams proving key. Piazza was responsible for the tying run in the fourth, when his groundout to third brought home Alfonzo, but that was all the Mets could get going against the four-time Cy Young winner. A Williams single put the Braves up, 2–1, in the fifth and Eddie Perez's sixth-inning homer off Mahomes made their lead two. The Mets lost, 4–2.

The second game looked better from the outset. Ventura walked to lead off the second inning versus Kevin Millwood, Hamilton singled him to second, and Robin scored on Cedeño's single. Mora chose the NLCS to launch the first home run of his major-league career, giving Rogers a 2–0 lead to carry to the sixth. It crumbled there, though. Brian Jordan hit one two-run homer and Perez hit another. Alfonzo doubled home Mora in the eighth to cut the Braves' lead to 4–3, but when Piazza had a chance to drive him in, Bobby Cox ordered him intentionally walked and Rocker struck out Robin to end the threat. The Mets returned to Shea down two games to none. Mike was hitless in seven at-bats.

Those Braves fans who attended the games at Turner Field were enthusiastic enough, but they did not form a capacity crowd. More than 5,000 seats went unsold each date. For Atlanta, the National League Championship Series was old hat. The Braves had been in every NLCS since 1991. The novelty had apparently worn off. Not so at Shea, where Mets fans were hungry for more playoff baseball and thirsty for Brave blood. Every player introduced was literally informed by close to 56,000 souls that they "SUCK!" Particular venom was expressed to Chipper Jones, whose given name of Larry was suddenly the best known moniker in New York. Word had gotten around that Mike Piazza called him Larry because he wasn't going to call a grown man "Chipper." Mets fans were as happy to greet their nemesis as "LAR-REEEE!" as they were disgusted by his "Yankee stuff" suggestion.

After Tom Seaver threw out the ceremonial first pitch, the home crowd could not have been more primed for the Mets to get even, but the nine innings that ensued were no match for the pregame fervor. In the first inning, Williams led off with a walk, Bret Boone grounded back to the mound, but Leiter threw the ball wide of first. Two on, nobody out. Williams and Boone took off for a double steal. Not only did they succeed, but Piazza threw the ball into center, which allowed Williams to score. Without benefit of a base hit, the Braves led, 1–0.

And that's how the Friday night game ended. Leiter gave up nothing else over seven, and Glavine blanked the Mets over the same span. Boone had attempted to score on a flyout to center in the first, but Mora, excelling from yet another position, threw him out at home. The collision at the plate, however, left Piazza with what was described as a "slight concussion," not enough to knock the catcher out of the game. Mike's two leadoff singles, in the fourth and sixth, led nowhere. A reshuffling of the Mets lineup—Olerud batting second, Fonzie third, Benny fifth and Robin sixth—amounted to zip. Rocker, challenging Larry/Chipper for Shea's disfavor, entered to a stream of profane invective and flying objects in the ninth. He had called Mets fans "stupid," which was a taunt almost as offensive as Jones's crack about New York team loyalties, but the worst insult of all was his pitching. Sticks and stones were irrelevant. The Mets' bats couldn't hurt him in Game Three, and the Braves led the best-of-seven series three games to none.

One more loss would do the Mets in, an ignominious ending to such an exhilarating season. No baseball team trailing by such a margin had ever come back to pull a seven-game series out, but the Mets couldn't think about what was impossible, only what was within their grasp. Game Four was thus yet another "most important game" of 1999, and they had a remarkable track record of winning those.

Zeroes were wild Saturday night, October 16, as John Smoltz attempted to lead the Braves to a clinch of their fifth pennant of the '90s and Rick Reed did his damnedest to prevent it. Nobody reached base for either side until the third, when Cedeño singled, but he didn't score. The first Brave on was Boone, via a single in the fourth, but he was cut down stealing by Piazza. Not until the sixth did a "1" appear on the Shea scoreboard. It was put there by Olerud, who homered with two out to give Reed the lead he needed.

Reed protected it in the seventh, but come the eighth, after Rick had faced the minimum 21 batters to record 21 outs, Brian Jordan and Ryan Klesko each hit home runs, on the first and third pitches of the inning. If the Mets couldn't overcome a 2–1 deficit in the next two innings, they were done.

So they overcame it, in their now trademark dizzying fashion.

Smoltz allowed a single to Cedeño to start the bottom of the eighth, got one more out and was then replaced by lefty specialist Mike Remlinger, a Met directly before and after the 1994–95 players' strike. Remlinger was inserted by Cox to face Matt Franco, who was announced as the pinch-hitter for Turk Wendell (who had replaced Reed), but when Valentine saw the southpaw, he called back Franco and went with Agbayani. After all that, Benny struck out.

But with Mora batting next (he'd replaced Rickey in left earlier, the mechanics of which left Henderson visibly unhappy, since the veteran had already trotted out to his position when Melvin appeared), Cedeño stole second. Melvin proceeded to walk, setting in motion another chain of changes, Rocker in for Remlinger and, per double-switch protocol, Seaver's old White Sox shortstop Ozzie Guillen replacing Walt Weiss. Mora and Cedeño successfully engineered a double steal, and Rocker, pitching to the lefty-swinging Olerud with first base open (he had handled him with ease in every previous encounter), gave up a bouncer that ticked off Guillen's glove and into center field.

The Mets' rabbits raced home, scored, and hugged high in the air, having leapt giddily at the realization that their runs had kept the Mets alive. It took a scoreless ninth from Benitez to confirm they'd done exactly that. The Mets were 3–2 winners and had, if nothing else, a little more life.

Oh, what life it would be.

TWENTY-SIX INNINGS
October 17, 1999–October 20, 1999

The 1999 New York City Marathon was scheduled to be run on November 7, its 26.2 miles expected to be traversed by tens of thousands of runners across five boroughs. No doubt for many of the participants it would be daunting, grueling, and at times seem impossible to endure.

But at least they'd have recent proof that such a challenge could be undertaken valiantly.

From late in the afternoon on Sunday, October 17, to a touch after midnight on Wednesday, October 20, a 26-inning marathon unfolded. It started in Queens and it ended in Atlanta. Measured conventionally, only one entrant crossed the finish line qualified to be declared the winner, yet anyone who witnessed every step of this last leg of the race that constituted the 1999 baseball season in Flushing knew in their exhausted bones that nobody, even those who ultimately came in second, deserved to be written off as a loser.

If not for "one of the more cheaper hits" John Rocker swore he'd given up in his "entire life," the one that allowed the Mets to prevail on Saturday night, Sunday in New York could have been fully given over to other sporting pursuits. Marathon training beckoned for the locals who planned to be among the more than 30,000 racing on foot in three weeks' time. For those who preferred four legs over two, Monarch's Maze galloped to an impressive come-from behind win in the Jamaica Handicap at Belmont Park. At the Meadowlands, horses of different colors, the blue-and-white clad Indianapolis Colts, did a nice of job of coming back themselves, making up a 13–0 deficit and defeating the New York Jets, 16–13 on a field goal by Mike Vanderjagt with 14 seconds left in the fourth quarter. To add injury to insult, Bill Parcells's squad lost not only their fifth game in six tries, but their third starting quarterback of the season, as Ray Lucas suffered a sprained ankle after getting sacked on the final play of the game. And, as if to remind one and all how close the second half of October is to winter, there was ice hockey at the Garden, where New York (the Rangers) topped Atlanta (the Thrashers), 4–1.

The world and the city were slated to move on to the usual concerns of autumn—lest anyone forget, the Yankees were engaged in their own League Championship Series, preparing to play the Red Sox in Boston Sunday night and planning to build on their typical two-games-to-one advantage—but Mike Piazza's Mets would not let go of anybody's attention so easily. They had made Shea Stadium the center of the sporting and metropolitan universe. After these past few weeks, you couldn't take your eyes off them. As first pitch approached at 4:09 P.M. on October 17, it couldn't be known how much more riveting an attraction they were about to become.

The initial steps the Mets took on their journey couldn't have been more encouraging. Masato Yoshii set the Braves down in order in the top of the first. Facing the great Greg Maddux, the also great Rickey Henderson reached on an infield single and, one out later, John Olerud, who wasn't so bad himself, homered. The Mets led, 2–0, and Henderson could enjoy a moment of non-controversy. After being removed from Saturday night's game rather clumsily by Bobby Valentine, Rickey made himself scarce in the dugout while his team was trying to keep its season alive. It didn't sit well with Turk Wendell, who singled him out as not truly part of the otherwise solid team effort the Mets were forging as they tried to overcome enormous odds and capture a pennant. Henderson, in turn, expressed some unkind words toward Turk before Game Five. With the Mets up two runs over one of the best pitchers in captivity, and Piazza following Olerud's homer with a single, family feuds hardly seemed to matter.

By the fourth inning neither did the 2–0 lead, which became a 2–2 tie, as Yoshii gave up consecutive doubles to Bret Boone and Chipper Jones and a single to Brian Jordan. With nobody out, he walked Ryan Klesko, which signaled the end of Yoshii's day. Orel Hershiser was summoned to stop the bleeding, and he was a human tourniquet, striking out Andruw Jones and Eddie Perez and grounding out Walt Weiss.

Fans of 2–2 ties were about to be in for a treat. Those who yearned for swift clarity probably should have chosen a day at the races. Monarch's Maze won his Sunday competition in just under a minute and fifty-two seconds. The maze the Mets and Braves would have to negotiate so one could emerge as king of the National League would be far trickier and run much longer. It wasn't for the fainthearted, never mind the faintheaded. If you valued your sanity, you shouldn't have been watching.

If you valued your body, you shouldn't have been playing. Piazza had apparently already decided he wasn't going to let a little or a lot of pain from inviting more. On top of the thumb that was forced into action in Game One and the "slight concussion" he took in Game Three, there was the matter of a knuckle sore from a Gerald Williams backswing he absorbed in Game Four. Throw in, for ill measure, his left forearm getting "nailed" in similar fashion by Klesko in Game Five, and he couldn't be blamed for "starting to feel like a piñata."

Yet, just as kids can't help themselves from high-sticking the papier-mâché figure that promises all sorts of sweet rewards, the players played on and the fans hung on their every move, of which there'd be plenty for hours, though none of it involved anybody crossing home plate.

Pitching and managing took over as Sunday afternoon became Sunday evening, overcast skies became wet ones and runners on base became runners left on base. The lights were on, the umbrellas, ponchos, and used popcorn containers provided protection against the elements, but nothing much could be done about the baserunners who didn't become run-scorers. That was the idea defensively, but it didn't do much to end suspense. From the bottom of the fourth through the top of the seventh, the two best or at least remaining teams in the National League put at least one of its players on every half-inning, yet nobody advanced past third base.

The Mets loaded the bases to no avail in the bottom of the sixth, and the Braves did the same in the top of the seventh after facing four Mets relievers in a four-batter span. Yoshii to Hershiser to Wendell to Dennis Cook (tabbed by Bobby V to pitch merely a portion of an intentional walk so as to coax Bobby Cox to remove Ryan Klesko) to Pat Mahomes got the Mets through seven. Maddux needed no help to get that far, but soon enough Atlanta dipped into its bullpen, too. Terry Mulholland threw a couple of innings. So did Mike Remlinger. On the Mets' side, John Franco replaced

Mahomes, then Armando Benitez followed Franco. By then it was extra innings, which almost seemed like an incidental detail. Mets baserunners became infrequent. The Braves kept getting guys on and Mets pitchers kept stranding them where they stood. Benitez gave way to Kenny Rogers in the 11th. Remlinger handed off to Russ Springer in the 12th. Octavio Dotel entered as the Mets' ninth pitcher in the 13th.

The 13th could have been unluckier than it was for Piazza, who was the target of the Braves' most direct attack on home plate since the fourth. In the sixth, Mike was part of a 2–5–1 double play when Maddux struck out on an attempted suicide squeeze and Klesko ran himself and his team out of the inning, but then it was Orel who made the tag. In the 13th, Keith Lockhart reached on a two-out single. When Chipper Jones lashed a ball down the right-field line, Lockhart took off, determined to break the tie. Melvin Mora, playing his third outfield position of the postseason, made another on-the-money throw. He zipped it to Edgardo Alfonzo, who relayed to Mike, and Lockhart was out, in Gary Cohen's estimation, by twenty feet.

That didn't mean he wasn't gonna try to take Piazza out with him. As onrushing runners had been doing forever, Lockhart decided to crash into the catcher in hopes of jarring the ball loose. Keith was unsuccessful in his primary endeavor, but he definitely put a hurting on Piazza, crashing into the same forearm that bore the brunt of Klesko's backswing many hours and innings before. When Mike batted in the bottom of the 13th against Rocker, he sensed he pulled something. He also struck out. Battered, bruised, and 1-for-6, Mike left after 13, giving way to understudy Todd Pratt.

Dotel pitched a scoreless top of the 14th, Rocker a scoreless bottom of the 14th (with a 14th-inning stretch in between). Octavio and the Mets couldn't hold the fort forever, though. In the top of the 15th, Lockhart, unfazed by his end of the collision with Piazza, tripled home Walt Weiss from second, putting the Braves up, 3–2. After dancing through baserunners (19 of them left on) and raindrops, the Mets had relented.

But not for long.

The Mets had coming up to start the bottom of the 15th, potentially their last half-inning of the year, Shawon Dunston, facing the sixth Brave pitcher, Kevin McGlinchy. He had never walked as a Met and he wasn't about to start now. But the .344 hitter wasn't going to make an out. Shawon was going to get a hit and he would take all night if he had to. He almost did. His at-bat lasted nine minutes, involved a dozen pitches and included six foul balls after the count reached 3-and-2. On pitch No. 12—matching his uniform digits the Brooklynite recognized as descended from Ken Boswell—Dunston did what .344 hitters do. He singled up the middle.

Then he stole second, because Shawon realized the Mets didn't have all night. The man batting behind him, pinch-hitter Matt Franco, walked quite a bit as a rule, particularly as a pinch-hitter (he drew 19 in 1999, a major-league record that proved many major-league records are kept). Not surprisingly, unless you counted the Mets' indefatigability as a surprise, Matt, who was batting for Dotel, walked. The Mets had first and second with nobody out . . . make that second and third with one out after Alfonzo bunted Dunston and Franco up a base. Fonzie would finish eighth in National League MVP voting (directly behind Ventura and Piazza), but the most valuable thing the budding star could do here was sacrifice himself. He did it as he did most everything all season: beautifully.

Olerud, who homered 14 innings and more than five-and-a-half hours before, wasn't going to be given the chance to become the first Met to drive in a run since the Jets were taking off their pads in defeat. Cox ordered John walked. Loading the bases with one out was sound baseball strategy, but it was not without risk. After all, McGlinchy was a rookie being trusted to secure a pennant and his next assignment was the cleanup hitter and famous home run-hitting catcher.

Pratt was up, naturally. If he repeated what he'd done to Matt Mantei eight days earlier . . . that was too much for the tens of thousands who'd persevered through all the raindrops and all the zeroes to ask. But if Pratt could just keep this game going, well, that would be a gift. It would also present Valentine with a challenge. To set up this final run-scoring opportunity, Bobby had replaced Franco with Roger Cedeño, also sound baseball strategy given Roger's speed. Except that Roger had sat out all the previous action due to back spasms incurred from celebrating a little too boisterously at home plate Saturday night. If the Mets got one run across and no more, Cedeño would have to hang around and play the field because he was the last man the manager plucked from his bench. Also, if this game saw a 16th inning, the starter from Saturday night, Rick Reed, was going to have to pitch. It was either Rick or Al Leiter, and Leiter, who pitched Friday, theoretically needed to be saved for Tuesday's Game Six in Atlanta, which was still just a theory. The Mets still needed a tying run.

They got it, on four balls. Pratt walked to first, Olerud to second, Cedeño to third, and Dunston home. The Mets and Braves were in a 3–3 deadlock.

Then Robin Ventura came up and, like the mojo he introduced into the Mets vocabulary, rose to the occasion. On the 482nd pitch of the game, thrown in its 346th minute, he hit a fly ball to right that kept going. "Back to Georgia!" Bob Costas declared on NBC as soon as the ball cleared the fence. No 16th inning would be necessary, but a sixth game definitely would be. The hit was, per Ventura's specialty, a grand slam home run.

Or was it? See, Cedeño ran home, Olerud to third, Pratt to second, but after Robin touched first, Tank rolled around and decided, *ah, the hell with it,* and hoisted the oncoming Ventura into the air. It wasn't in accordance with home run rules, but it was what every Mets fan in existence would have done at that moment had emotion been their third base coach.

Thus was born another phrase for the Mets lexicon: the Grand Slam Single. It should have been worth four runs and the Mets should have won, 7–3. Official scorer Red Foley, the Elias Sports Bureau, and the National League—a killjoy consortium if ever there was one—trimmed three runs from Robin's RBI total and called it 4–3, creating another one-run win for the never-say-die but always-say-travel Mets.

Back to Georgia they went.

* * *

Perhaps the Mets and Braves just didn't remember any other way to proceed. Maybe they'd forgotten that earlier in 1999 they'd played each other in 10–2 and 16–0 blowouts. It wasn't a month before that they exchanged 9–3 and 9–2 decisions. But that might as well have been in another millennium. These Mets and Braves of middle October were glued to one another. It would take a quart of nail polish remover to reduce the stickiness between them. The Braves figured they'd be going back to Georgia, sure, but to prepare to welcome a whole other wave of New Yorkers to Turner Field. The Yankees, with relatively few watching, beat the Red Sox in Game Four Sunday night. The Fox broadcast wasn't much viewed in the visiting team's home market because most eyes were still glued to NBC, which was airing its last-ever NLCS. The Mets, casually dismissed as New York's other team since 1996, drew more than six times as many viewers as the defending world champions as Game Five plowed into lore. More than half of the televisions on across the aptly named Metropolitan Area that were on when Ventura had his grand slam rebranded a single were tuned to Robin's exploits.

New York couldn't get enough of the Mets, even if the Braves had had enough and were ready for the Yankees, who clinched their series in Boston on Monday night while the National League took a breather. When the weary combatants returned to action Tuesday night, October 19, the Braves looked like they'd waited long enough to set their World Series date.

The Mets looked dead, which should have qualified as "what else is new?" news by now, but they looked seriously beyond resuscitation. The bottom of the first was a disaster. Leiter, probably a lesser bet on three days' rest than Reed (highly efficient for seven innings on Saturday) would have been on two. Al was not sharp. He hit Gerald Williams to commence the festivities, walked Bret Boone and, next thing he knew, both were stealing on him and Piazza. Not only were Williams and Boone successful, but Mike threw another ball into the outfield, and the Braves were leading, 1–0. Then Al hit Chipper Jones, gave up an RBI single to Brian Jordan, saw Andruw Jones reach on a fielder's choice to load the bases, and allowed a two-run single to Eddie Perez.

Six batters. Four runs. No outs. And more damage just up ahead, because when Pat Mahomes came on to retire Brian Hunter on a fly to center, it scored another run. The Mets left the first inning in a 5–0 hole, all but cadavered.

Somehow, there was no killing these Mets, no matter how on the verge of expiration they seemed to be. Their ace starter was gone; their star catcher was in pain and a slump; their task against Kevin Millwood (who'd handled them fairly easily twice during the season and once during the playoffs) was daunting on any 5–0 night, but ridiculous to contemplate on a night when the sturdy old Braves could at last smell the finish line and sold-out Turner Field wouldn't shut its chophole. Good luck coming back to life under those circumstances.

The Mets didn't necessarily have luck on their side, but they did have Mahomes, and Pat stood between the Mets and their imminent demise as he had done so often as the long man of choice in 1999. He gave Valentine four shutout innings, enough time for the Mets to start to forge a comeback . . . which they didn't do while he was on the mound. It was still 5–0 in the fifth when Wendell took Pat's place. Turk was just as effective, keeping the Mets within dreaming, if not exactly striking, distance.

Finally, something good began to happen for these Mets in Game Six. In the top of the sixth, Alfonzo doubled, Olerud singled, and Piazza lifted a fly ball to left field that was deep enough to score Edgardo. It was Mike's second run batted in of the series, and it set the stage for a little more offense. Ventura doubled behind him and Darryl Hamilton brought both John and Robin home with a well-placed ground ball. The Mets were no longer in a five-run hole. Two runs was a manageable and imaginable deficit.

Unfortunately, this was the moment the Mets bullpen, in the person of Wendell, bent. Turk started the bottom of the sixth by hitting Jordan with a pitch. His trip around the bases would end on a force at home, but the former NFL safety—Brian was a more effective two-sport Jordan than Michael ever was—didn't go lightly. After he took his HBP, a single and intentional walk loaded the bases. Turk got the ground ball he wanted, but when it was relayed to the plate, where Piazza received the ball standing with his foot on the plate, Jordan's gridiron instincts (not to mention his irritation at getting hit in the first place) took over. He tried to take out Mike like he was Ray Lucas in the Meadowlands. The effort didn't jar the ball loose, but it put yet another hurting on Piazza's body and snapped something in Mike's soul. Piazza cursed out the baserunner and admitted to spoiling for a fight. Jordan resisted responding. The Braves got in the next blow that counted anyway. Cook replaced Wendell and gave up a two-run single to pinch-hitter Jose Hernandez. After six innings, the Mets trailed, 7–3.

After six-and-a-half, the game was tied at seven.

There was not enough chloroform in the state of Georgia to fully embalm the Mets. Cox tried to put them to their eternal sleep once and for all by calling on not just another reliever, but John Smoltz. His Game Four starter was otherwise a spectator, so why not? The 1996 Cy Young Award winner had closed out Game Two. This was no time for pussyfooting. Bring in your best possible pitcher and get this thing over with.

Yeah, the Mets didn't care about anybody's credentials. Instead, their batters teed off as if they'd been redirected to Augusta. Matt Franco, pinch-hitting for Cook, doubled. Henderson doubled him in and took third on Alfonzo's ensuing fly to right. Olerud singled in Rickey to make it 7–5. Up stepped Piazza, whose signature across the 1999 postseason had been comprised of absence and ache. That was about to change.

On a 2–1 pitch, the player who had registered only three hits in 22 at-bats through the NLCS, Mike stamped his name on Mets playoff history:

"A drive in the air to deep right-center field," Gary Cohen called it. *"Back goes Jordan, back to the track, looking up, IT'S OUTTA HERE! IT'S OUTTA HERE! MIKE PIAZZA TIES THE GAME! PIAZZA TIES THE GAME WITH A TWO-RUN OPPOSITE-FIELD HOME RUN!"*

Like everything else about the Mets since he showed up on May 23, 1998, Mike had made it a whole new ballgame. They had only marginal hope as a franchise before he was traded to the team and here they were two wins from the World Series. They were down all night until he crushed Smoltz's delivery past the 390 mark in right-center and now, as Costas put it, they were "tied at seven, hoping for Game Seven."

Karma, Hollywood, and the kindest possible fate clearly wanted that Game Seven. The Mets took a lead of 8–7 in the eighth, but Franco couldn't hold it. They took a lead of 9–8 in the 10th (by which time a battered Piazza gave way once more to Pratt), but Benitez couldn't hold it. When it came to the Mets at Turner Field, the Braves were stronger than all conceivable forces. With Kenny Rogers on in relief in the bottom of the 11th, the Braves loaded the bases. Andruw Jones worked the count to 3-and-2. Then he walked. The Braves won the damn thing, 10–9. At 12:27 A.M. on Wednesday, October 20, the 1999 Mets ceased to exist as a competitive entity. Atlanta won the pennant.

But their vanquished rivals took possession of the legend.

* * *

To the participants and their fans, the World Series that followed would be a big enough to-do, though history would little note nor long remember many of its details. The Yankees swept the Braves, who had likely exhausted their reserves winning the NLCS war of wills. Only one of the games, the third, was particularly tight. "I'm just drained," Chipper Jones said in the Bronx after it was over. "I'm going home and sleeping for a week."

As home of the Braves, Turner Field got to host the introduction of the All-Century Team before Game Two, the payoff from the gala All-Star festivities in July. The fan vote produced a roster of twenty-five greats, with an expert panel commissioned to "compensate for oversights in fan voting" and select five more. All living honorees were introduced by Vin Scully, himself completing a half-century behind the mic. The process reflected baseball as it was viewed later rather than early in the century it endeavored to celebrate. For example, Mark McGwire, who added 65 home runs in 1999 to the 70 he slugged the year before, was tabbed by fans as one of the two flagship first basemen of the preceding hundred years, joining Lou Gehrig on a pedestal that consigned the likes of Hank Greenberg, Jimmie Foxx, and the recently retired Eddie Murray to the also-ran tier below. McGwire was one of four active players to be labeled All-Century, joining Ken Griffey, Cal Ripken, and Roger Clemens, who started and won clinching Game Four ("I think I learned what it feels like to be a Yankee now," the Rocket said upon earning the ring he'd craved from afar in Toronto). Not making the cut, by fan vote or panel selection, was Tom Seaver. His competition included Sandy Koufax, Bob Gibson, Walter Johnson, and Cy Young. It might have been the toughest lineup Tom had ever gone up against.

The last Mets word of the ending century came forth from one of those who drained the Braves en route to their date with the Yankees. Shawon Dunston, having just had his vision that "We're going to the World Series! We're going to play the Yankees!" ruptured by reality, stood in the visitors' clubhouse at Turner Field in the wee hours Wednesday, following the Game Six defeat, and addressed his teammates. The brief speech was not broadcast, but it was captured by *Daily News* columnist Lisa Olson, who reported Dunston told his comrades, "I am so proud to be a Met. . . . You guys made me believe again. You made baseball fun for me. I will never, ever forget what this team did."

His audience, according to Olson, was barely maintaining its composure before he spoke. When he was done, "Dunston's words put a quick end to whatever cool machismo the players were clutching." These were Mets who recognized what they'd achieved, even if the designations they'd receive in the record books—National League Wild Card; NLDS winner—reflected a road navigated only semi-successfully. The delight would have to be confined to the details, recurring flashes of ecstasy embedded within the emotions the players and the fans would have to summon on their own.

What a year it had been. And that was before the final month, from the moment they alighted in Atlanta with the division on the line until the instant they were compelled to vacate it, the pennant cruelly snatched from their grasp. There was one ball too many from a pitcher who shared a name with a country singer, yet nobody dared consider these Mets the cowards of Queens or Fulton or any other county. "I told them they played like champions," Bobby Valentine relayed to reporters, and it was probably the least controversial thing he'd said all through this Metsiest of Met rides.

After 26 innings when the composite score stood at 13–13, they all sure seemed champion-like, despite the fact that, as their manager acknowledged, "we don't have a trophy." Yankees fans would have another parade to attend. Mets fans would have to peer into the mind's eye and toss streamers in their dreams. Every one of their players deserved to be thought of as deserving: Dunston; Rogers; Benitez; Franco (both Francos); the bottomless bullpen; the Greatest Infield Ever (no question mark necessary); the replacements who were now stalwarts; the rookies who behaved like veterans; the Mets who'd been around since the team lost far more than it won; and the Mets who'd come aboard to push the team toward winning it all.

Even the fellas who reportedly decided to take refuge in a game of cards in the shadows of a mind-boggling game of baseball. In the right context, Henderson and Bonilla (both removed from Game Six anyway) playing hearts and fuming could be processed as the edge-of-the-millennium equivalent of Keith Hernandez giving up against the Red Sox and grabbing a Budweiser while Gary Carter batted with two out and nobody on in another Game Six. Together, the lot of 1999 Mets hadn't quite done all they set out to do, but they sure figuratively died trying. Those who rooted on every last one of them right up to the moment Bobby Valentine's gamble on Kenny Rogers failed would never forget the way these players knew how to hold 'em and only consented to fold 'em when it was irrefutable that the dealing was done.

The Met who could sit at the table and count his money the longest did no such thing. "Fans look at Mike," Dunston suggested after his farewell address, "and all they see is $100 million. He's set for life. He doesn't have to go through that beating. But he acted like he's making $100,000."

Ballplayers may not grasp everyday economics (a hundred grand as peanuts wouldn't have resonated so well in most precincts of Shea's upper deck), but Shawon's point was Piazza was as hungry as a long-term contractee as he was as a 62nd-round draft pick. "All he wanted to do," Dunston judged, "was play."

Now that there would be no Game Seven to strap everything on for, all Mike wanted to do was get away. Everything in Game Six—Jordan taking it to him, him taking it to Smoltz—had taken what was left out of him. Eschewing the team flight back to New York, he opted to rent a car in Georgia and drive off into the literal sunset, heading back to his home in California, hoping to mend physically and mentally from what he'd been in the middle of, what he'd borne so much of.

For everybody who cast his or her lot with Piazza's team, the stakes were so different from what they'd been before he arrived, even from when after he first settled in. The end of 1999, his first full year as a Met, was a veritable universe removed from 1998. The Mets hadn't seen deep October in more than a decade coming into this year. Now Mike and his teammates had driven their fans to the doorstep of the World Series. Had these guys somehow pulled out Game Six, there'd have been Game Seven. A hypothetical can be neither proven nor disproven, but it was impossible to comprehend the Mets not winning the game that was never played and moving on as the National League representatives in the fall classic. It was just as hard to believe the Mets wouldn't have put up a much stronger fight against the Yankees than the Braves had.

A genuine Subway Series, however, was still a dream at the close of 1999. That particular parochial baseball fantasy would have to wait for another race, another year, and another century.

AS THE WORLD TURNED
March 29, 2000–October 26, 2000

No Met season ever started earlier than 2000's. Earliest date. Earliest time. Least amount of patience to get on with the first 162 games and get to what was now understood as the good part. And the period between seasons was no time to stand still.

Kenny Rogers: off to Texas. Shawon Dunston: back to St. Louis. Bill Pulsipher: back from Milwaukee. Jesse Orosco: back from the '80s with his left arm still intact. Orosco's most famous out, of course, was the one he recorded versus a righty batter, Marty Barrett, to close the last World Series the Mets were in, the last World Series the Mets won, on October 27, 1986. Jesse struck out Marty, then flung his glove in the air. More than thirteen years later, the Mets were still waiting for another title to land. John Olerud took his three-season .315 batting average and flew home to Seattle as a free agent. Todd Zeile, veteran of more than a decade and seven different clubs, replaced him.

Like Ray Romano's character on CBS, everybody'd loved Olerud. The same couldn't be said about a Met who was under contract for 2000, Bobby Bonilla. His continued proximity to a manager he couldn't stand (and who couldn't stand him) was pretty much untenable by the second year of his second act, so Steve Phillips got creative in eliminating the "distraction" from the Mets' going list of concerns. Unable to trade Bobby Bo, the club reached an agreement to pay him off on a deferred basis. The GM had a grander scheme in the works to land Ken Griffey Jr., finalizing a deal with the Mariners a year before Junior hit free agency, but one detail couldn't be solved: Ken didn't want to come to the Mets. He was traded to Cincinnati for Mike Cameron instead and signed a very long-term contract with his dad's old club.

As a consolation prize, Phillips gathered two of the chips he was going to use to get Griffey—Roger Cedeño and Octavio Dotel—and turned them into Mike Hampton and Derek Bell from Houston. Mostly Hampton, the 22–4 southpaw who spearheaded the Astros' playoff drive in '99. Bell's contract was tossed in. The Mets accepted it graciously and slotted Derek in right field, next to Darryl Hamilton in center and Rickey Henderson in left.

Spring training had a few more moves left in it. Orosco, who was about to make curious history (imagine the closer from the 1986 Mets, who'd played with 1962 Met Ed Kranepool in 1979, pitching for the Mets in the 21st century), was swapped to St. Louis for utilityman Joe McEwing, only semi-ironically dubbed "Super Joe" for his versatility. Jay Payton, talked up as a big prospect since the 1995 yearbook projected him as the center fielder in 2000, finally made the team to stay after a series of injuries in the minors and a couple of cups of coffee in 1998 and 1999. And impressing beat writers enough to win the Johnny Murphy Award as best rookie in camp was non-roster invitee Garth Brooks.

The Johnny Murphy honor, named for the general manager who helped build the 1969 Mets, was real; it was won by Melvin Mora in the spring of '99, and goodness knew he proved himself authentic in the ensuing October. Garth Brooks, though, was only a little more genuine in baseball terms than Sidd Finch. The No. 1 country music star of the 1990s did love his baseball, and did wear No. 1 in actual exhibition games, which didn't count, so he could have worn his cowboy hat for all it mattered. Brooks was on hand in Port St. Lucie to help raise money for his Touch 'em All Foundation, just as he had for the Padres the spring before. The singer played a little third, a little first, and hit not at all (0-for-17). The award may have been presented in the spirit of fun, but Garth was no April Fool's joke. He couldn't have been. The Mets were long gone from Florida by April 1.

Their early start on the World Series required them to see more of the world than any contender before them. More than 6,700 miles separated Shea Stadium from the Tokyo Dome, yet the latter served as the site of the Mets' home opener in 2000. First official road game, too. Major League Baseball wanted ambassadors and found them in the Mets and Cubs, chosen (with their consent) to play the first regular-season games outside of

North America. MLB hoped to generate goodwill by showing off Mike Piazza and Sammy Sosa, but this was no goodwill tour. Unlike the Garth Brooks show, these games counted.

Recognizing the travel burden involved, the teams were scheduled to get going ahead of everybody else, on March 29 and 30, giving them a chance to play, return to the States, and presumably recover. Nothing could be done about the time of first pitch as it fell in New York, however. It was a night game for the crowd in Tokyo, meaning Mets fans in their native habitat needed to be up at 5:05 A.M. to get a gander at Hampton's debut ... which wasn't worth setting the alarm for: five innings, nine walks, and a 5–3 loss. At least it was light out by the time Piazza hit the first Met home run of the new millennium in the eighth. He can always say it flew across the International Date Line.

The second game of the trip started just as early and went characteristically longer. Rey Ordoñez broke his 101-game errorless streak with a miscue in the first. Zeile flubbed a throw in the fifth, leading to the only run Rick Reed gave up over eight. So much for the definitive Greatest Infield Ever. In the top of the 11th, tied at one, the Mets, as "visitors," loaded the bases with two outs for pinch-hitter Benny Agbayani. Despite his imprint on the 1999 season, Benny appeared to be the odd man out in the outfield once the stateside roster was set. But the Hawaiian was on the trip and came off the bench to give Tokyo a taste of Met magic. Benny belted a grand slam to conjure a 5–1 lead that Armando Benitez protected in the bottom of the inning.

The 1–1 Mets of 2000 had journeyed a great distance to start even all over again. There's probably a Far Eastern proverb embedded somewhere in there that applies to taking the first steps in a pennant chase that was brand-new yet felt like a continuation of the one they'd already been on.

* * *

Predictably, the Mets sleepwalked for a week or so before waking up and hitting the ball real hard. In a stretch of seventeen games that carried them to the end of April, the Mets won thirteen, several by scores that could have discombobulated Y2K software. The numerical overdrive began on a Friday night in Pittsburgh, when the Mets pushed four runs across in the

12th inning to win, 8–5, a margin largely attributable to Piazza collecting five hits, knocking in four runs and homering twice. In that one game, Mike raised his batting average from .265 to .350 (it had wallowed below .200 post-Japan). Two days later, the Mets won 12–9, with Mike going 3-for-4. The thunder rolled. Piazza and his team were off and hitting.

The scoreboard began lighting up like the pachinko parlors of Japan: 10–7; 8–3; 7–6; 15–8; 6–5. And that was before a weekend at Coors Field that culminated in consecutive wins of 13–6 and 14–11. As April turned to May, the Mets slacked off a bit—they dropped four straight on their first visit to San Francisco's new Camdenesque Pac Bell Park—but Piazza hardly stopped hitting. He was batting like his old Dodgers self, carrying an average that hovered in the .380s before settling for a nice, long stay in the .360s.

His power was still potent as well, best exemplified on a Sunday afternoon in May when the Mets were visited by Randy Johnson and the Diamondbacks. Johnson struck out 13 batters in 6 2/3 innings, but also allowed eight hits, every one of them for extra bases. Three of them, including a home run, were to McEwing, who immediately took on from this encounter the persona of giant-killer (or at least Snake handler). The only single the Mets produced all day was the one that won the game, off the bat of Bell, down the right-field line in the bottom of the ninth, and it was scored a single only because it ended the contest. With so much else going on in a 7–6 final, the lunar mission Mike launched was bound to get lost . . . sort of like it got lost in the green seats of Shea's third deck. In the third, with the Mets trailing by one, Piazza crushed a pitch from the Big Unit far and fair into the left-field mezzanine, a shot estimated at 492 feet. Randy might have scratched his head over being strafed by a Super Joe, but he could do nothing but tip his cap to the superstar.

"Piazza," Johnson conceded, "hit a ball that's probably still circling the stadium right now."

Mike finished the day batting .361, Bell .360, Edgardo Alfonzo .351. Yet the Mets were only four games over .500, 6 1/2 behind the Braves in third place, behind Montreal. The bursts of offense were astounding, but not enough about the team seemed settled. Its projected leadoff hitter, the greatest who'd ever played, essentially dogged his way out of town. Henderson had been unhappy since the '99 postseason, carped about going to Japan, and finally expended his last iota of goodwill not running hard . . .

really barely running at all . . . on a ball that hit the wall in left field. Rickey got only as far as first. He'd be released and wind up keeping company with Olerud in Seattle.

The outfielder who was anchoring a position adjacent to him when the season began in Japan, Hamilton, was lost to a foot injury a few days after the Mets returned to America. By the end of May, Rey Ordoñez and his three Gold Gloves headed for the sidelines with his left forearm broken from tagging a runner. Shortstop was now a Mets question mark for the first time since the age of Tim Bogar. Bogar had been traded for Luis Lopez, and Lopez for Pulsipher. Pulse got another chance to fly the Generation K flag as the Mets found themselves a little shy of reliable starting pitching as Bobby Jones floundered in his return to the rotation and Hampton struggled to find consistency in New York. The feel-good elements of Pulse's story didn't translate to positive results. Two starts yielded an ERA of 12.15, a demotion to Norfolk and, ultimately, a trade to Arizona for another recidivist Met, Lenny Harris. Ventura wasn't quite the Ventura of 1999. Zeile didn't resemble Olerud at all.

As the season went on, however, things began to sort themselves out, slowly if not surely. Mora was given a shot at shortstop. He hit better than Ordoñez ever did, but was shaky on defense. Payton really did become the center fielder of 2000. The leadoff spot, after some auditions went awry—notably that of 1998 first-round pick Jason Tyner—fell to Agbayani. Benny didn't fit the mold of the prototypical swift leadoff man, but he got on base, and besides, Valentine enjoyed casting against type (he also continued to raise the ire of Phillips, having given a talk in April at the University of Pennsylvania basically trashing most of his GM's offseason moves). Harris, an accomplished pinch-hitter, was a big help off the bench. Lefty Glendon Rusch, a little-noticed pickup in 1999, settled in as a dependable starting pitcher. Jones, determined to improve, accepted an assignment in the minors to ascertain what was wrong with him and hopefully get it fixed.

When the Mets arrived in the Bronx on Friday night, June 9, to start the Subway Series—not the one they wanted last fall, but the first of two MLB insisted be played in the heat of summer—the Mets had picked up the pace, passing the Expos for second place, sticking within conceivable reach of the Braves and, should it come down to consolation prizes, making a play for another wild card. The Yankees were, per usual, in first place, though not comfortably, and their Friday night starter, Roger Clemens, didn't look all that All-Century. His record was under .500, and his ERA had climbed over 4.00.

To begin the third, in a scoreless duel versus Al Leiter, Clemens faced the top of the Mets' order for a second time. Tyner, during his brief leadoff tryout, reached on an error. Bell, who hadn't stayed hot since the Randy Johnson game, walked. Following a passed ball, Alfonzo, who never cooled off, also walked. The bases were loaded for Piazza. There was nobody out and nowhere to put him

Mike, the big wheel in the Met offense, kept on burning. He took ball one and then creamed Clemens's next pitch, driving it over the center-field fence. Yankee Stadium sounded like Shea North as the Mets grabbed a 4–0 lead. Just as in their two meetings in '99, Piazza got the best of Clemens. His next time up, in the fifth, he singled. When he was due up in the sixth, with the Mets leading by seven, Joe Torre replaced his pitcher. Piazza batted against Todd Erdos. He singled again. The Mets won, 12–2.

In a battle of megastars, one surely outshone the other. Including one interleague game versus the Blue Jays, Piazza had crafted a .583 average versus the owner of five Cy Youngs and one World Series ring. Almost every hit was mammoth. It was less a rivalry than a twice-annual beat-down.

The next afternoon, the Yankees went back to the being the Yankees and pounded Jones and the Mets (hastening Bobby's Norfolk detour), 13–5. The rubber game, though, would have to wait. It rained on Sunday night in the Bronx, leaving the Subway Series tied for a month and one wet image behind. With the tarp on the field, Ventura grabbed one of Piazza's jerseys, fashioned a thin mustache, and copied Mike's practiced manner-isms. Robin splish-splashed his way around the covered bases, headfirst-diving into home and calling himself . . . er, "Mike" safe. Between Friday night's blowout and the third baseman's incognito tour de force, it might have been forgotten by Mets partisans how burdensome these games could be. They'd get their chance to be reminded in early July when in addition to welcoming their crosstown foes to Queens, they'd make up the rainout smack in the middle of it. A day-night doubleheader was scheduled, after-noon at Shea, evening in the other place. It was no ordinary solution, but these were never casual get-togethers.

* * *

On June 14 in Chicago, Piazza homered and drove in three runs. Two days later, in the Mets' next game, at Milwaukee, he homered and drove in a pair. Mike wasn't going to homer every day, but driving in runs was another matter. By late June, Mike geared up as an RBI machine. By the time the Mets welcomed the Braves to Shea for their first meeting since the 1999 night their lights went out in Georgia, Piazza had driven in at least one run in 11 consecutive games, eight of them Met wins. He couldn't have been hotter.

Yet Mike Piazza was not the hottest topic on the eve of the Mets' and Braves' four-game feud. John Rocker had seen to that the previous December when he spouted off in *Sports Illustrated* about just what he thought of New York, encompassing everything from its diverse population ("I'm not a very big fan of foreigners") to the mass transit line that connected Manhattan to Flushing. Rocker compared the ride on the 7 line to his imagined version of Beirut, car after car speckled by "some kid with purple hair, next to some queer with AIDS, right next to some dude who got out of jail for the fourth time, right next to some 20-year-old mom with four kids." The reliever considered the whole tableau "depressing." Shea security considered Rocker a target and instituted extra precautions to protect him from Mets fans and his own mouth, installing a canopy in the visitors' bullpen to protect him from projectiles. They couldn't stop vocal commentary, however, and he was greeted predictably on Thursday, June 29, when he entered the eighth inning to protect the Braves' 6–4 lead. He struck out Ventura, then grounded out Zeile and Payton. Despite two more Piazza RBIs, Atlanta won the opener.

That was depressing. So was most of Friday night. Shea was packed less to boo Rocker again than to take in the postgame fireworks. It was more or less the only thing worth hanging around for as the Braves scored five off Hampton and another three off Eric Cammack to take an 8–1 lead to the bottom of the eighth. Even the opportunity to boo Rocker was off the table as the wrestling-style heel nursed a callus on his pitching hand and would be unavailable to Bobby Cox.

A diehard would say there was plenty of reason to stay put besides the promised Grucci Brothers' colored light extravaganza. *It's baseball*, that fan would tell you—*anything can happen*. That it rarely does makes it all the more explosive when the unlikely comes to pass.

In the bottom of the eighth, the Mets scored a run to make it 8–2. The only problem was the run scored on a fielder's choice grounder, the second out of the inning. Piazza, who had singled, was on third at that point, but a six-run lead still looked pretty formidable. As did the five-run lead that remained when Zeile singled in Piazza. When Payton followed Todd with another single, the fourth of the inning, Cox decided to take no chances. He removed mop-up man Don Wengert (Kevin Millwood had pitched seven strong innings) and brought in de facto closer Kerry Ligtenberg.

Ligtenberg was out of control—literally. He walked Agbayani to load the bases. Then he walked pinch-hitter Mark Johnson. The Braves' lead was now 8–4. Mora walked, too. It was 8–5. The bases remained loaded. The third out remained elusive. Cox took out Ligtenberg and brought in Terry Mulholland, a pitcher who'd been around so long that he was a footnote in the story of the 1986 Mets. As a rookie for the Giants fourteen years before, Terry was on the mound, pitching to Keith Hernandez. Hernandez bounced a ball back to him. It got stuck in the pitcher's glove. So the pitcher tossed the glove, with the ball wrapped inside it, to first base. Hernandez was out. The Mets won anyway. Everybody had a good chuckle. Now, Mulholland needed one more out, by conventional means or otherwise, to end this increasingly serious Mets threat.

Instead, he walked Bell to make it 8–6. The crowd forgot it was waiting around for the Grucci family and leaned forward for their favorite sons.

Alfonzo singled. In came two runs to tie the game at eight. If nothing else, the Mets had come all the way back. But they didn't come this far to get only that far.

Piazza came up. He needed to see only one pitch. What happened to it was described by Gary Cohen:

"Bell is the lead run. He's on second, Alfonzo at first with two out. Eight to eight, bottom of the eighth. Incredible. Mulholland ready to go. The pitch to Piazza . . . swing and a drive deep down the left-field line . . . toward the corner . . . IT'S OUTTA HERE! OUTTA HERE! Mike Piazza with a LINE DRIVE three-run homer! Just inside the left-field foul pole! The Mets have tied a club record with a ten-run inning! And they've taken the lead . . . eleven . . . to eight! Piazza drives in a run for a thirteenth straight game, and the first time in *twenty-one years the Mets have put up a ten-run inning. They've done it against the Atlanta Braves, they've come from seven runs down . . . here in the bottom of the eighth inning. They lead it eleven to eight. Incredible!"*

Mike's swing took care of everything but Mulholland's glove. Or maybe in the frenzy that followed his giving the Mets an 11–8 lead Armando Benitez would hold on to, that went flying Charlie Brown–style, too. The Braves' lead and veneer of invincibility certainly took a hike. It was a comeback, a game, and a result that would have fit snugly within the wars of September and October 1999. And when July dawned the next day, the Mets seemed closer than they had all season to ensuring an encore in the autumn ahead. Greg Maddux was on the hill for Atlanta. New York wasn't impressed. A six-run second, capped by Piazza's two-run homer—meaning a fourteen-game RBI streak—made it 7–0 en route to a 9–1 romp. The foes were one game apart in the National League East standings.

Lest there be a moment to breathe and feel fulfilled about an enormous stride taken, the Braves won the finale on Sunday (with Piazza driving in a run for a 15th straight game) and the Yankees cruised back onto the Mets radar Friday. A tight pitching matchup between Leiter and Orlando "El Duque" Hernandez went the visitors' way, 2–1, Mariano Rivera flying out Piazza to start the ninth and Payton to end the ninth.

The appetizer cleared away, it was time for baseball history: Saturday, June 8, 2000, Yankees at Mets at 1:15, Mets at Yankees at 8:05. The last time something like this occurred was in 1903 between the Giants and Dodgers, except the Dodgers were known as the Superbas and Ebbets Field hadn't yet been built. The stadia on that occasion were the Polo Grounds and Washington Park. Also, the second game wasn't really a night game, because who had lights in 1903? For that matter, New York didn't yet have a subway system. This twenty-first century Subway Series within a Subway Series would include chartered buses and police escorts for the players to transport them between ballparks. It was Metrocards or Triborough traffic for everybody else. Goodness knows the basepaths were jammed with storylines all day.

In the top of the first game, the Mets caught a break when leadoff hitter Chuck Knoblauch got greedy and tried to take second on a single to center. Payton threw him out easily. Maybe it would be the Mets' afternoon. Or maybe not. A minor league fill-in umpire named Rob Cook—at Yankee first base coach (and ex-Met) Lee Mazzilli's urging—ruled first baseman Zeile had obstructed Knoblauch's path and awarded him second. Replays suggested there'd been no obstruction, but they were just pretty pictures that had no impact on an umpire's decision. With their break taken from them, the Mets fell behind, 2–0, detracting from what was supposed to be the big story of the matinee.

Dwight Gooden was back at Shea. His first tenure as a Yankee ended after 1997. He kicked around from Cleveland to Houston to Tampa Bay before landing with his old team if not his original team. Doc received a nice ovation from those Mets fans not too caught up in stewing over Cook's call. Gooden pitched five innings, not overpowering the Mets, but getting them out enough. He flied Piazza to center to end his assignment. Jones pitched pretty well after the first, going seven, but the Yankees won, 4–2.

Mets fans craved revenge in the nightcap, but so did somebody else, and he wasn't wearing a Mets uniform. Clemens had apparently had enough of Piazza taking him ever deeper, so to send a message (or worse), Clemens came up and in on the second pitch of the second inning at Yankee Stadium. It hit the batter on the bill of his batting helmet. The helmet went flying. The batter went down.

Mike hit the ground and lay flat on his back for several seconds. It didn't look good from either a physical or competitive standpoint. Piazza was able to get up, but he was leaving the game. Words like "groggy" and "gingerly" peppered Cohen's description of the scene. The first concern was for Mike's well-being. X-rays revealed a minor concussion. The next was, depending where you stood in the Subway Series, disgust or bewilderment with Clemens's actions. The old saying, "He's got better control than that," came to mind. The Yankee starter wasn't ejected. The Mets' starter, Rusch, delivered a tepid payback, plunking Tino Martinez on the rear end in the next half-inning; as this was an American League park, Clemens didn't have to worry about direct retaliation.

Ill will between the stars and their teams had escalated. Valentine recognized what he saw: "My player, who's had pretty good success against their pitcher, got hit in the head. I've seen him hit guys in the head before." Joe Torre brushed it off as essentially just one of those things: "I was thrown at many times." Between innings, Clemens tracked down Piazza, who was waiting for an initial examination inside the Stadium. He had phoned to apologize or at least check up on his victim. Piazza refused to take the call.

After Clemens and the Yankees won this game, 4–2, Roger insisted he meant for his pitch to be belt-high. "I'm glad to hear he's all right." Piazza, still dealing with a headache, declared his certainty that the pitch hadn't accidentally gotten away. "I don't want to say he intentionally hit me in the head, but I think he intentionally threw at my head . . . Roger Clemens is a great pitcher, but I don't have respect for him now at all."

The next night at Shea, in the ESPN finale that would close out the first half, the Mets got even as best they could. Phillips denied the Yankees use of the Mets' weight room. Hampton and Benitez combined on a 2–0 shutout. None of it was particularly satisfying. Mike Piazza, the Mets' best player, was out of action, struck by a fairly lethal weapon, felled by a completely unsympathetic character who also happened to be wearing a red cape of a uniform.

The Mets and Yankees were done playing for 2000, unless another unforeseen adjustment to the Subway Series schedule was going to be made. And as any rider of the 7 line could tell you, you never could be too sure when the next train might come rumbling down the tracks.

* * *

Piazza had been a fixture at every All-Star Game since 1993, a starter since 1994. He was enough of an institution that he'd taken to joining the ESPN crew that announced the Home Run Derby. He was elected yet again in 2000, but after taking that fastball to the helmet, he had to skip the festivities at Turner Field. The Mets were represented by Leiter and Alfonzo. Also on hand, albeit in the colors of other teams, were Oakland's Jason Isringhausen, San Francisco's Jeff Kent, and Boston's Carl Everett. Along with Fonzie, they were proof that the 1995 Mets may have been on to something.

Piazza was back in action when the second half resumed, and so was Steve Phillips. The GM may not have landed Griffey, but he made a deal for another Cincinnati superstar, Barry Larkin. Once again, though, the veteran in question said thanks/no thanks and vetoed the deal. Phillips kept looking for a more sure-handed shortstop than Mora. He decided he'd found him in Baltimore, trading Melvin to the Orioles for Mike Bordick. Within the same flurry of deadline activity, he sent two former No. 1 picks—Tyner and lingering Generation K afterthought Paul Wilson—

to the Devil Rays for Bubba Trammell (outfield depth) and Rick White (another bullpen arm). The Mets were locking and loading with the post-season in mind.

On July 27, after sweeping a doubleheader from the Expos, the Mets took possession of the National League wild-card lead. Three days later, the Mets celebrated Ten Greatest Moments day at Shea Stadium, a pregame gala preceding the Mets-Cards Sunday tilt, sponsored by Nobody Beats the Wiz. The organization hadn't done much to commemorate its past of late—no inductions in the team Hall of Fame since Keith Hernandez in 1997, still no revival of Old Timers' Day—but with a nice 1999 banner now plastered on the right-field wall alongside those marking 1969, 1973, 1986, and 1988, the franchise in its 39th season could take a moment from the present and toast a little history. Fans were asked to go online and choose what they thought were the best moments they'd ever experienced.

Winning it all in 1986 topped winning it all in 1969. It was hard to beat the two world championships. Recency bias won the Grand Slam Single third place. The "You Gotta Believe" Mets of '73 finished a relatively distant seventh, but it was enough to lure Willie Mays to the park as one of the ava-tars of that unforgettable collection of miracle workers. Tug stopped by. So did Tom Terrific, Le Grand Orange, Mex, and the Kid. Mets tradition was on display. It was Old Timers' Day without calling it such, reaching back to 34-home run man Frank Thomas to carry the banner (or placard) for the Original Mets. The creation of the Mets confounded Internet-era voting patterns and finished tenth. And speaking of creation, fans grateful that a big-name transaction went their way recognized the creation of the thor-oughly modern Mets by voting as their eighth-ranked greatest moment—one ahead of Pratt's walkoff versus the Diamondbacks—the trade that brought them Mike Piazza. Fortunately, this was one ceremonial gathering Piazza could and did attend; he was catching and batting cleanup in the game that would follow.

Mike said he was honored to be included, but indicated the rationale for his selection left him a trifle unfulfilled. "I wish," he said, "I would have hit a big homer or something, not just have been traded." As it happened, Tram-mell, in his first game as a Met, hit a big homer, just as Bordick had done the day before. Jones pitched like his old Fresno self and the Mets won, 4–2, sweeping the weekend series from the NL Central-leading Cardinals.

More great moments were ahead. Few beat the Mets in August. Twenty-nine ballgames played, twenty ballgames won. Bordick was the hoped-for defensive upgrade at short. Hampton had rounded into ace form. Leiter was enjoying a stellar season. Hamilton was back from injury, though center field was now mostly the province of Payton. Benitez continued to pile up saves. Bobby Jones had stabilized—Bobby J. Jones, that is; in an echo of the two Bob Millers from 1962, the Mets also had a Bobby M. Jones. The spirit of '62 lived on when, against the Giants at Shea, Agbayani handed a ball to a fan in the stands . . . while it was still in play. Evidence that 2000 was a whole other kind of year came when the Mets recovered from Benny's miscue and won that game.

At the core of it all, adjacent to Alfonzo, was Piazza—still hitting up a storm four-and-a-half months into the season, still giving it his all behind the plate. Mike was the DH that night in the Bronx against Clemens, but once the interleague portion of the schedule concluded, he was a full-time catcher, and he took that element of his game seriously. On a trip to Los Angeles, he showed just how much he put into his position when he went head over heels into the first row of seats at Dodger Stadium to catch a foul pop, never fearing the concrete that threatened his noggin.

While Piazza was throwing his entire body into advancing the Mets' cause, *Sports Illustrated* was featuring it on its cover again. "The Man," the magazine called him, hailing Mike as "the greatest hitting catcher ever and the heart of a team on a tear." The Mets, Tom Verducci wrote, appeared to be perhaps the "most balanced" team in baseball, while its cleanup hitter, according to batterymate Leiter, meant "everything" to its lately winning ways. At the time of mid-August publication, Mike was among the National League leaders in the all the glamour categories: .351 batting average, 31 homers, 97 RBIs. All that while guiding a strengthened pitching staff (its ERA was more than a run lower with Piazza behind the plate than it was with Pratt) and diving into front rows like he was one of the few catchers more famous than himself: Bob Uecker.

Mike was a favorite for his first MVP and the Mets were finally a first-place team when they got to the first of September, but each entity tailed off. Yet make no mistake about it. There were going to be playoffs. True, the Mets had to endure the indignity of the Braves clinching their sixth consecutive National League East title at Shea on September 26, but had their own reason to hug and high-five one night later when they nailed down the wild card, beating their nemeses, 6–2, and earning a trip to the postseason for the second straight year, a Met first. The players celebrated in relatively subdued fashion, knowing there were miles to go before they could truly howl with delight like the title characters in their new non-sequiturial fight song, "Who Let the Dogs Out?"

* * *

A more pertinent question had an answer by the time the 94–68 regular season ended on a five-game winning streak. Who would the Mets play in the National League Division Series? As the wild card, they'd get the out-of-division opponent with the best record, which turned out to be the 97–65 San Francisco Giants. Get by them and the first of two long-awaited rematches would be in sight. The Braves would be taking on the Cardinals. Assuming Atlanta beat St. Louis (the Braves had never lost an NLDS), the Mets could think about finally knocking off their archrivals . . . and then maybe do something about local bragging rights on a national stage.

But one miracle at a time. The Giants needed to be beaten first, and that would be difficult. While Piazza cooled in September—final totals a still very impressive 38–113–.324—he was surpassed in the MVP derby by a pair of San Franciscans. Barry Bonds, now thirty-six, put up perhaps his best year since his last award-winning season in 1993, socking a career-high 49 home runs, but finished second in MVP balloting to his own teammate if not great and good friend, Jeff Kent. The ex-Met who didn't go anywhere when he was traded to Cleveland for Carlos Baerga busted out when he crossed the Golden Gate. He was regularly putting up numbers at second base that were usually the province of corner infielders and outfielders. The BBWAA rewarded him with its Most Valuable honor, consigning Mike to third place.

Individual accolades were for later. For now, it was time to win the NLDS and a date with the Braves . . . or the Cardinals, one supposed. The Giants took a great leap forward toward making that appointment with presumably Atlanta by defeating the Mets handily in Game One, 5–1. Hampton, who'd finished the regular season strong, was ineffective and the Mets did nothing versus Livan Hernandez. In the third, right fielder Bell, who'd never really snapped out of his slump from late May, slipped on the Pac Bell

Park grass and suffered a high ankle sprain. It was enough to sideline him for
however much of the postseason remained.

The "if necessary" portion of this best three-of-five affair appeared dead
certain to kick in as Game Two—with speedy late-season call-up Timo
Perez taking over in right for Derek—wore on. Leiter was close to brilliant
for eight innings, nursing a 2–1 lead until Fonzie padded it with a two-run
homer off Felix Rodriguez in the top of the ninth. Valentine allowed Al a
shot at a complete game, but when Bonds led off the bottom of the ninth
with a double, he went to Benitez. No biggie; Armando had set a Met record
with 41 saves in 2000.

The biggies would come when Benitez gave up a single to Kent and
then, one out later, a three-run home run down the right-field line to J. T.
Snow. There'd be no save in the ninth, and the Mets could only hope for
salvation in the 10th.

If they asked, they received. With two out, Hamilton—something of a
forgotten man in this Mets new world in which the outfield was now comprised of Agbayani, Rookie of the Year candidate Payton (he'd finish third),
and Perez—pinch-hit and doubled. The next batter, Payton, stroked the
first pitch he saw from Rodriguez into center and drove home Darryl. The
reprieve was granted. The Mets led, 5–4. After Benitez gave up a leadoff
single to Armando Rios, Bobby V turned to the old closer, John Franco,
to get the job done. John was now a setup man, but this was no time to ask
for ID. Franco got two outs, still had a man on, and, on the seventh pitch of
a full count, froze Bonds—who'd just led the league in walks for the sixth
time in nine years—looking to end the game. It was a close pitch, but his
catcher, Piazza, pulled it in on the edge of the inside corner and secured the
biggest strike of the new century.

As Game Three was getting under way at Shea late on Saturday afternoon, October 7, the big scoreboard in right-center transmitted a bulletin
that required a moment to absorb. Someone had let the Braves out. The
Cardinals had swept mighty Atlanta. The Braves were no longer in the postseason and therefore no longer presented an obstacle to potential Met happiness. If two wins over the Giants could be secured, the road to the World
Series would steer fully clear of Turner Field.

Ah, but "if" can be a mighty long word come playoff time, and Game
Three would make for a mighty long adventure. The Mets knew how to

navigate those in October and their fans knew how to persevere through them. "The Mets go melodramatic in October," Roger Angell once observed. "It's in their genes." Experientially or at least spiritually, that could provide an edge. Or it would be nice if it did. Bonds and Kent were perfectly capable of upsetting karma's apple cart at any moment.

Rick Reed and Russ Ortiz exchanged zeroes for three innings. In the fourth, the Giants broke through, with Bobby Estalella and Marvin Benard serving as trigger men. Reed was fine thereafter through six, but the Mets didn't get to Ortiz until Rick was lifted for pinch-hitter Hamilton in the bottom of the sixth following a leadoff walk to Bordick. Hamilton singled, then so did Perez to put the Mets on the board. Mets relief pitching then took over, as it did in so many of the marathon sessions of October 1999. Dennis Cook grounded out Bonds with a runner on second in the seventh and Turk Wendell came in to strike out Kent to end the frame.

After Turk got the Mets through the eighth, they stitched together a one-run rally: hit-by-pitch; pinch-hit fielder's choice; popup; stolen base; and, at last, a double from Alfonzo. Piazza had a chance to drive Fonzie in from second for the lead, but Robb Nen struck him out. It was 2–2 heading to the ninth . . . and innings to be named later.

Franco and Bonds met again with a man on and two out in the ninth. John struck him out again (swinging). Nen responded by putting runners on first and second with two out. Bordick struck out to send it to extras. Benitez came in for the tenth, let Giants land on first and third, but flied out Felipe Crespo. Rodriguez pitched a perfect bottom of the inning. In the eleventh, Benitez blew the Giants away in order, on three swinging strike threes. Piazza started the home 11th with a single and was pulled for pinch-runner McEwing. The Mets loaded the bases, but Pratt, pinch-hitting for Armando, struck out to end the threat.

Rick White was the next Mets pitcher. He walked Bonds to begin the 12th, which was three bases less worse than what could have happened. The Mets' second Rick rolled from there, though, fanning Kent and Ellis Burks and eventually getting out of the inning. Aaron Fultz became the next Giants reliever in the bottom of the 12th and the latest to keep the game going. The top of the 13th ended with White stranding two runners as he popped Bonds up.

Game Three was past the five-hour mark. Its roots as a day game were long forgotten. It had grown much darker and much colder at Shea. Go much longer, and this baby could cross the International Date Line. Agbayani from Hawaii had a better idea. With one out, he drove a Fultz pitch somewhere in the direction of Alaska. It was a no-doubter walk-off home run that concluded a 3–2 Met victory in five hours, twenty-two minutes, and thirteen jubilant innings. Well, the ending was jubilant. Most of the middle was tension personified. "These are always nerve-racking," Piazza said as the Mets sat one win from the NLCS. "A lot of guys really couldn't swallow out there." Benny, though, ate up the chance to be the kind of hero Mike or Barry (0-for-5) usually was: "It's a great feeling to be 'The Man.'"

The man who would attempt to seal this series victory was a fella who missed the 1999 postseason altogether and appeared in danger of disappearing from 2000 at midseason. Bobby Jones was the only 1993 Met besides Franco to last into the new millennium. His fourth career loss was the '93 squad's 101st. He had looked at Mets from both sides now. He was going to have the chance to pitch them toward if not directly to the World Series.

On another wind-chilled late afternoon at Shea, after Kristi Jones promised Bobby Valentine (who'd considered Hampton or Glendon Rusch for the start) that her husband would pitch "the game of his life," the Mets enlisted their foremost symbol of positive thinking, Tug McGraw, to throw out the ceremonial first pitch. Ignoring the cold, he whipped off his jacket and revealed a shirt bearing the phrase he embroidered into the Mets fan consciousness twenty-seven falls before. The omens all insisted that a Mets fan had to Believe. Jones further steered 56,245 minds in an optimistic direction when he retired the Giants in order in the first, and then the second, and then the third. He was staked to an early lead in the bottom of the first when his fellow Fresnoian, Mark Gardner, gave up a two-out walk to Piazza and a two-run homer to Ventura, who circled the bases without incident. Bobby threw another perfect inning in the fourth, which set the forever no-hit-conscious Shea crowd to murmuring. None of the Mets' Ten Greatest Moments were no-hitters because no Met had ever thrown one. Wouldn't it be something for it to happen under these circumstances?

It would be something more familiar to have the effort broken up by an ex-Met, and, leading off the fifth, Kent did the dishonors, lining a double over the head of a not nearly tall enough Ventura. Perfection was gone and adequacy appeared to be eluding Jones. With one out, he walked Snow. With two out, he walked Doug Mirabelli, though that could be attributed to caution. Gardner was up next. Facing the pitcher with two out was a decent bet. Of course Giants manager Dusty Baker could have pinch-hit for Gardner. San Francisco needed to win to get the series back to Pac Bell where the Mets had lost all four in the regular season and barely escaped with a split in this series. Baker chose to stick with his pitcher, who hit .116 in 2000.

Bobby popped up his pal and got out of the inning. Mark rewarded his manager's faith by giving up back-to-back doubles to Timo and Fonzie, resulting in two more runs and a four-run Met cushion. Jones reverted to perfection from there. The sixth, the seventh, the eighth . . . nothing for the Giants. The Met lead remained 4–0 in the top of the ninth as Jones, who hadn't completed a shutout since besting Pedro Martinez in 1997, attempted to finish flawlessly. He grounded Benard to first, Bill Mueller to second, and was left only with the task of retiring the most accomplished National League hitter of his generation.

No problem. Bobby Jones induced a fly ball from Barry Bonds (.176 in the four games) to Jay Payton in center, sealing his one-hitter and sending the Mets to NLCS. The five-strikeout gem, featuring eight innings with no baserunners and one masterfully maneuvered so as to leave the bases loaded, earned Bob Murphy's utmost admiration. Upon calling the final out of this "magnificent game," Murph declared, "The Mets have never had a better game pitched in their thirty-nine year history than this game pitched by Bobby Jones." Bob had seem 'em all, including the one voted No. 6 in the Ten Great Moments promotion, Tom Seaver's "imperfect game," the one-hitter over Jimmy Qualls and the Cubs from the summer of '69. Jones's performance wasn't as overpowering as Seaver's, but it was proffered in the glare of the postseason with advancement to the next round on the line.

Besides, who would argue with Bob Murphy? Not Lenny Harris ("we're all about destiny"); not Todd Zeile ("we're made up of winners"); and not Piazza, who had just caught his first Met one-hitter, making him the first Mets catcher to direct one since Charlie O'Brien partnered with David Cone in 1991. Mike had handled two no-hitters in Los Angeles, though those bona fides rarely came up in conversation in discussing the greatest-hitting catcher of all time. What got noticed in a series like the one with the Giants was how well he hit . . . or much he didn't. Mike's stats in the NLDS: a

.214 batting average, no home runs or runs batted in. But there was plenty of presence. Walking in front of Ventura in the first inning of the fourth game was evidence that the Giants didn't want to let the Mets' best hitter beat them. And he didn't. But enough of everybody else on the Mets did, which is all that matters in a playoff series.

Like Bonds, who had played in five postseasons since 1990 and had never fully blown up, Piazza, save for that one electric swing against John Smoltz in 1999, had yet to prove himself the kind of offensive star in October he had been six months out of every year.

Unlike Bonds, he was about to have another opportunity in October of 2000.

* * *

The Mets and Cardinals were blood rivals in the second half of the 1980s the way the Mets and Braves were lately. The realignment of the National League into three divisions put an end to their organic enmity, but the NLCS reignited some dormant passions. Mets fans remembered the "pond scum" propaganda that percolated in St. Louis from the days Strawberry, Hernandez, and Carter went to baseball war with Smith, McGee, and Coleman. The casts were different now and the hype was situational, but the stakes were the highest they'd ever been between the two teams. Only one of them could win a pennant.

This was the first Cardinals team to make the postseason in the Mark McGwire era, but 2000 hadn't been much of a year for the man recognized the October before as Iron Horse Lou Gehrig's All-Century peer. A bad knee limited Big Mac to 89 games and 32 homers. He hadn't played the field since July, but would be available to manager Tony La Russa as a pinch-hitter. Another curious component of La Russa's roster was his starting pitcher from the first game of the NLDS, Rick Ankiel. Ankiel won 11 games as a rookie during the regular season, impressive enough to place second, just ahead of Payton, in the Rookie of the Year voting. Yet against the Braves, he fell apart as few postseason starting pitchers ever had. He walked six batters in 2 2/3 innings, which doesn't begin to describe his lack of control, for he also unleashed five wild pitches. The Cards battered Greg Maddux for six runs in the first inning, so St. Louis survived the historically horrible outing, but it definitely cast doubt on Ankiel's abilities and how they'd translate against the Mets.

The first game of the Championship Series, on October 11, matched ex-Astros Mike Hampton and Darryl Kile. Kile had no-hit the Mets seven years earlier. No hint of that 1993 dynamic revealed itself at Busch Stadium, as Perez, a .294 hitter as Derek Bell's replacement in the Division Series, doubled to lead off. A little Ankielish wildness snuck into Kile's repertoire as he wild-pitched Timo to third, then walked Alfonzo. Piazza came up and came through, with a double to left that scored a run and birthed a legend. For once Mike got hold of Darryl's pitch, third base coach John Stearns—wearing a microphone for FOX Sports—shouted for all to hear, "The Monster's out of the cage! The Monster's out of the cage!" The Monster is what the Mets called Mike behind closed doors, for the most obvious reason possible. "Mike's private nickname around the clubhouse is The Monster," Stearns would explain, "because it's frightening sometimes the way he hits."

The Cardinals may not have been spooked, but they should have been alarmed. Piazza was awake and so were his teammates. Ventura drove home Alfonzo with a sac fly to make it 2–0 before St. Louis could hit. Hampton proceeded to put Redbird batters to sleep, pitching seven shutout innings. Along the way, Fonzie drove in a run, Zeile and Payton homered, and the Mets prevailed, 6–2. Mike went 2-for-4 and eschewed monstrous hyperbole. "We're a confident team," he said. "But it's far from over. We've got to keep the hammer down and keep pushing forward."

La Russa gave the Mets a shove in the right direction for Game Two by starting Ankiel. Inside of five batters, the rookie walked three and threw two wild pitches. When the sixth batter, Agbayani, delivered the first hit, a double, to make it 2–0, his manager realized it wasn't going to be Rick's night and took him out. Britt Reames mostly kept the Mets off the board for 4 1/3 innings, but did give up Piazza's first homer of this postseason, a leadoff blast in the third. Leiter went seven and gave up three runs to leave the game tied at three heading into the eighth. The bullpens then traded shaky half-innings. Matt Morris and Dave Veres gave up two runs to the Mets, their last out coming when Piazza, who had been intentionally walked only to have Zeile drive in a run, was caught in a 7–5–6–4 rundown. Franco suffered a touch of the Ankiel, with a walk and a wild pitch in two-thirds of an inning, and Wendell gave up a two-out, game-tying double to J. D. Drew. McGwire emerged to pinch-hit with the go-ahead run on second, but Valentine saw La Russa's intentional base-on-balls to Piazza and raised it by putting Mark on first. Turk responded by striking out 1998 Met Craig Paquette.

The Mets broke the 5–5 deadlock in the ninth by threading together a Cardinals error, a sac bunt, and a Payton single. Benitez pitched a scoreless ninth, and the Mets took a 2–0 lead in the series, marking their first-ever five-game October winning streak. It was also the first time they'd won the first two games of a postseason series since the 1969 NLCS. Shea and a potential similar conclusion awaited. Thirty-one years earlier, the Mets took two in Atlanta and clinched the flag at home when the playoffs required only three wins. In 2000, though, there would have to be a detour. On Saturday the fourteenth, the Cardinals jumped on Reed, Andy Benes was sound for eight innings, and the Mets lost, 8–2.

There'd be no Mets sweep, but there'd also be no great shift in momentum. On Sunday night, after Jones spotted the Cardinals two runs on a Jim Edmonds homer in the top of the first, the Mets shook Kile and Shea. Technically, their fans did the shaking. While the Mets rattled off five doubles in their first six at-bats (Perez, Alfonzo, Piazza, Ventura, Agbayani), 55,665 commenced to jumping as if directed by Van Halen or the Pointer Sisters, depending on one's musical proclivities. The stands definitely vibrated and the ballpark was a house of pain to the visitors. More reasons for Mets fans to jump around emerged in the second when Zeile—the only batter to make an out amid the doubles parade—delivered a two-run two-base hit that threatened to wreck the thirty-six-year-old stadium's infrastructure. When Benny singled behind him to make it 7–2, Shea somehow survived, but not because the crowd had calmed down.

Jones wasn't on a par with the one-hit standard he set for himself versus San Francisco, but a five-run lead and a Monster of a catcher will forgive a lot. Will Clark, the old Giant, homered in the fourth to cut the Mets' edge to 7–3, but Piazza grabbed the run back on a dinger of his own in the bottom of the inning. Eric Davis, the old Dodger, ended Bobby's night with a run-scoring pinch-double in the fifth, and Rusch allowed two more of Jones's baserunners to score to make it 8–6, but the contemporary Cardinals never drew any closer. The Mets won, 10–6, and ended the evening one game from a National League flag.

On Monday night, October 16, the same date on which the Mets won their first World Series, the franchise ached to punch a ticket to its fourth. The vibe at Shea was more 1986 than 1969, as the Mets continued to dominate St. Louis, scoring three runs in the first and three more in the fourth off Pat Hentgen. Hampton breezed through inning after inning, making his acquisition from the Astros the essence of prescience. The Mets envisioned him furnishing that something extra that would push them beyond the National League Championship Series and he was bringing it.

Game Five simmered along into the bottom of the seventh, Hampton carrying the 6–0 lead toward a conclusion agreeable to the home folks, having permitted only three hits and one walk. Then, because it wouldn't be a Mets postseason affair without a little melodrama, things got a bit weird. La Russa decided his best bullpen option with the Cardinals' season nine outs from ending was Ankiel. In front of tens of thousands of unsympathetic souls (not that a few didn't cringe for the kid, given the scenario's competitive contours), the manager tossed his rookie into the fire. Unsurprisingly, Ankiel got burned, issuing two walks, two wild pitches and an additional run in two-thirds of an inning. An inning later, another episode out of the ordinary flared when Veres came high and tight to Payton one pitch, then hit him above the left eye with the next. Jay, an inning from the World Series after six years in the minors, saw blood and red, in that order. He charged the reliever, who claimed innocence. Benches cleared, as they will, though nothing came of it.

The Mets, up 7–0 and with decidedly bigger things on their horizon, couldn't be blamed for their sensitivities in this area. Four games earlier, Mike James followed his surrender of dingers to Zeile and Payton by dinging Bordick on the right thumb. Perhaps it was intentional, perhaps it wasn't, but the Mets' shortstop didn't start Game Two and wound up batting .077 in the NLCS; it was initially diagnosed as a bruise and Bordick returned to action, but subsequent examination showed it to be broken. And nobody had forgotten what happened to Piazza in July at Yankee Stadium.

But the best revenge is living well, and you can't do better for yourself than making the World Series. In the bottom of the ninth, the Mets took care of two ex-teammates, one ghost of a slugger, and a burden that had been building for several seasons. Hampton retired Paquette for the first out; pinch-hitter McGwire for the second; and Rick Wilkins, who started three games behind the plate for the Mets in the week prior to their trade for Piazza, for the third. Wilkins lofted a fly ball to center, where Perez, who had taken over for Payton, reeled it in uneventfully.

Except there was an event: Timo's catch clinched the Mets the National League pennant, their first in fourteen years. Hampton was their first-ever NLCS MVP; there was no award in 1969 or 1973, and in 1986 it went to Houston's Mike Scott for being impossible for the Mets to hit in the only two games they lost. Hampton proved similarly imposing to St. Louis, shutting out the Cardinals across 16 innings in Games One and Five. Great pitching beat great hitting in picking who was Most Valuable, because there was no discounting the hitting the Mets brought to bear in beating the Cardinals.

Batting averages don't tell all stories, but they illustrated the Mets' success pretty tellingly in their five-game victory: Alfonzo, .444; Zeile, an Oledrudian .368; Agbayani, .353; Perez, .304 less than two months removed from Norfolk; and, oh yeah, Mike Piazza, .412 on two singles, three doubles, and two homers. That made for a .941 slugging percentage. Throw in five walks—because nobody really wants to pitch to a Monster who has escaped his cage—and he was on base more than he wasn't. Not incidentally, when the final out was made, Piazza became only the third catcher in Mets history to rush out to the mound to greet a pitcher upon the capture of a National League flag. Jerry Grote, Gary Carter, Mike Piazza—quite the crouching and hugging pantheon.

After a dozen professional seasons, dating back to short-season A ball with the Salem Dodgers of the Northwest League, Mike was heading for his first World Series. "This is a very special moment," the superstar exulted as players hugged and champagne poured.

* * *

Nobody really doubted what was coming next. The Yankees, having cast aside the Oakland A's in five games in the ALDS, were one win from eliminating the Seattle Mariners of John Olerud and Rickey Henderson in six. With the Mets having completed their business on Monday night the sixteenth, the Yankees returned to Yankee Stadium the next night to do something quintessentially Yankee: win their thirty-seventh American League pennant. They trailed their Game Six by four runs at one point, but took the lead on David Justice's seventh-inning home run that spurred Michael Kay to scream over WABC, "Get your tokens ready! You might be boarding the subway!" And when the last out of the 9–7 decision was recorded, Bob Costas, broadcasting NBC's final baseball game (MLB's next contract granted FOX over-the-air exclusivity), invoked Sinatra: "Start spreadin' the news—New York, New York."

It was coming as surely as your next train is coming: sooner or later. The Mets had been building to the World Series and the Yankees were practically permanent occupants. Some on the Met side of town embraced the neighborly clash with characteristic humility. "All we are," Fred Wilpon blushed, "is the little guy in Queens trying to emulate the Yankees." Wilpon went back to the days when his Brooklyn Dodgers regularly tangled with (and mostly lost to) the Yankees in the Subway Series, the last of those in 1956. He was the co-owner of the team; he could afford to be romantic. Others, though, understood that the gap between a Subway Series and a regular World Series was one worth minding. During the NLCS, Franco dared to utter unneighborly thoughts. The Yankees, he said, had "had the spotlight for so long, it would be nice to have it all to ourselves in New York."

Nothing doing. The Mets were going, the Yankees were going, everybody would have to step in to let the doors close behind them and leave the rest of the country on the platform to watch in wonder.

If history was to dictate the outcome, there'd be no reason to go through the turnstiles. The Yankees, in existence fifty-nine years longer, had not only qualified for thirty-five more World Series than the Mets had, but they'd won twenty-three more. This Series, however, wasn't being played between 1923 and 1999. It was 2000, and the Mets had been the better team. The Mets won more games—94 to 87—and had sliced through their postseason so far in more convincing fashion. The Yankees endured a dreadful September, losing thirteen of fifteen to end their regular season. Emblematic of their slip if not fall from grace was the season Cone compiled. One of their most reliable October weapons since 1996, David went 4–14 with a 6.91 ERA during the season and pitched one inconsequential inning in the playoffs.

On the other hand, there weren't a lot of firsts among the Yankees when it came to making the World Series. Their roster was jammed with those used to playing ball in late October, whether for the Yankees or somebody else. Along with Cone, Clemens, Pettitte, Jeter, Williams, Posada, Rivera, and so forth, there was Justice, Jose Canseco, Denny Neagle, even Doc Gooden still hanging on (he pitched more against Oakland and Seattle than Cone had). For all the talk about Ruth, Gehrig, DiMaggio, and Mantle, the Yankees didn't get by on ancient history. They swept the last two World Series and won the final four games in 1996. The lavishly successful recent kind of history provided preface enough.

A clean slate awaited both teams in Game One, Saturday night, October 21. Leiter and Pettitte kept it blank for quite a while, though the Mets assisted the Yankee starter at an instantly critical juncture. Perez led off the top of the sixth with a single. Two outs later, Zeile launched a fly ball to deep left that looked to all of Western civilization like a two-run home run. Timo thought it did, and he started trotting. Todd didn't exactly motor around first, either. A 2–0 lead was in sight, pending the formality of both runners crossing the plate.

Thing is, the ball's flight came up a little short of the stands. Fan hands that might have reflexively reached out and inadvertently created interference controlled themselves. The ball stayed on the players' side of the wall and thus remained in play. Justice fielded it off the top of the wall and relayed it to Derek Jeter, who had stationed himself along the left-field line. Jeter threw on the mark to a plate-blocking Jorge Posada. Perez, who required an instant or more to determine that what Zeile hit wasn't a home run, sped up and slid, but not fast enough, not soon enough, and not safe enough. Perez was thrown out.

Lost opportunity. Not lost World Series, but a chance to take a lead on the Yankees not cashed in could be registered as a loss within a game that was still in progress. And when Justice doubled in two runs in the bottom of the sixth for the first scores of the game . . . well, let's just say that unless he did something wonderful soon, all Timo Perez did to get the Mets to the World Series was in danger of getting forgotten.

The Mets demonstrated resilience. In the seventh, one-out singles from Payton and Agbayani and a walk to Pratt—catching while Piazza took advantage of the DH rule in the American League park—set up Bubba Trammell, pinch-hitting for Bordick, to drive in two runs. Trammell had played far less than Bordick, but at the moment was the more valuable dead-line acquisition. One out later, with Jeff Nelson subbing for Pettitte, Fonzie pushed home a third run on an infield single.

Leiter protected the 3–2 lead in the seventh. Franco did the same in the eighth. In the top of the ninth, the Mets had a golden chance to extend their edge. Mariano Rivera hit Pratt with one out. Kurt Abbott, Bordick's replacement, doubled Tank to third. Perez grounded to second. Had Todd broken on contact, he probably could have scored. But Tank didn't roll and he wound up stranded where he stood. The same one-run lead would be handed to Benitez in the bottom of the ninth.

Armando's first batter was Posada. He flied out. His next assignment: Paul O'Neill, the "warrior," in George Steinbrenner's estimation. Fittingly enough, O'Neill battled through a ten-pitch at-bat that eventually became a walk. One out, but one on and more to come from unlikely sources. Luis Polonia singled O'Neill to second. Jose Vizcaino, the mid-'90s Met who resurfaced as a Yankee mid-season, singled them both up ninety feet. Chuck Knoblauch flied to left, which scored O'Neill to knot the night at three. The Mets' first World Series game since they defeated the Red Sox to win it all in 1986 was going to extras. It would stay there until the 12th when Vizcaino bested Wendell with the bases loaded. Jose's single gave the Yankees a 4–3 win. Seeking the brighter side of darkness, Valentine reasoned, "We came with very little World Series experience, and we got a lot of it in one night."

It probably wasn't enough to prepare them for the experience on deck for Game Two. In the probable pitchers listings, the names printed were Hampton for NY (NL) and Clemens for NY (AL). But where everybody's attention was focused, the second game shaped up as one pitcher versus one hitter: Roger Clemens versus Mike Piazza. No offense to NLCS MVP Hampton, but few outside of his immediate family were interested in how he'd handle the Yankee lineup. For that matter, nobody was fixated on how Clemens would approach Perez, Alfonzo, or any other Mets batter. The last time a Game Two was so breathlessly anticipated because of two principals, it was when Clemens faced Gooden in 1986. That clash of titans was an aesthetic dud. The Rocket was mediocre, the Doctor was dismal, and the final was 9–3.

The Monster had not necessarily been caged since breaking out in the NLCS. As designated hitter, Piazza went 1-for-5 in his first World Series game (on Sunday night, he'd catch). Clemens's recent sample size filled more of a mixed bag. He wasn't very good in two losses to Oakland, but was spectacular in his one start versus Seattle. In Game Five of the ALCS, he allowed one hit, walked two, and struck out 15 in the 5–0 shutout that nudged the Yankees toward their clincher. Of course, none of those games came in the heightened atmosphere of an intracity World Series and none of the batters he faced owned the loudest of .583 batting averages against him nor took one of his fastballs off his batting helmet a few months earlier.

So this would be different.

Clemens got two strikeouts to begin the game. He then worked Piazza to a 1–2 count before drawing a foul ball out of him. The pitch shattered Mike's bat. Mike had taken a few steps toward first before realizing it was foul. Roger took a piece of the bat, the barrel, and fired it in the general direction of Mike. It skipped in front of Piazza's feet.

Yes, it was different. To the entire world, the pitcher who (intentionally or not) beaned the hitter in their last encounter was now taking aim at him with a whole other type of potentially lethal weapon. Who throws chunks of bats at the other team, for cryin' out loud? Piazza, still steaming from their July encounter, did not take the wooden message lightly . . . not that anybody could figure out what precisely Clemens was communicating.

Cohen on WFAN: "I don't know what Clemens had in mind."

Joe Buck on FOX: "That was surprising."

Buck's partner Tim McCarver: "In my view, right now, Roger Clemens is dead wrong."

Piazza was pretty sure his opponent was up to no good, and quickly veered toward his nemesis in anger after what Buck described as the "jagged, pointed, sharp piece of wood" bounced past him. Their exchange boiled down to:

"What's your problem?"

"I thought it was the ball."

Why Clemens would throw a ball at a baserunner's feet is up for debate, but what was clear was the pitcher was amped beyond the norm, even taking into account the extraordinary circumstances and setting. Many years after this World Series was history, Torre revealed Clemens broke down and cried between innings, swearing it wasn't his intention to throw anything at Piazza. In the moment, though, tempers rather than tears were on display. A little New York baseball convention broke out around the mound once Piazza neared Clemens in search of answers. The Mets left their dugout, the Yankees theirs, and the umpires showed up as well. If this was the moment viewers were tuning in for, it was an anticlimax. No fight, no ejection, and everybody back to their corners.

Piazza grounded out on the next pitch. Hampton, with his own World Series start to worry about, didn't retaliate. The Yankees reached him for two runs in the bottom of the first and another in the second. Clemens, meanwhile, channeled his emotions into overwhelming the Mets, striking out nine of them and giving up only two hits in eight innings. By the time he exited, the Yankees led, 6–0.

Nelson entered to record the final three outs, but the notion that it would be routine eluded the Mets. Suddenly, they decided to hit back the only way that could hurt the Yankees. Fonzie singled. Mike homered. Ventura singled. Nelson left. The mighty Mariano came on, got one out, but then gave up a single to Agbayani. A passed ball put runners on second and third. Rivera cut down Robin on a ball hit back to him, but Payton then sent a ball out of the Stadium, and, unbelievably, the Mets trailed by a run. More believably, they ended Game Two that way, losing it, 6–5.

Torre, who didn't win three World Series and get halfway to a fourth by not defending his players, stood up for Clemens's reasoning, whatever it was, amid the postgame media inquisition. "Why would he throw at him?" Joe rhetorically asked reporters, assuming a pitcher who generally showed no qualms about throwing at batters would not want to risk ejection from such an important game. On the Mets' end of the debate, John Franco wasn't buying what Torre or Clemens ("I was fired up and emotional and flung the bat toward the on-deck circle where the batboy was. I had no idea that Mike was running") were selling. "I think he knew what he was doing all along," the senior Met said, "and is coming up with excuses."

As for the batter who took a ball off the batting helmet in July and the barrel of a bat in his path in October, Piazza summed the situation succinctly and indisputably: "It was just so bizarre."

* * *

If business was short of usual in Game Two, Game Three promised baseball in the realm of the normal, though that might not do the Mets any good in the World Series. The Yankees had now won 14 consecutive games while vying for a championship. Their starter in the third game would be

Orlando Hernandez, undefeated in eight postseason decisions. The Mets needed to disrupt the norms that had come to define autumn in New York.

Carryover from that five-run ninth on Sunday night was minimal. El Duque was dominant on Tuesday the twenty-fourth, striking out 12 Mets in 7 1/3 innings. But Ventura did tag him for a leadoff home run in the second, and Piazza's and Zeile's doubles in the sixth added up to another run. Reed pitched effectively himself, fanning eight Yankees in six innings while allowing individual runs in the third and fourth. The game remained 2–2 into the bottom of the eighth, and Hernandez kept pitching. After striking out Ventura, Zeile singled and Agbayani doubled. The Mets had a late-inning lead. Unlike Saturday night, they padded it, with pinch-hitter Trammell scoring pinch-runner Joe McEwing with a sac fly off Mike Stanton. Benitez preserved the 4–2 score to confirm the World Series was not yet over.

The winning pitcher was the Mets fan from Bensonhurst, John Franco. Perhaps he'd have been among the 55,299 making noise in the stands had he not been needed in uniform. Not everybody in the stands was rooting for the Mets in this Subway Series, but the majority was true to the black, orange, and blue. "A lot of people don't like to play here," said Zeile, who had morphed into a Flushing favorite. "The field . . . there's planes going overhead . . . we feel comfortable here. It's loud."

It would be loud when Game Four started, but it was the vocal minority speaking up, and it said something that didn't require the kind of interpretation Clemens's first-inning hijinks had three nights earlier. Jeter led off versus Jones with a first-pitch home run that seemed to suck all the hard-earned Met momentum straight out of the Series. It was one run, but it was a rather declarative keynote statement. Worse yet, from a Mets standpoint, the Yankees kept finding ways to add amendments. O'Neill's triple set up a second run in the second and Jeter set the table the same way in the third. He scored on a fielder's choice and shoved the Mets into a three-run ditch.

Perez had done little since getting thrown out at home in Game One. He had been scouted to within an inch of his life by the Yankees, who comprehended all his tendencies and pitched accordingly. It worked for the most part, but here he led off the home third versus Denny Neagle with a single. After Alfonzo grounded out, Piazza, who hit a foul home run down the left-field line in his first at-bat, got the Mets back in the game with a shot into the Picnic Area seats. Three-two was a negotiable deficit. Torre certainly recognized what one swing from a superstar could do, for when Piazza came up again in the fifth—two out, bases empty—he pulled Neagle and inserted the heretofore forgotten man of the Yankee dynasty, David Cone.

The same David Cone who'd pitched to an ERA that scraped seven in 2000, but also the same David Cone so intrinsic to three world championships in the past four years and, yes, the same David Cone who was the toast of the Conehead section at Shea in the late '80s and early '90s. Cone was thirty-seven. He was being asked to retire No. 31. Mike had homered off Neagle in the third after almost homering off Neagle in the first. "Piazza," Torre would explain, "is one of the few players that's in scoring position when he's in the batter's box." By removing Neagle, Torre showed he wasn't taking any chances. But by exchanging him for an arm whose best days had disappeared with the turning of the century, he was risking plenty.

This matchup between a former Cy Young winner and a perennial Silver Slugger was all baseball, no sideshow. Unfortunately for the Mets, Piazza was as successful against Cone in Game Four as he was versus Clemens in Game Two. Mike popped up to end the inning, and the Mets never made up that last bit of ground. They didn't put anybody else in actual scoring position and lost, 3–2. Elimination loomed the next night.

Leiter and Pettitte were at it again in Game Five. Al was perfect for the assignment, both for his repertoire that confounded Bomber bats and the heart-laden sleeve he wore whenever he pitched. Mets fans' anxieties required a surrogate for them out on the field. Leiter cared like they did. Perhaps everybody in uniform took it as personally as Al, but nobody seemed to show it more. His face could have been the scoreboard. It would always tell you how the game was going.

The game was going fine for the longest time. Bernie Williams reached Al for a home run to lead off the second, but a little good luck in the bottom of the inning (a mishandled bunt and a slow roller) led to two runs and a 2–1 lead. The starters returned to their zero-yielding ways until the sixth when Jeter delivered a solo home run. It was 2–2 and remained that way into the ninth, an inning Valentine left Leiter in to start and hopefully conclude.

Tino Martinez struck out swinging, as did O'Neill. Leiter was still strong. He pitched Posada to a 2–2 count and then threw a knee-high fastball that nicked the inside corner if you were watching via FOX's center-field camera, but missed if you were home plate umpire Tim McClelland. Ball three gave Posada just enough life. On the ninth pitch of the at-bat, the Yankees catcher walked. Scott Brosius then singled. Valentine stuck with Leiter to face Luis Sojo, the second baseman who replaced Pettitte in the batting order via double switch in the eighth.

The very first pitch he saw—the 142nd Leiter threw—he offered at. Sojo clubbed the ball fair into the grass a few feet in front of the plate. It bounced once, then bounced a second time under Leiter's swiping glove, then bounced again in front of the infield dirt, a bit to third base side of second. Alfonzo charged from the right, Abbott from the left. Each dove. Neither could reach it. Its next bounce was from the back of the basepath into short center field. It was less bouncing than rolling by the time Payton rushed in to scoop it up and fire it home in the hopes it would beat Posada there. Payton's throw carried him into the air. As he fell to the ground, Piazza waited slightly up the third base line to receive it.

He never got it. The ball Sojo hit and Payton threw glanced off Posada and bounced away, into the Mets dugout, allowing Brosius to come around. The "thirty-eight hopper," to use an expression that was not literal yet wholly evocative, produced two runs. Leiter attempted to don a mask of stoicism, but that was not his brand. He had just pitched his heart out. All it got him was the chance to be the losing pitcher in the last game of the World Series and his heart shattered somewhere on the mound . . . right around where Sojo's single bounced by.

Five different Mets—Leiter, Alfonzo, Abbott, Payton, and Piazza—landed on their knees in their attempt to cut off the go-ahead runs. Now, all prayers said, it was time to jump up off the grass and the dirt and make one final stand for 2000.

Rivera came in to keep the Mets grounded. Hamilton pinch-hit for Franco, who had replaced Leiter to get the third out Al thought he had when he almost struck out Posada. Hamilton fanned. One down. Agbayani, however, walked on four pitches. The Mets had gotten to Mo in Game Two. Maybe they could do it again. The two batters you'd want up in such a situation were lined up, just as they were that night at the end of June when coming back against the Braves was turning from inconceivable to actually happening.

First, Alfonzo. While Edgardo (who'd had an uncharacteristically awful offensive Series) batted, Benny took second unaccosted. When Edgardo flied to O'Neill in right, Benny took third. His run by itself didn't matter much, but if the next batter could get ahold of one, this thing would not be over.

Mike Piazza came up. He took one strike and then swung. Off the bat, it was a far different story from the one Sojo improvised. No bouncing. It was a fly ball traveling. It looked good and it was going deep, perhaps as deep as so many balls had flown in this hyper homer era.

But then, as if to remind one and all that William A. Shea Municipal Stadium, particularly 'neath the cover of October skies, tended to play as a pitcher's park, it died. When it fell into Williams's glove in front of the warning track in center field, so did the 2000 Mets. They lost the game, 4–2, and the World Series in five. Each of the other losses was by one run, but what bonded all four was that they were losses. Coming close four times was admirable, but it wasn't sufficient to send the Series back to the Bronx for a sixth game, a second shot at Clemens, and one more chance to keep going. The season that started earlier than all the others didn't last long enough.

The noise Todd Zeile so enjoyed at Shea was absent following Piazza's bid to tie the score came up short. There were certainly enough Yankees fans on the premises to make themselves heard, but those who cheered the Mets on through these five games . . . and the two playoff series before them . . . and the 162 games before those . . . and, really, the two years that led up to and into 2000 were left in silence if not exactly shock. They had fallen to the Yankees, whose expansive assortment of rings (their followers would be happy to fill you in on the revised size of their permanent collection) attested to the opposition's formidability. The Mets had tiptoed around the Braves, knocking off the Cardinals, who were kind enough to elbow aside the Atlanta obstacle they themselves could never quite dislodge, but the other brick wall in their lives refused to budge.

Yet it did say nice things before heading out of Queens and on to its next Manhattan parade. "The Mets are, in my opinion, the best team we've played in my years here," World Series MVP Jeter declared. Steinbrenner, who no doubt would have made the lives of all Yankees miserable had they dared to lose to their neighbors, magnanimously added, "The Mets gave us everything we could want."

Mets fans were left thinking almost the same thing.

WITH HIS HELP
April 3, 2001–October 7, 2001

Mike Piazza was a catcher who wasn't shy about serving as a pitchman. Among other goods and services he endorsed were ESPN's *SportsCenter*, Pert Plus shampoo, Claritin allergy medication, and, alongside '80s sitcom alien Alf, the 10–10–220 telephone deal (ninety-nine cents per call up to twenty minutes, seven cents a minute thereafter). In the summer of 2001, New Yorkers saw Mike assume the role of spokesman for a product nobody could doubt he used himself: Mets baseball.

In the ad, Mike leaves his Manhattan apartment building just as he might in real life and is wished good luck by his doorman. As he begins to walk the streets, everybody he runs into offers a piece of advice on his swing, his throwing, and his general ballplaying ability. One straight-out-of-central casting Sweet Old Lady warns him, "You just gotta win, because it's killing my husband." The tagline to the spot tells Mets fans, "With your help, they could be champions." Piazza, in the midst of another All-Star season, was the last Met the citizens of Gotham needed to coach, but when the subject was the Mets, what other player were you going to think of?

Truth in advertising was on display. Mike was living in Manhattan. His ballclub definitely needed assistance. Fans were more than happy to dispense it. But the way they were playing for most of 2001, there was no sign they could come close to doing what they had done the year before.

When Ralph Kiner and Mr. Met raised the 2000 National League Champions flag up Shea Stadium's center field pole prior to the April 9 home opener, the residual vibes from the best parts of the previous October were still in the air. This was a celebration of a pennant, not a recrimination for not winning the World Series. The 2000 Mets who were still 2001 Mets—a group that most notably did not include Mike Hampton, who took a massive free agent contract with Colorado because, he swore, they had great schools out west—drew cheers. The inevitable new additions (one of whom wasn't Alex Rodriguez, despite offseason buzz that indicated the all-world shortstop was a perfect and perfectly eager match) were applauded as well. One of them, flamboyantly wristbanded Tsuyoshi Shinjo, won the crowd over immediately by belting a home run off the Braves' Jason Marquis. Piazza, having entered his tenth major-league season, the minimum for Hall of Fame consideration, burnished his credentials by hitting two homers. The Mets rolled over Atlanta, 9–4, a week after taking two of three at Turner Field, and all looked Amazin' on a sunny afternoon in Queens.

Cloud cover moved in shortly thereafter and stalled over Shea. The National League champs, supplemented by Shinjo from Japan and a pair of new starting pitchers (Kevin Appier and Steve Trachsel replacing the departed Hampton and Bobby Jones), could not get untracked in April. Or May. The Mets didn't string together three consecutive victories until May 25, which pulled them to six games under .500 and nine games out of first place. As the cute "with your help" commercial entered heavy rotation, it became apparent the Mets were going to need more than a few friendly tips to rejoin the pennant race.

Piazza took one very big swing on Sunday night, June 17, the end of the first of the two feeding frenzies better known as the annual Subway Series. Now that the Mets and Yankees had played for all the marbles, the regular-season matchups lost a little luster, but they still filled the ballparks and they still meant plenty to those filling them. The first two games of the Shea set went the Yankees' way, so it was critical that the Mets not get swept. All that mattered to the Yankees was not pitching Roger Clemens, lest he have to stand in the batter's box and worry about getting hit.

Joe Torre held Clemens out and the Yankees rolled toward a sweep, carrying a 7–2 lead into the bottom of the eighth. Finally, the Mets woke up. They cut it to 7–5 and had runners on first and third when Shinjo—who co-starred with Benny Agbayani in his own commercial (Tsuyoshi translating advice a sushi chef's hitting advice for Benny)—hit a grounder that threatened to turn into an inning-ending double play. At the cost of pulling his quad muscle, Shinjo slid into first to beat the relay, which allowed the Mets to continue the rally down only one. Piazza came up as the go-ahead run . . . and became the go-ahead run after drilling a three-run homer off Carlos Almanzar deep into the late night. Mets dignity was preserved, 8–7.

"We were frustrated, our fans were," Piazza perceived. "At least they can walk out of here with some pride." Mike would make Mets fans proud again three weeks later, breaking up a scoreless tie in the Bronx with an RBI single in the 10th off Mariano Rivera. The Mets won that game, 3–0, their only victory in the second Subway Series of the season.

When the All-Star break came, the Mets were 13 under and 13 out. As skipper of the defending pennant-winners, Bobby managed the National League team in Seattle. Piazza was back behind the plate and Rick Reed made the squad, too. It appeared to be the last time anybody would associate the 2001 Mets with the World Series. Before July was done, the front office pretty much gave up on the concept of the Mets as contenders and began to dump salary.

Reed, All-Star status notwithstanding, was traded to Minnesota for out-fielder Matt Lawton. The Mets needed a right fielder/leadoff hitter because Timo Perez had gone back to Norfolk, never really having recovered from his disastrous World Series. Darryl Hamilton, often dealing with injuries and intermittently feuding with Valentine, was released. Todd Pratt, who hit the home run that won the 1999 NLDS and transformed the grand slam that defined the 1999 NLCS, was sent to Philadelphia. The Phillies became two-time trading partners in July when the Mets unloaded the stalwarts of their bullpen, Turk Wendell and Dennis Cook, receiving mainly Bruce Chen, a young lefty starter who'd come up with the Braves.

They were breaking up that old gang of Bobby V's, and it was disorient-ing. On the last Saturday afternoon of July, Wendell came out of the bull-pen at Shea for the Phillies. Fans conditioned to enthusiastically greet his appearances over the previous four years indeed roared wildly after his sec-ond pitch. But the cheers were for Robin Ventura, who hit it out of the park for a game-winning home run. When Piazza did the same to Rheal Cormier in the bottom of the ninth the next day, there was no confusion. Cormier had no history with the Mets, and Mike was Mike.

* * *

Back-to-back walk-off home runs should have given the Mets some momentum. It didn't, typical of 2001, when a couple of steps forward were inevitably neutralized by at least as many steps back. As of August 17, the Mets' 2001 season was over. Then, because there was no rule against it, the Mets started to win. They took the final two games of their trip in Los Angeles, the second of them on a pair of Piazza homers. When they returned home to face the Rockies, Mike got the best of his 2000 batterymate Hampton (not greeted warmly by the 28,510 in attendance). His second-inning home run not only extended the Mets' lead to 5–0, but went in the books as Piazza's 300th as a catcher. Aside from the round-number milestone, the homer broke a tie with Lance Parrish and put Mike in fourth place overall among slugging catchers. Yogi Berra was six ahead in third place, with Johnny Bench (327) and Carlton Fisk (358) waiting up the road.

Ever since he missed time to injury in early 1999, the subject of Mike switching to first base to preserve his bat against the wear and tear of receiving recurred now and again. Conceivably, he could have been John Olerud's replacement in 2000, but the Mets went with Todd Zeile and Piazza continued on as the greatest-hitting catcher in baseball history. Still, he was getting older—in early September he'd turn thirty-three—and defense, particularly his arm, was never his calling card. When Gary Carter was at Shea for his induction into the Mets Hall of Fame, he took great pains to compliment what Mike did well behind the plate. "He still receives the ball well, calls a good game, and he's the greatest hitting catcher of all time," Gary said while, in the same breath, drawing comparisons between Mike's poor numbers on steal attempts and the notoriously bad throwing of second basemen Steve Sax and Chuck Knoblauch. Plus the Mets had replaced Pratt with Vance Wilson, a young catcher who didn't hit much, but was renowned for his defensive acumen.

For now, though, Piazza wasn't about to be nudged from his post, and the Mets, diving into a thirteen-game homestand, were playing like their season wasn't finished. They pounded Hampton and took two of three from the Rockies, then three of four from the Giants, two of three from the Phillies, and two of three from the Marlins. Their margin from first place was down to 8 1/2. Neither the Braves nor Phillies were having a banner season as they fought for first place. The Mets had a series at the Vet coming up and, later in the month, six games versus the Braves. They were 65–72, which didn't exactly advertise postseason aspirations, but stranger things had happened in baseball. The 1973 Mets, no fan in Flushing required reminding, entered September substantially under .500 and began October clinching a division title.

Enough was happening to not dismiss "You Gotta Believe" instincts out of hand. Piazza's 31st home run got the Mets going in the first inning on Labor Day in Philadelphia, and his double was part of a five-run ninth that fueled the 10–7 victory that touched off a three-game sweep. "If we get within a few games, so be it," Piazza said, reflecting on the Get out of Mediocrity card the Mets seemed to have printed for themselves, "but right now, we're just having fun." Five nights later, the Mets found themselves riding a six-game winning streak, having scored three in the ninth to beat the Marlins in Miami, 9–7. The fun was ongoing. They had rushed to within a game of .500 and seven games of first. Everything that had not gone right from April well into August was now clicking. They'd taken seventeen of their previous twenty-one games heading into the Sunday finale at Pro Player Stadium. Despite losing that last game in Florida on September 9, their momentum was undeniable and their hopes tangible heading to Pittsburgh for a series scheduled to begin after an offday on Monday.

* * *

The next time the Mets played, their game couldn't have mattered less. Baseball couldn't have mattered less. Sports couldn't have mattered less.

There were no ballgames on Tuesday, September 11, 2001, destined to become the most recognizable date in modern American history. Four commercial airliners were hijacked by terrorists. Two were flown into the World Trade Center. One was flown into the Pentagon. Another crashed in a field in Pennsylvania before it could reach its presumed target in Washington, DC. These brazen attacks resulted in previously unimaginable tragedy. Nobody was sure how many thousands were dead.

Nothing could any longer be termed unimaginable, though placing import on "the loss column" seemed beyond fathomable. New York was part war zone, part wake. The Twin Towers were gone from the skyline, their literally smoldering remains all anybody could focus on. Of course there'd be no baseball on September 11, not in New York, not in Pittsburgh, not anywhere. MLB postponed all games through September 16, deciding it would pick up its routine the next night and grafting the unplayed week onto the back end of the schedule.

With all civilian flights grounded, the Mets rode by bus from Pittsburgh to New York. They were New Yorkers like everybody else, stunned, saddened, angry. Because their jobs made them celebrities, they put their fame and fortune to good use before resuming their fun and games (or even thinking of how they could). Players visited Ground Zero, the site of the rubble of the buildings that had been destroyed, wishing well to those digging through the horror of what remained. They made their way to hospitals and firehouses, consoling survivors and comrades of those who'd been lost trying to save lives or simply stay alive. Led by a fully dedicated Valentine, they set up alongside Red Cross volunteers in the Shea parking lot, a staging ground for necessary supplies to be funneled to the rescue and recovery—more recovery than rescue, it turned out—personnel. Each Met, along with several former Mets, pledged a day's pay to the New York Police and Fire Widows' and Children's Benefit Fund, a group set up by Mets icon Rusty Staub years before, a resource never needed more than now.

Then, back to baseball. On September 17, the Mets were supposed to play at home, but Shea was still being used for more pressing purposes, and besides, New Yorkers weren't ready to file into a ballpark and redirect their attention to anything resembling a distraction. Another adjustment to the schedule was made and the Mets returned to Pittsburgh, where the crowd was sparse, the mood was solemn, and the outcome seemed irrelevant. The Mets, wearing baseball caps bearing the logos of the agencies whose members put the lives of others above their own, beat the Pirates, 4–1. The backwards helmet Piazza wore while catching read NYPD.

MLB initially permitted a one-night tribute, but the Mets stuck with the caps. NYPD, FDNY, PAPD, OEM, and EMS became intertwined with the usual NY. It was an excellent fit spiritually and, oh by the way, the Mets swept three from the Pirates. On the eve of their (or anybody's) first ballgame in New York since September 11, they had cleared the .500 hurdle and moved to within 5 1/2 lengths of first place. The playoff chase was still a secondary concern, but their upcoming opponent was Atlanta, the very team they were trying to run down. They couldn't do it in 1998, 1999, or 2000, but 2001 was all of a sudden a very different year.

And September 21, 2001, was a very different night at Shea Stadium. It was unprecedented in mood and tone. The fact that it was open for baseball probably deserved to be marked down as a municipal victory. Ten days after downtown Manhattan's most recognizable landmark was successfully targeted for destruction, 41,235 people were willing to stream into as public a gathering spot as Queens had. Security was dimensions tighter than it had been when the goal was merely protecting John Rocker from the surlier elements of a partisan crowd.

Rocker was gone from the Braves, traded to Cleveland at midseason. The usual bile attached to a Braves visit to Shea was absent. There was nothing usual at all unfolding. The pregame, usually the understated hum of reflex ritual, was given over to intense remembrance and mourning. Bagpipes played. Diana Ross performed "God Bless America." Marc Anthony sang the national anthem. Small flags that had been handed out were waved. Red, white, and blue trimmed each uniform. A memorial ribbon in those patriotic colors fronted the permanently darkened World Trade Center section of the miniature skyline that topped the scoreboard. The Mets and Braves lined up as they had on opening day, but when it came time to play ball, there was no routine retreat to opposing dugouts. Instead, the rivals sought one another out to shake hands and hug. They'd go at it on the field, but they, like the thousands in the stands and the millions beyond the ballpark, understood they were in this thing together.

Somehow a baseball game commenced and proceeded, Chen pitching for the Mets, Staten Island product Marquis for the Braves. The teams exchanged runs in the fourth. Atlanta scored theirs on an error by Piazza, but Mike doubled and crossed the plate on Shinjo's sac fly to tie it at one in the bottom of the inning. In the eighth, the most New York of the New York Mets, John Franco, entered the game. His father had worked for the Department of Sanitation, a piece of biography continually reinforced by the orange T-shirt he wore under his jersey. "I am one of them," John said of those who had sought to rescue anybody who could be rescued at Ground Zero. Facing the Braves in relief of Chen, he put two runners on base after recording two outs. Armando Benitez followed and gave up a double to Brian Jordan to break the tie. The Braves led, 2–1.

Steve Karsay, a Queens boy, came in to pitch for the Braves. Lawton led off by grounding out. Edgardo Alfonzo, winding down a subpar season, worked a nine-pitch walk and was removed for pinch-runner Desi Relaford. This brought up Piazza. The same Piazza who lived in Gramercy Park, not too many blocks from the World Trade Center. The same Piazza who was moved to tears by the bagpipes before the game. The same Piazza whose NYPD helmet couldn't be missed when he crouched.

It was a function of the batting order that Piazza was up at this moment with the Mets down by one with one on in the eighth. Hits, walks, outs . . . he was due up third in the inning. Alfonzo walked, so Piazza was going to hit. Nothing mysterious about that. Consider, though, the kind of hit it would take to put the Mets ahead here on a night devoted to the idea that New York—or "New York, New York," as Liza Minnelli serenaded an impromptu kickline of firefighters and police officers during the seventh-inning stretch—was determinedly resilient. It was just an idea at this point. The city was still groping to find its bearings.

A home run was necessary for New York's team to take an immediate lead. A home run was by no means a rare bird in baseball in 2001, just as it hadn't been in the years prior. The sky had been filled with them. For the second season in four, the all-time single-season home run record was being seriously pursued. Barry Bonds hit three on the Sunday before September 11 to bring his total to 63. The night before the Mets and Braves came together in New York, Bonds hit his 64th. Mark McGwire's platinum standard of 70 was within his reach.

There was only one Bonds, but he wasn't the only hitter for whom home runs were common currency. Sammy Sosa had made 50 home runs unremarkable; 2001 marked his fourth consecutive season with at least that many. Two other players, Alex Rodriguez of Texas and Luis Gonzalez of Arizona, were en route to clearing 50. Nine men would total 45 or more.

The Mets didn't have any of those guys, but home runs could be and were hit by anybody in the course of the season. Lawton, by no means a renowned power hitter, had been with the Mets only since late July and had hit three. Fonzie, despite a batting average that had muddled below .250 for months, had hit 15. The cleanup hitter Ventura was up to 20. Shinjo had 10. Elsewhere in this Friday night lineup, Todd Zeile had nine; Jay Payton, recipient of a showstopping hug from Minnelli, seven; and the comically light-hitting Rey Ordoñez, three. Joe McEwing, sainted as Super for slaying

Randy Johnson, had pinch-hit for Chen in the seventh with seven home runs in his back pocket.

Every one of these Mets who'd batted against the Braves in the first baseball game in New York since New York had been attacked theoretically could have hit a home run between the first and the eighth innings. None did. Then again, none of them was the Met who would leap to mind as the obvious candidate to do so on a night like this. That Met was up next.

Because when the subject was the Mets, what other player were you going to think of?

Mike Piazza took a strike from Karsay. Then he took a swing. Over Fox Sports Net New York, Howie Rose had the call:

"And it's hit deep to left-center ... Andruw Jones on the run ... this one has a chance ... home run! Mike Piazza! And the Mets lead three to two!"

Usually Piazza's trips around the bases at Shea were musically accompanied. A button would be pushed and the "HEY!" from "Rock and Roll (Part 2)" or the closing licks from "Won't Get Fooled Again" would score the moment. But, again, this night wasn't the usual at Shea Stadium, so when Mike's long ball—his 34th of the year—clanked off the center field camera platform and he broke into his trot, all you heard was cheering and yelling and the rustling of those little flags. Rose's partner, Fran Healy, used uncomfortable language in light of what had been on everybody's mind for ten days when he immediately observed, "This place exploded! It's been waiting to explode all night," but perhaps that was the point. For a moment, the grief over what became of those airliners and those buildings and all those people could coexist with a little happiness, a little excitement, and a little sense that the things that were considered important before September 11 could maybe be considered at all. It was a game in a town that had no headspace for games. But the home team was winning and the home team's best player was, to use another term whose application to athletes had fallen out of favor, the hero.

How could the place not explode? Or at least take a deep breath and express an emotion that wasn't complete sadness? The TV cameras found several men in uniform. Not baseball uniforms, but dress blues. They were gentlemen represented on those caps the Mets were wearing, owning every reason to be grim, but Piazza's home run wouldn't permit them to be. The feeling may have been fleeting in the face of all else that surrounded their lives, but clearly they were happy. "Shea Stadium," Rose said, "has something to smile about."

A home run that can do that is one that will stay with the player who hit it and everybody who experienced it. "I'm just so happy I was able to come through in that situation and give people something to cheer about," Piazza said after the game. "That's what they came out here for, to be diverted a little from their losses and their sorrow." Fittingly, the homer represented the difference between winning and losing in the moment, too. The Mets held on to beat the Braves, 3–2, and inch to within 4 1/2 games of first place. It still wasn't the biggest deal in the world, let alone New York, but in September of 2001, if you were so disposed, you couldn't help but form a grin from it.

* * *

There would be another Met win over the Braves the next night, pushing the Mets another game closer. On Sunday, September 23, Benitez was handed a three-run lead to protect in the ninth inning and, with it, a chance to sweep Atlanta and trim the distance between the Mets and first to 2 1/2. For all that had been written and said about how a New York rife with divisions needed the Miracle Mets in 1969, it was impossible to believe any city and time could use a team and a stretch run like this one more. The Mets coming all the way back on the Braves would be more than a baseball miracle. It would be a mitzvah. The Mets' demise in August had not been much exaggerated and New York had since been through like nothing that could have been envisioned. A stampede on first place might have only accomplished so much for the municipal psyche, but it sure would have been Amazin' to have discovered how much.

It was not to be. Benitez gave up a two-run homer to Jordan and a run-scoring single to B. J. Surhoff. In the 11th, Jordan belted another home run, and the Braves went on to win, 5–4. New York was reminded that not every story writes itself to custom specifications. The Mets sucked up the loss, traveled to Montreal and swept the Expos. Piazza delivered a three-run pinch-double that helped set the club up for one last stand at—where else?—Turner Field. The 79–74 Mets, winners of twenty-five of their previous thirty-one, trailed Atlanta by three as they began a three-game series down south.

They never drew any closer, losing without fanfare on Friday the twenty-eighth and then suffering the worst of blows (relatively speaking) on Saturday the twenty-ninth. This time, Armando was asked to protect a four-run lead and couldn't. The Mets' edge melted from 5–1 to 5–4. Valentine switched out Benitez for Franco. Franco walked his first hitter, then gave up a grand slam to Jordan, whose first name might as well have been Larry and nickname could have been Chipper. The Mets lost, 8–5, and were officially eliminated from contention three nights later at Shea.

Baseball continued, as baseball will. If the scene of September 21 didn't confirm that iota of resilience—"it told the rest of the country and the rest of the world what New York is about," Piazza had said—nothing could. But baseball continuing also meant the mundane business of playing out the string for a team that, for the first time since the final few games of 1997, had nothing driving them to the wire. The home games postponed after September 11 were being made up in front of tiny crowds amid a homestand that exemplified going out with a whimper. "God Bless America" continued to be performed. "Take Me Out to the Ball Game" and "Lazy Mary" went into storage for the duration. Baseball was still figuring out if it could be baseball like it used to be.

Elsewhere, Bonds caught and passed McGwire (who was about to unexpectedly announce his retirement), establishing a new single-season high of 73 home runs, or more than twice as many as Piazza's Mets-leading 36; Rickey Henderson, these days a Padre, broke Ty Cobb's career record for runs scored *and* collected his 3,000th hit; Cal Ripken and Tony Gwynn played the final games of their illustrious careers; and the Yankees tuned up for yet another postseason. Though it was the Mets who were most visible in the aftermath of September 11, it was the Bronx Bombers who'd carry the Big Apple's banner through October and into November. They'd wear the same first responder caps the Mets first made so visible, but only during batting practice. On November 4, their run of consecutive world championships ended at the hands of the Arizona Diamondbacks in the ninth inning of the seventh game of an absolutely scintillating World Series. If nothing else, Yankees fans in New York were granted an absorbing and extensive distraction, and, when it was over, Mets fans were, at last, freed from having to hear anything new about "the rings, baby."

Perhaps such relief was a sign that New Yorkers were going to get on with being New Yorkers after all.

PART V
ARE WE IMMORTAL YET?

AS ERAS END
April 1, 2002–October 3, 2004

Theodore White wrote about politics, not baseball, yet in his final book, he raised a point as applicable to America's national pastime as it is to elections. White recognized that firsts were fairly easy to identify, but lasts tended to be elusive. The author of the *Making of the President* series wondered, for example, if anyone could identify "the last time or place anyone took a gold eagle or sovereign from his purse and slapped it on the table to pay for dinner" or "the last company of archers" directed into battle under the belief that "a well-drawn flight of arrows could overmatch a volley of bullets." No such records are kept, not even by Elias.

Baseball is kind enough to leave a box score behind after every ballgame and a veritable box set of them after every season so we know exactly the last times a pitcher pitched, a catcher caught, and a slugger slugged, and for whom. Still, it can be harder to define precisely that player's time in terms of context and team. Mike Piazza remained a Met after 2001, but the Mets as defined by Mike Piazza began to fade in 2002 and were done by 2005.

It wasn't as obvious as the Kremlin ordering the dismantling of statues and changing the names of cities. Piazza's image graced the cover of pocket schedules. Merchandise bearing his name and number remained for sale. He was, in his fifth season as a Met, the most recognizable Met to Mets fans and the public at large.

But more and more, these Mets ceased being the Mike Piazza Mets, the Mets Piazza drove to heights previously out of reach. Some of that was a function of losing more than winning, but it also reflected the ever-changing cast around him. The Mets of 1998 to 2001 shuffled through personnel as

well, but they achieved enough to be bronzed in memory. To recall Piazza
at the most intense and unforgettable of moments was to evoke by association the men who were on base or on deck when he doubled into the gap,
the men who nodded at the sign he put down and fired strike three into
his mitt, the men who greeted him at home plate or in the dugout after a
home run.

Those men began to disappear en masse as 2001 slipped into 2002. In a
way, team history was rebooting if not repeating itself. A decade earlier, the
Mets had tried to prop up a faltering contender with a thorough houseclean-
ing and the import of big, impressive names. That it backfired then didn't
necessarily mean it couldn't rekindle Mets fortunes now. But it backfired
nonetheless. Three terrible and terribly embarrassing seasons for almost all
concerned trudged forth.

Roberto Alomar and Mo Vaughn were acquired. They bombed. Jeromy
Burnitz and Roger Cedeño were reacquired. They also bombed. Chemistry was off all around. "A team of strangers" is what a clubhouse observer
labeled the 2002 Mets. Piazza's numbers remained good. He hit a home run
off Roger Clemens, though the bigger story that day was Piazza's pitcher,
Shawn Estes, didn't plunk Clemens (he tried; and he did homer off him).
The other big stories surrounding Piazza were sidebars to game action. He
chose to tell the media he wasn't gay when a story broke alleging he was.
He didn't have to get mad at Keith Hernandez, now a broadcaster for MSG,
but he did when Hernandez observed (based on copious evidence) that the
Mets had quit. Mike and Keith made up, which was nice, considering they'd
been teammates of a sort, each named to the Mets' 40th Anniversary All-
Amazin' team by the fans.

The Mets themselves weren't amazing and finished last. Bobby Valentine was fired. Art Howe was hired. Fred Wilpon thought the new manager "lit up" a room. The Mets brought in Tom Glavine from the Braves,
Mike Stanton from the Yankees, and Cliff Floyd, the former Marlin. They
dimmed some more as 2003 got under way, soon getting Steve Phillips
fired. Mo Vaughn's arthritic knee knocked him out for the year. Needing a
first baseman, Howe told reporters he planned to change Piazza's position.
But he neglected to tell Piazza first. As Mike was beginning to take ground
balls, the "plan" went awry. He absorbed a horrific groin injury while batting in San Francisco in May and was sidelined for three months. His first

base tryout was limited to a single inning on the night the Mets honored the retiring Bob Murphy. The Mets finished last again.

In 2004, it was basically more of the same. Mike caught long enough and slugged well enough to pass Carlton Fisk for most home runs hit by a catcher. It merited a curtain call in May and a night in his honor at Shea in June. Fisk, Johnny Bench, Yogi Berra, and Gary Carter all swung by. Then Mike returned to first base, which wasn't really his bailiwick. The Mets swept the Shea half of the Subway Series and moved to within a game of first place in July, but contention wasn't really their bag, either. Every good sign—such as the promotion of promising rookie third baseman David Wright—was countered by a fistful of bad ones—such as the trade of pitching prospect Scott Kazmir for injured starter Victor Zambrano. They finished next-to-last. Howe was fired. Jim Duquette, who had replaced Phillips, was replaced by Omar Minaya.

Heading into the last year of his contract, all that remained of what would be remembered as the Mike Piazza Mets was Mike Piazza.

GOING IN STYLE
April 4, 2005–October 2, 2005

In the 2004 film *Sideways*, Virginia Madsen as Maya could as easily be talking about a ballplayer as a bottle of wine when she broaches the subject of "steady, inevitable decline." It's the peak of flavor that the palate cherishes. For Maya and Miles (portrayed by Bart Giamatti's son Paul), it is the '61 Cheval Blanc. For baseball fans who wish to indulge in the pouring of immortality, it is inevitably the Ruth of '27 or the Gibson of '68 they fetch from the cellar of memory, not the Babe or Bob from when the sips were nearing their last. Ted Williams, in Ed Linn's biography *Hitter*, scolds a Texas Rangers pitcher who, in 1991 at Fenway Park, brings him a picture to autograph. The photo shows the former Teddy Ballgame "looking unfashionably portly, in a Washington uniform" from his managing days. Ted is offended: "Where did you get that lousy picture? I'm not going to sign that."

The pitcher comes back the next day with a picture of Williams homering, from 1949. *That* Ted signs. Tom Seaver, still part of the Channel 11 broadcast team in 2005, tells stories in which Jerry Grote is his catcher and Gil Hodges is his manager—you don't hear much about John Stearns and Joe Frazier, let alone Junior Ortiz and Frank Howard. The canonical tales of Dwight Gooden's greatness are primarily limited to 1984 and 1985; Doc won plenty of games for the Mets in the years after, but it wasn't the same, so why be impolite and delve into, say, 1991? Yet as the backs of Topps cards of esteemed veterans can attest—and as Maya herself said regarding the wonders of *vino*—a baseball career "is actually alive, and it's constantly evolving and gaining complexity. That is until it peaks."

The Mets of 2005 still had Mike Piazza, but it had sunk in that he wouldn't be and couldn't be the Mike Piazza of 1998 to 2001 anymore. For the first time since he'd started a season with them, they didn't print a pocket schedule with his picture on the cover. These were the Mets of headline-grabbing free agents Carlos Beltran and Pedro Martinez and talented youngsters Jose Reyes and David Wright. The immediate future belonged to others.

* * *

Piazza was, however, the starting catcher and cleanup hitter on opening day once again. The first base experiment was forever over. Old Mets second baseman and new Mets manager Willie Randolph—honing his skills in recent years as a Yankee coach under Joe Torre—strived to instill his idea of professionalism in his new charges. He instituted a rule about facial hair. Piazza cooperated, shaving the scruff that covered his face in 2004 and losing his mustache. There was no rule about mustaches, but the ever self-aware Piazza (who hit his hallowed September 21, 2001, home run with frosted blond hair) explained, "I don't want to look like a seventies-style Burt Reynolds." His mullet had been reshaped since he came over from the Marlins. His goatee had come and gone. But the mustache had been such a trademark that in his early Met years, the TV cameras at Shea always managed to find this one kid in a Piazza jersey who had one drawn above his upper lip.

Mike, who'd managed to make black look like as native a Met color as blue and orange, might have to reach for the razor more often, but he could leave that first baseman's mitt in his locker for good. After an unsuccessful attempt to sign slugger Carlos Delgado, Doug Mientkiewicz, who the previous October cradled the final putout of the Red Sox' first world championship since 1918 (and then was slow to give up the ball that symbolized the 86-year struggle), was brought in to play first. He was never in Piazza's class as a hitter, but he was an actual first baseman. Mike could thus return to the only position he ever wanted to play. He'd be backed up by another newcomer, Ramon Castro.

The New Mets (as Beltran hopefully dubbed them) got off to a frighteningly familiar start, losing their first five on the road. Then Martinez and John Smoltz (15 Ks) dueled deep into the first Sunday of the season in Atlanta, Pedro outlasting his opposition, with Beltran, Wright, and Cliff Floyd each homering late for a 6–1 complete game win. Randolph could at last smoke the fancy victory cigar Piazza had given him before the season began.

The 1–5 Mets were, in a blink, 6–5. They swept the Astros (including a game started by Roger Clemens) in their series at Shea, then took two from the Marlins, the first a one-hitter from top 2001 draft pick Aaron Heilman, the second after a packed house cheered Pedro and booed Al Leiter. Leiter was as much of the great millennium times in Flushing as Piazza, but now he was the enemy.

Late-career Martinez, as Gary Cohen put it regarding his reputation, was not a diva, but a maestro. Floyd, fully healthy and playing every day in left, was off to his best start as a Met. Wright continued to grow and Reyes continued to run. Beltran's start was a little slower, but there was no denying he made the team much more formidable by his presence. Castro proved an ideal backup catcher, offensively and defensively (Pedro certainly liked throwing to him), which was fortunate, because Piazza was having a tough time getting untracked. The greatest-hitting catcher in baseball history didn't break .250 for good until June. While the Mets kept a toe in the wild-card pool through the spring and into summer, the man who was synonymous with catapulting them into contention in an earlier time struggled. Randolph dropped Piazza out of the cleanup spot in May and began slotting him sixth in July. Mike was voted onto the All-Star team, joining Beltran in the starting lineup, but the selection seemed to be a reflex action on the part of fans.

He was old. He was slower than ever. He couldn't throw runners out. He wasn't hitting much. But he was still Mike Piazza. And, as the reality set in that he wouldn't be around at Shea much longer, appreciation for who he'd been and who he occasionally still could be preempted darker impulses. With less than three months left in his Met tenure—it was agreed by all concerned he wasn't coming back in 2006—no Met was more popular in Flushing.

Applause arose regularly. Standing ovations. Curtain calls. They didn't exactly occur in a vacuum. It helped that Piazza began to hit. In his first 17 games after the All-Star break, Mike seemed reborn: 5 HR, 19 RBIs, .305 BA. He started only sixteen games of the twenty-three the Mets played in this span, but it was a judicious use of a diminishing resource. Piazza was thirty-six and Castro was capable. No sense draining Mike's battery.

The renaissance didn't last, but the affection didn't falter. Mets fans gave Mike the farewell tour the franchise had never really given anybody. The Mets didn't provide that kind of tableau. Their greats were elbowed from the picture, mostly, usually nudged out a side door. As was the case with those who made 1969 and 1973 so memorable, no 1986 Met got to properly tip a cap as a Met and ease into the sunset. No Met from 1999 and 2000 was given that courtesy, either. When fans wanted to applaud John Olerud and Edgardo Alfonzo, they waited for them to return as a Mariner and a Giant in 2003. Robin Ventura made the mistake of visiting as a Yankee in 2002. When he hit a grand slam (not a single) at Shea as a Dodger in 2004, it was good for a four-base ovation that served as his *au revoir*. By homering in the final at-bat of his career, in his second go-round as a Met, Todd Zeile made himself a nice day at the end of '04, of which John Franco was offered a third of an inning, but that seemed more like serendipity than a brilliantly executed bon voyage. After seven seasons of grunting and grimacing inning by inning, Leiter became just another Florida Marlin. Some of it was business getting the best of sentiment, but sentiment rarely got a seat at the table unless it grabbed itself a chair.

So what Piazza was getting wasn't exactly a last ride around the league—he wasn't retiring—but for the first time in the forty-four year history of the Mets, somebody was being sent off in style. It was the least that could be done for someone who so defined who the Mets had been for so long.

When Deputy Chief of Staff Josh Lyman dreamed of a trip to spring training on *The West Wing*, he told the White House press secretary, "Mike Piazza is going to be standing in the batting cage. He's going to turn and see me. He's going to say . . . 'Dude.'"

When Grandpa Hugh on *The Sopranos* tried to convince A. J. he couldn't be Italian if he didn't eat his artichokes, the young man shot back, "So what, Mike Piazza eats nothing but artichokes? I mean, that's dicked up."

When Doug and Carrie Heffernan's trip to Shea went awry on *The King of Queens*, they wound up in a holding cell—"Mets jail"—and kept involuntary company with a drunk yelling just one word: "PIAZZA!"

Mike played himself in the romantic comedy *Two Weeks Notice*, foiled in catching a foul ball by Sandra Bullock ("Hey, next time go to a Yankees game"). He considered doing the same in a Ben Stiller vehicle tentatively titled *Go to Hell, Mike Piazza,* but the movie never got made. He was seen hitting a home run in the time-traveling romcom *Kate & Leopold.* He appeared on *The Apprentice* as part of a scheme to sell toothpaste. "PIAZZA 31" showed up on the back of Dennis Quaid's young son in *Frequency.* Fred Armisen as Weekend Update roving reporter Tom Jankeloff on *Saturday Night Live* strolled Central Park in a "METS 31" windbreaker. "Piazza, New York catcher, are you straight or are you gay?" asked Belle and Sebastian in a song written out of admiration for the ballplayer—"the catcher hits for .318 and catches every day"—and as a comment on the media's more gossipy tangents.

Belle and Sebastian would be categorized under indie pop, not quite Mike's cup of tea. His taste for heavy metal was well known and legitimate enough to earn him a seat alongside genre maven Eddie Trunk on New York's Q104.3 FM whenever he wanted it. His budding oenophile tendencies were familiar to readers of *Wine Spectator.* His right-leaning politics were also a matter of record. "The GOP has invaded the island," he giddily announced to his teammates as the 2004 Republican Convention took up residence in Manhattan. A year later, he found meeting Rush Limbaugh "like meeting George Washington."

Rooting for Mike Piazza, though, was a nonpartisan phenomenon for eight seasons. From his freewheeling bachelor days to the settling-down phase he entered upon marrying model and actress (and former *Playboy* playmate) Alicia Rickter early in 2005, he was part of the Mets fan extended kin. When a player sticks around as long as Piazza had and has such an impact, it's less about gawking at a celebrity than it is looking out for his best interests. Hopefully you're not so delusional to think you know the guy personally if you don't, but after you watch him year after year and listen to him to expound thoughtfully on a regular basis—Mike was not gregarious in his manner, but certainly not tight-lipped—your proprietary stake in his well-being transcends whether he's still hitting .318 or is catching every day. You just want everything to be all right for him.

After all, he's done so much for you.

* * *

Piazza, New York Catcher, took a foul tip to his glove hand off the bat of the Pirates' Freddy Sanchez on August 16 at Shea and the result was a reminder of why the Mets had tried to steer him toward becoming Piazza, New York First Baseman. Mike suffered a hairline fracture in his left wrist and had to spend several of his final precious weeks as a Met on the DL. In his absence, the ballclub made one final push for the wild card, culminating in a thrilling 6–4 win at Shea over the team they were chasing, the Phillies, on August 30. The Mets trailed by one with two on in the eighth when Castro stepped up and blasted a three-run homer off Uggie Urbina. It was the kind of dramatic blow Mets fans were used to seeing delivered by another of their catchers.

September was less kind. The Mets fell into a losing rut reminiscent of the Art Howe reign and they quietly withdrew from contention, even dipping into last place for a while. By the time Piazza returned to action on September 10, the Astros were on the verge of their second consecutive wild card and the Cox/Smoltz/Chipper Braves—enjoying a transfusion of fresh blood from rookies Brian McCann, Kelly Johnson, and Jeff Francoeur—maintained their usual vise grip on traditional first place. Acorns grew to oaks during the span of Atlanta's divisional dynasty. It seemed impossible that at the end of Piazza's Met tenure, the Braves remained uninterrupted champions of the National League East, though it was true. They no longer won playoff series as a rule (or even as an anomaly), but during the regular season, they couldn't be slowed. In 2005, the Mets were still banging their heads against Turner Field's cruel walls, losing eight of nine in the recalcitrant house of horrors. The devil simply refused to get up and out of Georgia.

The Mets of Willie Randolph, however, were not the Mets of Art Howe, and they rebounded late. It wasn't enough to inject themselves back in the race, but they did rise above .500 to stay and they did make sure to leave the ex-Expos, the Washington Nationals, as lone occupants of the NL East basement. Nevertheless, on September 27, when Houston defeated St. Louis, New York's day in the wild-card derby was officially done. Mathematical elimination ensured Mike Piazza would leave the Mets with only two postseasons under his belt. Those affairs from 1999 and 2000 had endured as memorable if not wholly satisfying, and except for a few swings (and the barrel of one bat flung toward him), it couldn't be said they wholly belonged to him in the way a handful of superstars have taken over a fistful of autumns. But it was understood they never would have transpired without him, and

Mets fans would always have a home in their hearts for those Octobers and the sublime regular seasons that preceded them.

It was all expressed as best as it could be at Shea Stadium on the final Sunday of 2005, October 2, Mike Piazza's last game as a New York Met. He'd enjoyed a productive week leading up to the finale, knocking two balls out of RFK Stadium on September 25 and launching one 450 feet to left at Shea four nights later. The latter lunar mission, off Sunny Kim of the Rockies, was his nineteenth of the season and the 397th of his career, placing him, for the moment, at 44th all-time, one ahead of Joe Carter, one behind Dale Murphy. It was his 220th as a Met; only Darryl Strawberry, at 252, had hit more. The Mets won, 11–0, with Piazza catching Tom Glavine's complete game shutout. It was the first Glavine had thrown all year and the first Mike had caught from beginning to end.

Chants of "One More Year!" greeted every move made by a batter who would total no more than 62 runs batted in for 2005. "I'm glad they feel that way," the catcher said. "It's nice to know you're wanted." But this, by mutual consent between team and player, was going to be it. Randolph, who Jeff Torborg started at second base in his final game in the majors a dozen years earlier, recognized the emotional weight the day carried and not only inserted Piazza behind the plate (ironically, Sundays traditionally belonged to his backups) but slotted him fourth in the lineup. Mike was the Mets' cleanup hitter once more. Hitting in front of him were Reyes, Beltran, and Floyd; behind him came Wright, first baseman Mike Jacobs, right fielder Victor Diaz, second baseman Anderson Hernandez, and pitcher Victor Zambrano. Because MLB was trying to raise funds for victims of Hurricane Katrina, the Mets' batting helmets were adorned with the Red Cross insignia. On Piazza's, it appeared to be acknowledgement of all the scrapes and bruises, physical and otherwise, he'd absorbed since arriving at Shea on May 23, 1998.

Piazza couldn't do for the inconsistent Zambrano what he'd done for Glavine three nights before. The Mets fell behind, 2–0, in the first, 4–2 in the third, and 11–3 by the top of the seventh. Despite the strains of his vintage walkup music, Jimi Hendrix's "Voodoo Child (Slight Return)" filling the air each time he batted, Mike did not fulfill the fantasies of those who hoped he'd hit home runs 398, 399, and 400 on his way to destinations unknown. He grounded out three times against sinkerballer Aaron Cook. The lifetime .311 hitter was batting .251.

The score, the oh-fer and the less-than-stellar current-season stats were of little concern to the paid attendance of 47,718. One more victory would have been swell (the Mets, with 83 wins, their most since 2000, were trying to clinch sole possession of third place) and nobody would have minded No. 31 going deep one more time, but Mike Piazza had given his all already. The idea in the crowd this Sunday was to give back.

Who knew how many high fives were exchanged across eight years because Piazza had just done something worth slapping palms over? How many 31s on how many T-shirts and jerseys were worn on how many chests and backs? How many posters of Mike in mid-swing were tacked or taped to how many walls in and around New York? How many kids were lured to Mets and baseball fandom because Mike came up to bat with runners on base and came through? How many adults, raised on Seaver or Gooden, had their Metropolitan passions reignited because of a moment from 1999 or 2000? How many people had no idea who any other Met was but perked up to the name Mike Piazza? He was a galvanizing figure ten days after September 11, 2001 . . . and, as soon as six and a half innings went into the books on October 2, 2005, he was going to be one again.

When Matt Holliday flied to Carlos Beltran for the final out of the top of the seventh, public address announcer Alex Anthony directed fans' attention to DiamondVision. Up came a montage of Mike's biggest moments, set to "The Great Divide," a song by Creed front man Scott Stapp. There again on the big screen was the front man for the Mets, catching and throwing, hitting and slugging, winning and trying. All the big swings, all the moments forever enshrined in memory. In the gauzy prism of recollection, there was no Brave, no Yankee, nobody who could stop Mike Piazza.

The video ended, and nobody could stop Mike Piazza's acolytes, all the 31s in the stands, rising in unison, roaring and clapping without interruption. Piazza, never the effusive curtain call type, would have to take a bow, not for having just done something specific, but simply for having been who he'd been for the previous eight seasons.

He did, climbing out the Mets dugout with his shin guards still on. It wasn't enough. The applause overflowed like the plumbing tended to in the upper deck men's rooms. He blew a few shy kisses. He raised his arms about three-quarters of the way up. He made the "Aw, sit down" gesture, maybe leavened with a humble slice of "We're not worthy." He ducked back into the dugout, figuring he could turn off the faucets of affection if he stopped showing his face. He miscalculated. Nobody wanted to sit. Nobody wanted to stop. Nobody cared about the Mets playing the Rockies. Hell, the Rockies stood in front of their dugout and applauded, just as the Mets stood in theirs and did the same.

The seventh-inning stretch/tribute went on for more than seven minutes, an eternity in baseball. "That's when you know you've done something," Wright marveled. "That's when you know you're 'The Man' in New York." You don't see games put on pause that long unless an outsize occasion demanded it. You'd see it for Cal Ripken or Hank Aaron breaking unbreakable records. All Mike Piazza was doing was completing the terms of his contract. Perhaps this was a celebration of everybody having gotten their money's worth.

Eventually, the game had to be shifted out of park and driven toward its finish. Reyes made the last out of the bottom of the seventh, which meant Piazza would be due up in the bottom of the eighth. Except Randolph decided, with the Mets down by eight, there was no point in attempting to extract any more bang for the franchise's buck. Mike, who couldn't help but be emotionally spent by the reception he'd just soaked in, took his position one more time to start the eighth, but after warming up reliever Shingo Takatsu, he found himself replaced by third-stringer Mike DiFelice. The choreography allowed Mets fans, though disappointed there wouldn't be one more at-bat, one more chance to shower him with adoration. And that they did.

While they stood again and applauded again, he rose from his crouch, removed his mask, flipped his helmet around to its front side and revealed as enormous and boyish a smile as he'd ever displayed on the field at Shea Stadium. His 14th major-league season was over. His time as a New York Met was over. He was thirty-seven years old with whatever was left of his baseball future unspoken for. Yet, somehow, Mike Piazza never looked younger.

SLIGHT RETURN
August 8, 2006–September 29, 2013

The San Diego Padres are perhaps the most reliably unreliable set of dressers in major-league history, changing their uniform ensemble more often than some franchises change socks. Along with their sporadic (at best) involvement in postseason play, their recurring shifts in color and motif perhaps explain how, outside of their own sphere of influence, they've rarely elicited strong emotions. How can you get agitated for better or worse about the Padres when you can barely remember what they look like?

Yet come the summer of 2006, New York Mets fans swooned at the sight of a single San Diego Padre. When they looked past his sand brown pants, navy blue top, and downright bizarre No. 33, they recognized one of their own.

That was Mike Piazza. They'd know him anywhere.

Life went on for team and star following their amicable parting in 2005. The Mets went out and traded for a demographically similar catcher, Paul Lo Duca—originally a Dodger, later a Marlin, always Italian—and he was, in his way, the right man in the right spot at the right time for these Mets as Piazza was eight years before. Paul didn't hit for Piazzaesque power, but he fit neatly in the revised scheme of things. By midseason, Lo Duca was on the cover of *Sports Illustrated*, surrounded by the rest of the top of the order from the fearsome even newer Mets assembled by Omar Minaya. Lo Duca, dubbed "Captain Red Ass," was joined in the offseason by another ex-Floridian, Carlos Delgado. With David Wright, Jose Reyes, and the notice-ably more comfortable Carlos Beltran, "the intrepid Mets" were tearing up the National League East, leading the pack by a dozen games and burying, at last, the Atlanta Braves' divisional dynasty. Each Met on the magazine's cover, sans Delgado, was elected to start in the All-Star Game.

Piazza finished a distant second to Lo Duca, though that was mostly name recognition at work. He went altogether unselected, as NL manager Phil Garner took twenty-two-year-old Brian McCann of the Braves as Lo Duca's backup. It marked the first time that a healthy Piazza wasn't asked to the All-Star Game. Nevertheless, Mike was doing fine for himself after signing a one-year deal with San Diego the preceding winter. He, like Lo Duca, was the starting catcher for a first-place ballclub. His mustache and goatee were back even if something was off about his digits. Piazza couldn't be 31 for the Padres, because that honor would always belong to Dave Winfield, for whom the number was retired in 2001. Dave went into the Hall of Fame that year "as a Padre," to use the phrase bandied about talk radio, choosing his San Diego roots (back from when San Diego wore brown and gold) over his longer and more famous association with the New York Yankees. That mini-controversy came a year after Carlton Fisk picked his first team, the Red Sox, over the team for whom he played longer, the White Sox, and two years before Gary Carter was inducted as an Expo instead of a Met.

Carter hadn't exactly chosen the Expos, who were on baseball's endangered species list by 2003. "If the Expos are no longer in existence, how is that going to be beneficial to me and my family when we have an opportunity to be part of a family that will be around a long time?" Gary rhetorically asked when he won induction after his sixth year on the ballot. "My heart is always going to be in New York," he added, though he would take great pains to also say, "I'm so honored and proud to represent the Expos" as well as, "It would be nice to have a split for the hat, if there was a position for that."

When Carter entered alongside Eddie Murray (also not as a Met), the Hall had already taken the prerogative of final say out of the players' hands, lest it become a bargaining chip rather than an accurate reflection of immortality. The last straw was word, albeit never explicitly confirmed, that Wade Boggs had a clause in his Tampa Bay Devil Rays contract related to his going in as one of theirs when his big day came. Boggs was a Tampa native, but a D-Ray for all of two years at the end of his 3,000-hit career. Not surprisingly, when Boggs made the Hall in 2005, he, like Fisk, was crowned for posterity with a Red Sox cap. For anyone looking ahead to five years beyond Piazza's final game, a potentially disconcerting trend was at work. The first-team syndrome, connecting Hall of Famer with franchise of origin, seemed to be the prevailing fashion trend in Cooperstown.

On August 8, 2006, Piazza, in whatever duds he was decked out, remained very much active, and all that the crowd of more than 46,000 at Shea cared about was he was in their midst again. The Padres were in town for three games. Mike would start two and rest the third. On the first night, the Mets played him another video salute before first pitch (this one set to the Beatles' "In My Life") and even cranked up the Hendrix for his first at-bat. This was no slight return to the fans who rose and applauded as they had ten months earlier. When he singled in the sixth off Steve Trachsel, he was applauded again. The Mets were ahead in the game and way ahead in their division. Generosity of spirit could abound.

The next night Piazza was cheered for doing the most Piazza thing he could do: homering off none other than Pedro Martinez. It cut the Mets' lead from 4–0 to 4–1 and won him a fourth-inning curtain call . . . a curtain call in Padre colors at Shea Stadium. Mike, wary of showing anybody up, reluctantly complied because it was what the fans wanted. "You don't see that a lot," he admitted. A second home run off his former batterymate flew out of Shea in the sixth to close the Padres' gap to 4–2. There were still cheers, but maybe not as effusive as those that greeted the previous dinger. They loved their Piazza, but they were more invested in their first-place Mets. Mike drove one more ball deep before the night was done, in the eighth. Two runners were on base and, for an instant, it looked like drama overload. A third home run? To beat the Mets?

Nah. Beltran caught it at the warning track and Mike didn't have to find out what kind of fury he might have wrought had he scorned Mets pitching a little too much. Instead, though the Padres were swept, he could leave New York in a good mood. "It was a nice opportunity for me to say hi to all the fans that made my experience here amazing, something I'll obviously cherish until the day I die," he said. "They'll always be a part of me."

The next time the Mets saw Mike Piazza was in June of 2007. He was an Oakland A now, signed by Billy Beane, the GM celebrated for his smarts in the 2003 book *Moneyball*. Beane, the outfielder the Mets long ago traded for Tim Teufel (the same Tim Teufel who, as a Padre, grounded to the Dodgers' John Candelaria in 1992 with September call-up Mike Piazza behind the plate), kept budget-constrained Oakland a postseason contender more years than not by plugging undervalued assets into a Motel 6 roster. It was strange to consider Piazza, not far removed from completing a $91 million contract in New York, as fitting that particular bill, but Beane signed him as his designated hitter for one year.

Mike was less DH than DL, getting hurt in early May, but he did make the A's interleague trip to Shea in late June and did receive another standing ovation from a crowd that never stopped valuing him. Piazza returned to the lineup in the second half of the season, but Oakland was out of the race. The Mets appeared to be cruising toward a second consecutive division title, but the bottom fell out of their September, and they were surpassed by a new archrival, the heretofore dormant Philadelphia Phillies. Lo Duca slumped. Delgado slumped. Reyes slumped. In his final start, on the last day of the season, with everything on the line, Tom Glavine completely imploded, surrendering seven runs in one-third of an inning against the Marlins to ensure the Mets would not repeat.

Three thousand miles away, in Oakland, the A's were playing out the string versus the AL West champion Angels. They began the bottom of the ninth of their 162nd game tied at two. Piazza led off against reliever Chris Bootcheck with a single. Manager Bob Geren removed him for pinch-runner Shannon Stewart. Stewart scored. The A's won.

Piazza never played again. The A's didn't send Mike and his 427 home runs—396 as a catcher—off as the Mets had. He wasn't "The Man" in Oakland, just another rental. When, with 2008 already in progress, he decided to retire, he sent out a statement that thanked every team he'd played for and offered kind words for all who constituted, at one point or another, his home fans. Piazza saved his most heartfelt words for last: "I have to say my time wouldn't have been the same without the greatest fans in the world. One of the hardest moments of my career was walking off the field at Shea Stadium and saying goodbye. My relationship with you made my time in New York the happiest of my career and for that, I will always be grateful."

It read like a plaque cap pledge if you were so inclined to see it that way. Not that it was wholly up to Piazza, but he'd certainly signaled on whose side he stood in his mind, and now it figured to be simply a matter of time. Mike Piazza's final game was September 30, 2007. His name would be printed on Hall of Fame ballots after five full seasons from there had passed. Set the clock for January 2013, then. Who could deny the greatest-hitting catcher in baseball history?

* * *

Piazza's grip on the Mets fan imagination tightened in absentia. His 9/21/01 home run was voted the second-greatest moment in Shea Stadium history, even more momentous than the winning of the 1969 World Series (Buckner-Mookie finished first). When it was time to Shea Goodbye, as the Mets put it, it was Piazza who served as catcher to Tom Seaver in the ceremonial final pitch that closed the old ballpark on September 28, 2008, a scene that eased a little the sting of blowing another playoff spot in another Game 162. They recreated the tableau to open Citi Field a little more than six months later. When the Mets began to get serious about adding some team history to their new home—which arrived as an eerie update of Ebbets Field—one of the first touches was a mural along the left-field concourse of Piazza celebrating having just taken Trevor Hoffman deep in 1999.

Mike, in the flesh, was front and center at Citi on September 11, 2011, the tenth anniversary of the terror attacks. The Mets were solemnly marking the occasion before their game against the Cubs. Several 2001 Mets, plus a couple of close-enough alumni (John Olerud, Matt Franco), returned to Flushing to visit firehouses, thank first responders, and encourage fans to take part in volunteer efforts. Every year on this date for a decade, America was asked to remember what happened (as if it could forget) and within ten days, every media outlet in New York inevitably revisited the story once more from the angle of Piazza's home run. In 2011, the impulse was acted upon twice. On May 1, when news broke that Osama Bin Laden was finally captured and killed in retribution for 9/11, the Mets happened to be playing the Phillies on *Sunday Night Baseball*. The connection was coincidental but too obvious to ignore in the sidebar sense. Cue the tape of Piazza taking Steve Karsay over the wall once more.

The home run was Mike's foremost Mets legacy. He seemed to understand what it meant. "In that particular moment," he reflected a decade removed from his swing of swings, "people just really wanted something to cheer about. It was a blessing for me to be part of it. I'm so fortunate to have been in that situation and to have come through."

The Mets turned fifty in 2012. They gave their outfield fence a make-over, replacing the grim shade of soot with an intrinsically soothing shade of Shea blue. Basics were back, as orange and blue were given primacy in the team color wheel. The black caps, jerseys, and dropshadows were removed from the wardrobe except for two occasions: John Franco's induction into the team's Hall of Fame and Edgardo Alfonzo Bobblehead Day. It was almost as if somebody was paying attention to detail. Even Banner Day returned for the first time in sixteen seasons, albeit as a pregame procession and not between games of a scheduled doubleheader as the Good Lord (or Bill Shea) intended. The first-prize entry in this golden anniversary year portrayed a long-haired batter wearing No. 31 and hitting a ball marked "9–21–01," which left the Stars and Stripes trailing behind it. And if that was too subtle, the pre-2001 skyline stood in the background *and* there was text that identified the scene as

THE HOMERUN THAT HELPED HEAL NY
GOD BLESS AMERICA! LET'S GO METS!

Fifty years necessitated a Fiftieth Anniversary team. This one, unlike the "All-Amazin'" squad from the fortieth, was picked by a panel of writers and broadcasters. Time's march meant some previous incumbents were unseated. Wright replaced Howard Johnson at third, Reyes was in for Buddy Harrelson at short, and Beltran got the nod over Mookie Wilson in center. Seaver was still the right-handed pitcher and—although everybody missed Gary Carter, who had passed away over the winter after succumbing to a brain tumor—Piazza was still his catcher. The Mets revealed the composition of the team at the 92nd Street Y in Manhattan in June. Every living player named was either on hand or sent in a video clip expressing gratitude. The only member of the golden circle who stayed completely out of sight was Piazza. Considering the presentation was destined to air repeatedly on SNY, Mike's absence wound up enduring as a glaring omission.

If there was a hint of estrangement, it didn't last long. Just before the All-Star break in 2013, the Mets announced Mike would be inducted into their Hall of Fame at season's end, and to whet the fans' appetite, he showed up at Citi Field as part of that July's All-Star festivities and played in the celebrity softball game. He not only hit two home runs to power the National

League's victory, but he caught the last out, a pop-up from Bernie Williams, the same Yankee who caught Mike's last out in the 2000 World Series. Luis Sojo was nowhere in sight.

The Mets were, as had been their custom since moving into Citi Field, long out of the playoff hunt when the last day of 2013 rolled around, but on Sunday, September 29, they had a sellout crowd anxious to see Piazza honored on his own turf and to grab for themselves one of the giveaway black PIAZZA 31 T-shirts, a hot item eight years after Mike first kissed Shea good-bye.

On this gorgeous Queens afternoon, prior to their game against the Brewers, the Mets did the induction right, laying out the Met carpet not just for Mike and his family and friends, but a passel of Met legends who spanned the generations, from Al Jackson and Ed Kranepool through Ed Charles and Harrelson, on to Rusty Staub, Gooden, Wilson, and Keith Hernandez, and into the age of Piazza via Franco and Alfonzo. Al Leiter showed up by video from the set of MLB Network, where he had to track last-day playoff machinations. All the 2013 Mets stood attentively in the dugout. David Wright, the first captain since Franco, made himself available to catch the catcher's first pitch.

The day resonated with echoes from that final Sunday in 2005, except here, Mike, who entered the field to the strains of "Voodoo Child (Slight Return)" once more, spoke. It was a celebration of personal accomplishment, but also a bonding experience. Ironically, it might have taken putting on one of those Padres uniforms for Piazza to understand what it meant for him to be a Met. His defining moment in New York, he said, wasn't the home run of September 21, 2001, or any specific slice of 1999 or 2000. It was "when I came here in 2006 with San Diego. You guys cheered for me and you pulled for me, and that just shows what we have and what we have shared." The Mets, he added, "are in my prayers. I'm pulling for 'em, I love this team, I think the future looks good and we are gonna pull for 'em and get this team to the next level, right?"

As 2013 wound down, the Mets were trying to poke their necks one game ahead of the Phillies. Third place was on the line, but not much of a third place. A win on Mike Piazza Mets Hall of Fame Day would end their year at 74–88, the same record they dragged into winter in 2012 (while two stolen bases clinched the league lead for Mets leadoff hitter Eric Young Jr., the son of the Dodger who pinch-ran for Mike in his major-league debut). But these Mets had some young pitching worth monitoring, and, besides, if Mike said they were on the rise, it was coming from a good source. There was no impulse among the 41,891 clutching their PIAZZA shirts to disagree with him. Mike was one of their own. "I'm very, very proud to be a New York Met," he declared at one point, before closing his speech with "God bless the Mets." What really cemented the association was Piazza's solidarity not so much with the organization or even his fellow players, but with those in the stands who had a tough time letting him go in 2005 and had kept welcoming him back since 2006.

"They say that you can count your true friends on one hand," Mike reflected. "This is where you guys are—right here." He raised his right index finger.

The Met icon. The Mets fans. One and the same.

THE STRENGTH TO BE THERE
March 17, 2005–October 30, 2015

T he luck of the Irish was not with Joe McEwing on St. Patrick's Day 2005, the day he was released by the New York Mets. Super Joe saw it coming—the club had augmented its corps of utility players during Omar Minaya's first Hot Stove season—yet it was nonetheless hard to say good-bye. McEwing joined the Mets in 2000 and helped them make the World Series. He hit only 15 home runs in five Met seasons, but he racked up an impressive list of victims: Randy Johnson, Andy Pettitte, Kerry Wood, Tom Glavine (twice), and Mike Hampton.

Plus, not only was he the consummate supersub, but he was just as versatile in the clubhouse, acclaimed as extremely popular with his teammates, especially the only one who'd been on the club longer than he was. The best-known Italian-American member of the 2005 Mets was sorry to see McEwing go. "It's a sad day," Mike Piazza said in rainy Port St. Lucie that March 17. "He was so unselfish . . . the biggest cheerleader we had. It's a reality check. People come and go in the game. You learn that. But this is a loss for the organization."

There ended up being no spring game that St. Patrick's Day and there was about to be no McEwing. There was a television in the clubhouse, though, and before the rain canceled the Mets' outdoor activities, it was tuned to some doings in Washington. With no disrespect intended to Super Joe, time would reveal that what some of the players watched before switching over to March Madness coverage would inflict a greater reality check on Mike Piazza's legacy than any given teammate's release.

March 17, 2005, was the day that the House Government Reform
Committee held a hearing into the use of steroids in baseball. Members of
Congress cited an array of mental and physical dangers that faced youngsters who followed the pros' example. They also invoked the integrity of the
game. For baseball people, this was becoming an industry issue of the highest order. A few players in the Mets clubhouse looked in, including Piazza,
who regularly expressed interest in politics and government. "I'm just as
curious as anybody," Mike said. "Maybe something good can come out of
it. Obviously there's a lot of hysteria right now and it's a hot-button topic.
Hopefully, when the dust settles, we can move forward."

The congressional hearings weren't the first time performance-enhancing drugs had drawn the attention of the baseball public, but critical mass
was gathering through the spring of 2005. The flashpoint was the publication of a book by the old Oakland Athletics Bash Brother Jose Canseco,
Juiced: Wild Times, Rampant 'Roids, Smash Hits & How Baseball Got Big.
Chock full of names and accusations, it pulled PEDs into the spotlight. Canseco listed as users himself and a fistful of high-profile former teammates.
The best known and most accomplished was Mark McGwire, the savior of
the summer of '98, the man who surpassed Roger Maris, the inspiration
for the Mark McGwire Highway in Missouri, the slugger the fans hailed as
a peer of Lou Gehrig's when they elected him one of two All-Century first
basemen.

That century suddenly felt like a very long time ago. It wasn't the first
instance McGwire or anybody else was suspected of steroid use. Big Mac
wasn't too happy when that AP reporter noticed the Androstenedione
sitting in his locker at Shea Stadium in 1998 while he was smashing the
50-homer barrier. Andro was legal and not restricted by baseball. McGwire,
like a lot of athletes, worked out religiously. And those home runs he and
Sammy Sosa were hitting were credited for saving baseball after the strike.

The middle and late 1990s were indeed homer-happy days and the
good times kept rolling into the 2000s. All those records that had been so
far out of reach for so long just kept falling. The players were bigger than
ever and they were hitting balls farther than ever. It was great theater and
boffo box office, so not too many questions were asked. Eventually, though,
something just seemed too wrong to ignore about how charged up baseball
offense had become. Ken Caminiti, who had finished ahead of Piazza for

the 1996 NL MVP, stepped to the fore in 2002, admitting to *Sports Illustrated*'s Tom Verducci that he was a steroid user and he wasn't the only one. The story was credited for easing PED testing's entry into the next Basic Agreement. Until then, MLB turned a blind eye toward steroids and the players union didn't care to focus on it. (Testing of minor leaguers had begun the year before.)

In 2003, two years after breaking McGwire's record (and a year before Caminiti died of a heroin and cocaine overdose), Barry Bonds testified in a grand jury investigation of the Bay Area Laboratory Co-Operative, or BALCO, and the phrases "the cream" and "the clear" crept into the baseball lexicon. By the time Canseco's book came out, the topic was familiar and innocence was diminished, but there the visual of the procession of retired and active big leaguers—Canseco, McGwire, Sosa, and Rafael Palmeiro among them—testifying before Congress was as powerful as any swing any of them had ever taken.

Palmeiro, one of the players Canseco identified in his book, adamantly denied any involvement with PEDs: "I have never used steroids, period." To underscore his point, he defiantly wagged his index finger. Canseco maintained his book's claims of rampant steroid use throughout baseball, while Sosa had his lawyer read a statement of denial upon his behalf. It was McGwire, though, who made the most lasting impression with a phrase he repeated, "I'm not here to talk about the past." Mark was four years retired, seven years removed from his record-setting season and noticeably smaller than he'd been at the peak of his power. The past was why he was called upon. The past is what baseball is built upon. What baseball players had been built upon in the '90s and '00s was the matter at hand. But McGwire stayed as mum as he legally could.

The credibility of slugging, of believing what was being seen, grew shakier. MLB toughened its penalties for failing a PED test. Among the players who failed one in the summer of 2005 was Palmeiro. He'd hit more than 500 home runs and collected more than 3,000 hits, but this rebuttal to his denial effectively ended his career. In their 2006 book, *Game of Shadows,* Mark Fainaru-Wada and Lance Williams set out an array of evidence showing that Bonds—a far bulkier physical specimen than he'd been when he first excelled for Pittsburgh—had been deep into HGH, Human Growth Hormone. Bonds, reportedly resentful of the attention McGwire and Sosa were receiving circa 1998, was now nearing Hank Aaron's career home run record of 755. There was little public appetite to cheer him on.

In December of 2007, the Mitchell Report was released. The result of twenty months of investigation into PED use yielded a slew of names that, if you got them from a box of baseball cards, you'd have felt pretty good about your haul. Superstars, stars who wanted to be super, journeymen who wanted to hang on . . . they were all there. The epidemic transcended team affiliation. There were three catchers who'd played for the Mets: Todd Hundley, Todd Pratt, and Paul Lo Duca. There was Lenny Dykstra, who got bigger as a Phillie than he was as a Met. There were hitters and pitchers, infielders and outfielders. There was Bonds and there was Roger Clemens, the men who'd been winning MVPs and Cy Youngs by the armload as they aged. Bonds had 762 home runs, Clemens 354 wins. For more than twenty years, no matter how their personalities struck teammates, reporters, and fans, there was no denying how dominant they'd been. But there was every reason to wonder what made them stay so dominant for so long. Each was active in 2007, but wouldn't be in 2008.

In 2009, a report surfaced claiming Sosa, who'd also been out of the game since '07, had failed a steroid test in 2003, back when those test results were supposed to remain anonymous. Alex Rodriguez's positive test under those circumstances had emerged earlier in the year. Come 2010, McGwire, about to rejoin the Cardinals as hitting coach, finally addressed the past. During an interview aired on the MLB Network, he admitted to Bob Costas that he, in fact, had used steroids. He also said he didn't think it impacted his surge in home run production.

McGwire saw his name removed from what had been his highway in Missouri, but he wasn't too sullied to be barred from baseball altogether. He went into coaching without incident. Several of the high-profile players who were active when their names were linked to PEDs rolled on in their careers fairly uninterrupted. A couple, like Jason Giambi and Gary Sheffield (who hit his 500th home run in 2009, as a Met), came to be treated as elder statesmen. Andy Pettitte said he took HGH to help in elbow recovery and soon his connection to the issue faded. A-Rod was a magnet for controversy, but after a while, his 2009 scandal dissipated from view. Some players were simply more likable than others; some had been granted forgiveness because forgiveness is an easily dispensed commodity, especially if there are games to be won. People, even ballplaying people, are entitled to correct their mistakes and go about their business. Baseball had gotten more serious about education, prevention, and detection by the 2010s. It was easy enough to dismiss "the steroid era" as a time when "everybody was doing it." There was also an era, prior to 1947, when not everybody was welcome to play in the majors. Baseball learned and moved forward.

* * *

There was one component of baseball, however, that wasn't so forgiving, wasn't willing to move on and was conditioned to talk about the past. Those who decided which players were elected to the Hall of Fame took the steroid era very seriously. Irony of irony, they were the same people who didn't seem to care very much about it while it was flourishing. These were the members of the Baseball Writers' Association of America, the beat writers and columnists who covered baseball closely and, by codified tradition, were entrusted with conferring immortality once a player was eligible for official consideration for the Hall.

The same writers whose positive coverage of the home run explosion of the 1990s had a chance to correct what they thought were their own mistakes. Had they been too giddy about McGwire and Sosa? About Bonds and Clemens? Had most of them not looked deep enough into why some players had grown so much and how their statistics were out of alignment with the numbers that had come before? Had not they wondered how some of the greats got only greater as they aged past what was usually considered a player's prime? Had it not occurred to them that while some players earned their mega-contracts the old-fashioned way, others "cheated" to garner their fortune?

Well, they were going to think about it now and they weren't going to take any chances . . . which is where Mike Piazza, merely a viewer of the congressional hearing of St. Patrick's Day 2005, comes back into the story. Because of McGwire (and Sosa and Palmeiro) casting so much doubt on slugging, almost anybody who had slugged exceptionally when offensive production had become extraordinary just *had to be* considered suspect.

Piazza was not involved with the BALCO investigation. He was not mentioned in the Mitchell Report. He wasn't accused by Canseco or subpoenaed by Congress. His name hadn't leaked from any secret results. He was never known to have tested positively for anything untoward.

But he was suspect. Because almost everybody who hit a lot of home runs was. Plus there were whispers. Whispers weren't evidence, but they did make a sound. It didn't amount to volumes of noise during his career, but if you wanted to make a case once he was retired . . . well, the specific nature of that groin injury in 2003 was sort of unusual. And somebody thought acne on his back mysteriously cleared up around the time MLB testing began. And where did the hair on his back go, anyway? And how does a kid drafted in the 62nd round become the greatest-hitting catcher in baseball history? He worked out, didn't he? Didn't all those guys "work out?" Some writers saw signs that could be connected to steroid use and the whispers grew loud enough to be heard.

You could bet your asterisk he was suspect—that will happen when people decide to suspect you. But you'd lose your asterisk if you wanted to enter cold, hard evidence that Mike Piazza used anything illegal or did anything unethical in making himself the player he became. Mike didn't wag a finger or dismiss the past, but he also responded to suspicions by saying, in essence, nope, I didn't do that. He had used over-the-counter Andro— not then classified as an anabolic steroid—as part of his workout routine in the '90s, but in the memoir he published in 2013, he said he phased it out before MLB and the FDA banned it.

It's certainly not beyond the scope of possibility that Mike Piazza actually did what he was suspected of. But no tangible evidence was ever produced. The man played in Los Angeles and New York most of his career. He didn't have trouble landing in headlines. If there was a smoking gun that linked Piazza to performance-enhancing drugs, it's difficult to believe it wouldn't have appeared by the time he was eligible for the Hall of Fame in 2013.

And if it had appeared, it still wouldn't have erased what he accomplished. It might bathe those accomplishments in a different light, but those pitches he hit were never coming back, and the roar the crowds let out on his behalf would still reverberate in memory. That, too, is what happens when you talk about the past.

* * *

McGwire got nowhere near the Hall of Fame when he first appeared on the ballot in 2007. Cal Ripken and Tony Gwynn sailed in. Like Mark, Cal and Tony retired in 2001 after fabulous careers, beloved by virtually everybody in the game. Tony was an All-Century finalist at Fenway, Cal an All-Century honoree in Atlanta. McGwire was both of those things. He also retired in 2001, so this was his first Hall election, too. He'd swatted 583 home runs across 16 seasons, fifth-most in major-league history when he was finished playing.

Nobody cared. Or if they cared, they cared only about PEDs. McGwire wasn't going to be a Hall of Famer despite his numbers. It was the same story for Palmeiro when he came up for consideration in 2011. Others went in—including two Met teammates of Piazza's, Rickey Henderson and Roberto Alomar—but anybody whose stock-in-trade was power suspected of being supplemented by something in a bottle could forget about it. The informal five-year rule that said you had a pretty good idea of who was a lock for the Hall as soon as he became eligible went out the window.

What happened to both McGwire and Palmeiro should have braced fans for what was coming in 2013, when maybe the most impressive group of first-time candidates since the very first Hall of Fame election in 1936 went on the ballot. It was the debut year of Sammy Sosa and Barry Bonds, Roger Clemens and Curt Schilling, Craig Biggio and Mike Piazza.

Or, more accurately, it was the year of Jacob Ruppert, the Yankees owner who brought Babe Ruth to New York; Hank O'Day, the umpire who cost the Giants a pennant via his handling of Cub chicanery (a.k.a. Merkle's Boner) in 1908; and Deacon White, catcher, 1871 to 1890. Those were the choices made by the Pre-Integration Veterans Committee. As can be inferred by the name of the group that chose them, none was alive at the present time, which is certainly no disqualifier in a sport that lives to honor its history. But recent history usually carries substantial sway at Hall of Fame time. The five-year countdown had always primed fans to know who was likely going in next.

Nobody who hung 'em up in 2007 made it in 2013. Not surprisingly, Cooperstown attendance in 2013 was estimated to be in the neighborhood of friends and relatives of the descendants of the honorees. Let's just say there was plenty of room to be had on the grass at Clark Sports Center, a stark contrast to six summers before when Ripken and Gwynn drew somewhere upwards of 70,000. It wasn't exactly stunning that Sosa, Bonds, and Clemens, for all their accomplishments, were getting bypassed. They'd been in the PED news far too much, and the writers' dismissal of McGwire signaled they shouldn't expect a call from Jack O'Connell, secretary-treasurer of the BBWAA, the guy who spreads the good word to the winners every January.

Schilling, who also testified before Congress in 2005 (he said steroids weren't much in use, a tune he changed later), was one of the great postseason pitchers of his or any time, but wasn't necessarily an automatic choice under any circumstances. Biggio passed 3,000 hits in his final season with Houston, which is usually all it takes to be elected, but, well, there were whispers. Plus, he was a teammate of Jeff Bagwell, a star slugger who was also still waiting after a third year on the ballot. Association seemed to come with a side dish of guilt. Bagwell was suspect, though there was no evidence offered. Nor was there any where Biggio was concerned.

And Piazza? He drew 57.82 percent, not bad for a first-timer in general and fourth overall on the 2013 ballot behind only Biggio, avatar of clutch pitching Jack Morris, and Bagwell. He fell under the cloud that enshrouded his generational peers, just not as much of it. Mike easily outpointed Bonds, Clemens, and Sosa, which was hardly the goal where he was concerned. In his book *Long Shot*, Piazza (with Lonnie Wheeler) wrote, "Election to the Hall of Fame would, for me, validate everything." The book came out the same winter as the first vote. There was no startling PED admission within, but there was a preference stated for when his validation arrived: "I hope to go in as a Met."

The hope remained on hold by the time the paperback version was published in 2014. Piazza missed again, this time with a slightly higher share of 62.17 percent. The writers elected on the first ballot two Atlanta pitchers who gave Mets fans fits, Greg Maddux and Tom Glavine (his fit-giving wasn't confined to his days as a Brave), along with Frank Thomas, who preceded Piazza as Oakland's DH after his distinguished career with the White Sox. The Big Hurt was an outspoken critic of PEDs and was never suspected of injecting or ingesting anything out of bounds. Those three went in with a trio of managers: Joe Torre, Bobby Cox, and Tony La Russa. "The Monster" busted out of his cage against La Russa's Cardinals, while Cox and Torre directed teams that foiled Mike's in 1999 and 2000.

In 2015, Biggio, who came up two votes shy the year before, made it, joining three hurlers who sailed in on the first ballot. Nobody would argue against Randy Johnson, John Smoltz, or Pedro Martinez (the fourth of Piazza's Mets teammates to go in before him), but between this class and the one before it, a person could get the impression that the 1990s and 2000s were an era defined by pitching and managing. The Hall of Fame's role in presenting baseball history as it happened, at least inside the Plaque Gallery, was taking a beating from writers who withheld their votes from some of the most dominant players of all time.

There was no plaque for admitted baseball gambler Pete Rose after all these years, but he was the anomaly of the modern game, the exception that proved an overriding rule. Since 1992, it was a little odd to consider the player with the most hits wasn't in Cooperstown, but that was an easily understood dropped stitch in the sport's otherwise breathtaking tapestry. All the other indisputable greats were represented.

It was getting harder to take the chronological narrative Hall of Fame membership implied seriously. What exactly happened over that decade and a half the writers were rejecting? At the highest levels of the game, Biggio could double and Thomas could homer, but otherwise, apparently hurlers and skippers held forth almost unchallenged.

The Famescape had grown murky. Known or linked-to PED users were being penalized for what was perceived as unfair play, a fair enough response by the writers, even if the numbers posted in their day weren't going anywhere. The '90s happened. The '00s happened. Bonds, Sosa, and McGwire really did roam the earth and trample the record books. Elbowing them aside denied reality. The standings from those years stood. Nobody was picking apart every roster of every team and retroactively subtracting championships based on however many hits were recorded by however many hitters and pitchers were suspected of using. Statistics had advanced by the 2010s, but they hadn't advanced that much. Besides, the plaques seemed to fit more and more words on them every year. Surely there was space for a clarifying sentence like "admitted to using steroids" if applicable.

Biggio transcended the whispers in 2015, but not Piazza. He had edged his way closer—69.95 percent, more votes than any of the non-electees on the ballot—but not in. While the postmortems from those who rejected him rationalized that "innocent until proven guilty" didn't extend to the conferring of baseball's highest honor or fretted they'd wind up with Mark McGwire Highway–sized egg on their face should damning evidence suddenly surface years after the fact, the Mets, under chief operating officer Jeff Wilpon's name, issued what had become their annual statement of support and encouragement. "We are confident that in the not too distant future, Mike Piazza, the top offensive catcher in the history of baseball, will take his rightful place in the halls of Cooperstown," the boilerplate read. "We look forward to celebrating that day with him, his family, and our fans, when it happens."

Until it happened, Mike was keeping busy. He had a young family to tend to in Miami, a locale that offered geographic proximity to Port St. Lucie, which came in handy when the Mets invited him to camp as a guest instructor. Mike tutored the catchers, most prominently rookie Travis d'Arnaud, who couldn't have been happier with the arrangement. Travis was a Southern California boy who looked up to Piazza the Dodger and called the coaching he was receiving in the spring of 2014 "a dream." By 2015, dreams were coming true for d'Arnaud and everybody in a Mets uniform. After six consecutive losing seasons, the club won a division title and the pennant. Catapulting them toward the postseason was a Piazzaesque deadline deal they made for slugger Yoenis Cespedes, the biggest in-season difference-maker they'd come up with since Mike seventeen years before.

For the first World Series game in Citi Field history, the Mets needed someone to throw out the first pitch. They asked their catcher from their previous Fall Classic appearance. Piazza donned a Mets jersey for the occasion. No. 31 took to the mound on a chilly October night and, in rolled-up shirtsleeves, delivered a ball to backup backstop Kevin Plawecki. Mike always had hit strikes better than he threw them, but as was the case in his halcyon days, his mere presence improved the Mets' fortunes. The club had dropped the first two games of the Series in Kansas City, but after Piazza accepted another ovation, the home team went out and throttled the Royals, 9–3. It turned out to be their only win, but, as in 2000, Mets fans felt a degree of gratification for coming close.

Maybe next year one of their own would finally go all the way.

IN AS A MET
January 6, 2016–July 30, 2016

Jeff Idelson barely had to clear his throat. Almost as soon as the president of the National Baseball Hall of Fame and Museum opened the envelope containing the results of BBWAA voting shortly after 6 P.M. Eastern Standard Time on January 6, 2016, discerning viewers tuned into the MLB Network could infer the news he was about to deliver. "As we both know," Idelson said to host Brian Kenny, "one of the hallmarks of winning baseball teams is strength up the middle, and thanks to the baseball writers, the Hall of Fame just bolstered its roster in a very big way."

"Up the middle" means four positions: center field, shortstop, second base, and catcher. "A very big way" implied more than one player in that subset had been elected. The wait for what Mets fans had wanted to hear since 2013 had been long enough to allow for the instinctive parsing of the most innocuous of introductory sentences. They knew who was on the ballot, who played where, and whose time had come.

"Our first new Hall of Famer," Idelson continued, "set a standard behind the plate, hitting for power and average, launching four-hundred twenty-seven home runs, including a record three-hundred ninety-six as a catcher, posted a three-oh-eight lifetime batting average..."

To paraphrase Dorothy Boyd in *Jerry Maguire*, he had us at "behind the plate." The wait was over, the doubt had dissolved, the rationalizations for aversion to election were reduced to statistically insignificant and—pending confirmation of one more breathlessly awaited announcement—the biographical detail that had been affixed to every mention of Tom Seaver for nearly a quarter-of-a-century had been deleted. Idelson didn't have to say any more to confirm Seaver was no longer the only player to go into the Hall of Fame as a New York Met. The Franchise was about to have company.

But please, Mr. President, go on.

". . . including one two-hundred hit season in Nineteen Ninety-Seven, when he became the first player who was *primarily* a catcher to reach the two-hundred hit mark. Incredibly *durable* behind the plate, leading the National League in putouts four times and assists twice. Drove in one-thousand three-hundred and thirty-five runs, a twelve-time All-Star, winning MVP honors in his hometown of Philly in Nineteen Ninety-Six, he earned ten Silver Slugger awards, he was the Nineteen Ninety-Three Rookie of the Year. From Norristown, Pennsylvania, drafted in Nineteen Eighty-Eight in the *sixty*-second round, the thirteen-hundred ninetieth pick overall, today . . . he calls Cooperstown home.

"Mike Piazza, welcome to the Hall of Fame."

Geez, you were left to wonder, with a résumé like that, what took the Welcome Wagon so long? Every home run hit, every run driven in, every honor earned except this one was already banked in 2007. Cooperstown couldn't have opened its doors one or two or three Januarys before?

Then you remembered it pretty much ceased to matter. The process was slow and flawed and needed to be repaired for whoever else matched the description of "surefire Hall of Famer except for suspicions," but a fourth-ballot Hall of Famer attracting 82.95 percent of the vote was, at the end of the day, every bit the baseball immortal as a Hall of Famer elected on any ballot. When Ralph Kiner died in 2014, Seaver remembered him as "an inner-circle Hall of Famer." That Kiner had to wait until his fifteenth and final appearance on the writers' ballot to make it had nothing to do with his larger story. Piazza was one of them now. He was with Seaver, with Kiner, with Griffey.

Oh yes, the "big way" Idelson alluded to regarding strength up the middle was a nod to the other player elected. Ken Griffey Jr. was in on his first try, to the surprise of absolutely nobody. Griffey played 22 seasons, belted 630 homers, owned the American League in the last decade of the twentieth century, and never aroused suspicions of a PED nature. His vote total, however, was noteworthy beyond simply crashing the 75 percent barrier. Four-hundred forty writers cast ballots. Three of them left off Junior. Nobody else did. That made his share of the vote 99.32 percent, topping

Seaver's 98.84. Seaver holding that record since 1992 was the only reason a percentage of Mets fans obsessed on vote totals to the second decimal. Nobody had gone in more closely to unanimity than Tom Terrific. Ken now took over that record . . . though Tom still held it among pitchers.

The FRANCHISE POWER PITCHER WHO TRANSFORMED METS FROM LOVABLE LOSERS INTO FORMIDABLE FOE was these days, when not residing permanently on his plaque, a Napa Valley vintner. As proprietor of Seaver Family Vineyards and a fellow Hall of Famer, Tom begrudged Griffey not one iota of his election by near-acclamation. "There was going to be a time when somebody broke it," Seaver said of the son of his Cincinnati teammate, "and rightfully so in Junior." He was also prepared to share the In as a Met mantle with Mike: "I think it's terrific, wonderful. Mike was a helluva player, a great offensive player, and it's nice to have him. It's great."

Every Piazza specific Idelson rattled off—his draft slot, his rookie season, his All-Star MVP, his two-hundred hit year—related to the catcher's days as a Dodger, but Mike got his way plaquewise with the powers that be. On MLB Network the night the results were announced, he tipped his hand by emphasizing "the special place I have in New York City with these fans" who had done "nothing but embrace and honor me." And at the Hall of Fame press conference in Manhattan the next day that reunited the two "So Good . . . So Young" *SI* cover boys from 1994, the catcher threw out the other bulletin Mets fans had been waiting to hear.

"As far as my hat," he said of how he would portrayed for all of eternity, "I want to be very clear and say that as much as I loved comin' up with the Dodgers and will always cherish my time there, I'm gonna go in as a New York Met."

The next sound you heard was an entire fan base canceling the group therapy appointment it had made just in case Mike said different. For all the suggestions that baseball is a metaphor for life or America or whatever, baseball is mostly a metaphor for baseball, and baseball is a sport, a competition. Even in retirement, sides must be chosen. Mets fans wanted to be certain who was with them and not against them.

Conversely, Griffey, who unwittingly blew his best chance to go to a World Series when he passed on the chance to be traded from Seattle to New York in late 1999, and instead embraced the opportunity to go home to Cincinnati, gravitated back to his professional roots and announced he'd go in as a Mariner. "Out of my twenty-two years," Griffey would say upon his induction, "I've learned that only one team will treat you the best, and that's your first team." Mike begged to differ. His statistics weren't quite as spectacular in New York as they were in Los Angeles (age will have that effect on a catcher, even the greatest-hitting one), but his legend took on new dimensions in his second full-time city, a place that would always finish first in his heart. "I feel like the fans here truly brought me into their family," he said. "Every time I've come back, I've been so incredibly honored from the response."

* * *

The second player to go in the Hall of Fame as a Met would have another second coming his way in the summer of '16, and it was, in its way, every bit the honor that Cooperstown's call was. On January 25, the Mets announced No. 31 would be retired on Saturday, July 30, six days after the upstate induction ceremonies. The Mets planned to make a weekend of it, giving away replica Piazza jerseys that Friday night and a Piazza bobblehead on Sunday afternoon. The doll would be modeled on Mike's reaction to hitting his 1999 walk-off homer against Trevor Hoffman (who missed Hall of Fame induction on his first ballot in January by thirty-four votes).

If anything could be more special than a Met going into the Hall of Fame, it was a Mets player having his number retired. Except for that one time in 1988, it just wasn't done. Out above the left-field fence, on the original oversized "Great Wall of Flushing" (not to be confused with the defense Fonzie and Rey-Rey provided back in the day), every number the Mets had honored was displayed, though sometimes you had to squint between revelers on the Party City Deck and maybe past a poorly situated trash can to make them out.

There was 37 for Casey Stengel, who essentially invented the Mets. His record as manager was crammed with last-place finishes, but the Ol' Perfesser's personality, perspective, and propaganda propelled the Mets to the top of New York's baseball consciousness. Of course 37 was retired for him, becoming the first number to be framed in 1965.

There was 14 for Gil Hodges, who elevated the previously hopeless Mets to a world championship and died tragically young less than three years later. Gil remained the beau ideal of Mets skippers forever after. Of course 14 was retired for him, its memorialization made official on Old Timers' Day in 1973.

In the non-Mets category, there was 42 for Jackie Robinson, in 1997, displayed in Brooklyn Dodger red and blue. In the non-number category, there was SHEA, a 2008 tip of the hat to Bill Shea, the attorney who worked the levers of power until New York was granted a National League franchise to replace the two it lost. It was a nice consolation prize with which to acknowledge the late lawyer whose Stadium was about to be demolished. In the not-exactly-retired but nobody took it down category was a replica of the memorial patch worn in 2014 to remember Kiner, Met broadcaster for fifty-two seasons, which is to say all of them until he died. The Mets had worn and hung something similar for Gary Carter in 2012, but KID 8 was removed from the wall by 2013.

And, obviously, there was 41, synonymous with Seaver. You couldn't issue it to the next righty up from Tidewater in 1977 after Tom was traded or 1984 when he got away again. It wouldn't be overstatement to surmise there would have been a riot. The day the Mets retired 41 (and inducted him into their Hall of Fame), the summer after he called it a career, was a huge deal. There was Kiner and Bob Murphy introducing guest after guest. There was a letter for Murph to read from President Reagan. There was a veritable flotilla of gaudy gifts for him and his family: artwork, jewelry, cases of wine, skiwear to be enjoyed on a trip to the Alps, the Oldsmobile Cutlass Supreme convertible he was driven onto the field in . . . no Don's daughter ever came away from her wedding with a grander haul. There was a song recorded by WFAN's Suzyn Waldman and layered over a video montage on DiamondVision. Borrowing the melody from "Take Me Out to the Ball Game," it wished to *see Forty-One out on the mound/that effortless motion/ mechanics so sound.*

Mostly, on July 24, 1988, there was Tom, explaining to Shea Stadium that "I came to a decision a long time ago, that *if* my number was ever retired, there would be one way that I wanted to say thank you to everybody— everybody that's here on the field, everybody that's in the stands, everybody that's home watching on television. If you allow me just one moment, I'm gonna say thank you in my own very special way, and if you know me, how much I love pitching, you'll know what it means to me."

With that, Tom practically sprinted from the microphone set up at home plate to the mound, stood on the rubber, and bowed in every direction toward everybody inside Shea.

It was hard to top a number retirement like that, both in terms of who wore the number and how he expressed his gratitude, so maybe that's why, despite some worthy candidates—especially among those who forged 1986—the Mets never made a move to retire another player's number over the next twenty-eight years. Every franchise retires numbers as it sees fit. Some are more generous or less discriminating about it than others, depending on how you view matters. In some places, long and meritorious service is enough. In others, a one-team career that ends in Cooperstown is the stringent criterion. The Yankees, Mets fans will remind you, retire numbers like your local Firestone dealer re-tires Buicks. They've had a raft of greats, to be sure, but only so many Ruths, Gehrigs, DiMaggios, and Mantles. If that's your standard, then, well, the Mets had Seaver, period.

That *was* the Met standard from 1988 to 2016. It took Mike Piazza making it to Cooperstown to amend it.

* * *

Sunday, July 24, 2016, induction day in Cooperstown, New York. More than 50,000 have descended on the middle of nowhere. The ever-vigilant 7 Line Army alone has chartered thirteen buses and is ferrying 700 fans up from Flushing. The throng for Mike Piazza and Ken Griffey will be estimated as the second-biggest an induction weekend has drawn. Only 2007's, for Cal Ripken and Tony Gwynn, brought in more.

Griffey got more votes. Piazza, however, is second to none in attracting adoration. The Clark Athletic Center lawn is a lush shade of blue and orange. Even some black left over from the late '90s. Commissioner Rob Manfred gets to do what Bud Selig never did across twenty-two summers in office. He reads from the text of a plaque that has been crafted by the Pittsburgh-based Matthews International Corporation bronze division and topped by the image of a man in a New York Mets baseball cap. It's not quite the same-style cap Seaver went in with because, in Mike's day, the Mets wore an alternate version more often than not—but the curly NY is clearly visible. So is the facial hair from his prime, Willie Randolph's 2005 directive notwithstanding. Matthews and the Hall work very closely together on these babies. Sculptor Tom Tsuchiya sees the "classic Mike Piazza look" as one featuring a goatee, "the Fu Manchu kind of look. Not the bleach-blond."

Piazza dyed his hair on a road trip to Chicago in 2001. "I was getting a little bored," he explained at the time. "Figured I'd liven things up a little bit. I figured the worst thing it could do was change our luck a little bit." The luck transcended the look. The dye was washed out long ago. Mike is permanently rooted in Cooperstown.

MICHAEL JOSEPH PIAZZA
"Mike"
LOS ANGELES, N.L., 1992–1998
FLORIDA, N.L., 1998
NEW YORK, N.L. 1998–2005
SAN DIEGO, N.L., 2006
OAKLAND A.L., 2007

The team mentioned third comes in first when it comes to crowd reaction.

Manfred reads aloud that Mike was a "a durable and prolific power-hitting catcher." The numbers come tumbling out: 427 career home runs; the 396 as a catcher; 100 games caught 11 times; four times leading the National League in putouts. Rookie of the Year in 1993. An All-Star 12 times, the game's MVP in 1996.

Then the heart of the matter:

"Led Mets to the 2000 Subway Series, and helped rally a nation one year later with his dramatic home run in the first Mets game in New York following the 9/11 attacks."

Those are the specific credentials that will endure for all to read and all to see. Mets fans know there was more. There was what the trade in 1998 signified. There was how the ride through 1999 thrilled them. There were dozens of moments before 2000 and dozens more after 2001, and, blanketing all of it, the notion that was always sinking in: *My god, we've got Mike Piazza. Mike Piazza is on our team. Ooh, Mike is due up this inning. I wonder what Mike will do."* But even if Piazza was larger than life in Flushing, his plaque is the same size as everybody else's in Cooperstown. The fans who cared most and knew best would have to pass along and pass down the rest of the details on their own.

No doubt they would. They'd been doing so for nearly two decades.

When Manfred finishes reading, Mike poses with the plaque. The *MIKE PI-AZ-ZA!* chant of yore goes up. Shea lives.

Piazza thanks the commissioner. He thanks the BBWAA. He thanks Idelson and the rest of those who administer the Hall. He acknowledges his 2016 classmate. "Kenny," he says, "it is an incredible honor to be going in alongside of you," joking, "about the only thing we have in common as ballplayers are two arms and two legs."

He begins to weave into his story the men who are now his peers, his fellow Hall of Famers, particularly the ones on the stage behind him. To Mike Schmidt, from his hometown Phillies, "I watched you as a child, I celebrated with you, and suffered with you." To Johnny Bench, whose National League catcher's home run total he surpassed, "You will always be the best of all time . . . although maybe I hit the ball just a little better to right field."

Soon there are names every seasoned baseball fan will recognize and names that mean something mostly to Mike. It takes a little while to get to what many in the crowd would unabashedly refer to as the good part. The segue comes when Piazza mentions his "lifelong friend and agent," Danny Lozano, and remembers the time he told Florida's temporary Marlin he was about to become a New York Met.

A cheer goes up.

"It was actually the last team that I had imagined wanted me," Mike swears, "but it was the most amazing experience any human being could have."

He thanks Steve Phillips. He thanks Fred and Jeff Wilpon. He lavishes praise on "a colorful, unpredictable manager named Bobby Valentine." He commences to drilling down on the subject of "playing in New York. Actually, Queens." Queens draws a louder reaction than New York. It makes sense. The heart of the borough seems to have been transplanted here today.

- "When I was traded, there was a gutsy, not so big in stature, but big-hearted left-handed pitcher named Johnny Franco." Mike thanks him for "unselfishly" giving him his No. 31.

- "The first game I caught for the Mets that year was pitched by an intimidating yet cerebral left-handed pitcher with a devastating slider named Al Leiter." Mike's biggest honor, he says on the day he is honored for the ages, was "to catch one of his best-pitched games, a one-game playoff in 1999 against the Cincinnati Reds, in which he didn't shake me off one time." With that nod, the 1999 Mets are inducted, too.
- "I was also very fortunate to play with some incredible teammates in New York. Edgardo Alfonzo comes to mind. *Mi pana.*" That's Spanish for pal. "A great fielder, a clutch hitter. Many times I can remember him picking me up when I failed to come through." Mike singles out the 2000 Fireworks Night game against the Braves, when he himself capped off the ten-run eighth inning with a three-run homer, but "Edgardo actually had an amazing two-strike hit that tied the game and allowed me to relax and feel more confident at the plate knowing we were tied." Fonzie played enough years to merit inclusion on a Hall of Fame ballot but the committee that makes those decisions left him off when his chance came around in 2012. Fonzie deserved better. And he just got it.

Finally . . . well, not finally, because he will have plenty heartfelt to say a bit later on behalf of his faith and his family (along with the San Diego Padres and Teddy Roosevelt—Piazza is nothing if not thorough), but at last, Mike gets to his kindred spirits.

"How," he asks, "can I put into words my thanks, love and appreciation for New York Mets fans?" Maybe it's just allergies afflicting the former Claritin spokesman, but Piazza can be seen working a handkerchief when he finishes his question. *MIKE PI-AZ-ZA!* spreads through the crowd like pollen.

"You have given me the greatest gift and have graciously taken me into your family," he continues. "Looking out today at the incredible sea of blue and orange brings back the greatest time of my life. You guys are serious."

In 2016, Mike remembers 1998. "We didn't get off on the best foot," he says, "but we both stayed with it. At first, I was pressing to make you cheer and wasn't doing the job. You didn't take it easy on me, and I am better because of it."

If proof is needed, he is accepting induction into the Hall of Fame as he speaks. "The eight years we spent together went by way too fast," Mike laments. "The thing I miss most is making you cheer." If provoking cheers is what he wants to do, he's going to succeed with the following appraisal:

"No fans rock the house like Mets fans. You are passionate, loyal, intelligent, and love this great game."

Well, it takes one to know one. No Met ever exuded those qualities more than Mike Piazza. Tom Seaver never said those things about Mets fans when he was on this stage twenty-four years before, but he had a different temperament and it was a different, less interactive time. It took the trauma of being traded to Cincinnati to elicit from Seaver the sentiment, "As far as the fans go, I've given them a great number of thrills and they've been equally returned." Tom was from the Ted Williams school of, as John Updike put it, "gods do not answer letters." Mike, on the other hand, liked to tweet. Tom was as articulate a player as New York ever knew, but ultimately he preferred to let his pitching speak for him. The mound, after all, was where he took his bows at Shea. He appreciated the chance to pitch and was happy to let you watch. Piazza was, at heart, a fan. A fan of metal. A fan of the Mets. He lived to rock the house from wherever he happened to be standing. He demonstrated a rare gift that allowed him to step back and appreciate being appreciated. And he appreciated who he was and what he'd come to mean to so many.

"To be only the second Met to enter the Hall of Fame, following Tom Seaver, brings me great pride and joy," Mike adds as homage to one Met who isn't there today (Tom, dealing with the ongoing effects of Lyme disease, is said to find traveling cross-country difficult), and takes care to remember "I truly enjoyed Gary Carter's company" for another who fits that description in a sadder way. "He was a wonderful man, a great player, and I miss him."

The Mets portion of Mike Piazza's Hall of Fame induction speech wouldn't be complete without addressing the home run he is best known by, the home run that caused the jersey he wore then to be fussed over long after the bases were circled (its auction a few months earlier caused a back page fuss in New York), the home run that rated singular mention on his plaque. For a moment, he brings a joyous crowd back to the grimmest of days, to the period directly after September 11, 2001. Given all he is recalled so deeply and lovingly for, he must go there.

"To witness the darkest evil of the human heart and witness that as it tore many loved ones from their families will forever be burned in my soul,"

Mike says. "But from tragedy and sorrow came bravery, love, compassion, character, and eventual healing. Many of you give me praise for the two-run home run on the first game back on September 21 to push us ahead of the rival Braves. But the true praise belongs to police, firefighters, and first responders who knew that they were going to die, but went forward anyway."

The zeitgeist of the fall of 2001 insisted calling a baseball player a hero was to trifle with the term. It was still a valid thought fifteen years later. But a ballplayer who could leaven a tragic moment then and place it in proper perspective now . . . well, he could probably do more than hit to right.

* * *

The next week, the Cooperstown magic is transplanted back from whence it came. The timing is exquisite. The upstate New York hamlet may be closer to Queens than it is to Griffey's Seattle, but it's not especially close to the city. The recent extension of the 7 train will take a person only as far as 34th Street–Hudson Yards, over on the West Side. Better to shuttle Piazza to Citi Field and give another 42,707 a slice of the immortality pie.

It's a damp Saturday evening on July 30, but the rain moves out for Mike. Nobody will have to dress up as a Piazza impersonator and flop around on the tarp. Robin Ventura isn't available for such showmanship tonight anyway. He is, these days, managing the Chicago White Sox. Joe McEwing is one of his coaches.

Not so many years have passed that you can't find former teammates and contemporaries of Mike Piazza on major-league rosters. The Mets have several. David Wright and Jose Reyes (the latter having returned to town weeks earlier) are 2016 Mets, though each is on the disabled list tonight. Jerry Blevins was a September call-up with Oakland during Mike's final month as a player, a lefty reliever for the Mets now. Kelly Johnson, rookie from the last of the divisionally dynastic Braves, is a wise, old Met utilityman. Bartolo Colon was pitching for the Indians when Mike was catching for the Dodgers. Not only is he still pitching nineteen seasons later, he's a 2016 All-Star and, most legendarily, a late-career slugger, having launched his first home run in May, leaving him only 426 behind Mike.

Carlos Beltran, who batted in front of Mike as a Met in 2005, is a Yankee, at least until Monday's trade deadline. Adrian Gonzalez, who batted behind Mike as a Padre in 2006, is a Dodger with eyes on the playoffs. His home games are being called by Vin Scully, just as Mike's and Fernando Valenzuela's and Steve Garvey's and Sandy Koufax's were in Los Angeles and just as Roy Campanella's were in Brooklyn. But Vin, eighty-eight, says he's finally prepared to walk away from the game he's broadcast since 1950 and will do so when 2016 is over.

While Scully is winding down his sixty-seventh consecutive season behind the mic, the Mets are trying to make it back to the postseason for a second straight October. Given all their injuries—not just to aging David and Jose, but much of their vaunted young pitching—they're finding first place ever harder to see. After dropping their Friday night game to the Rockies, Terry Collins's Mets are 7 1/2 behind Dusty Baker's Nationals and trailing Don Mattingly's Marlins, too. The wild-card race is muddled. The Mets are mathematically viable, but just one of five teams battling for two spots, and at the moment, they have only the fourth-best record within that group.

Time is always marching on in baseball, and the 2016 Mets are no exception. Travis d'Arnaud, Piazza's prize pupil from a couple of springs before, has gone from bright hope of the catching corps to the subject of trade rumors. Td'A, in the social media shorthand of the era, is hitting .238 and showing zero power. Justin Ruggiano, a journeyman outfielder, has just journeyed from the minors to join the club on Piazza's big night, replacing Reyes, who had been trying to play with a strained oblique. Did they even have obliques when Piazza played? Reyes is a Met in 2016 by weird circumstance, to phrase it kindly. He'd been suspended after domestic violence charges the previous fall and his then-employer, the very same Rockies the Mets are facing this Saturday, eventually let him go. The Mets picked him up. He's proved a solid citizen and decent addition thus far . . . and become the starting third baseman in Wright's absence. Nobody saw that coming.

Nobody saw a player like Piazza coming to the Mets when Mike started making a name for himself in 1993. Not until a week, maybe two, before it happened had anybody seriously seen Piazza himself coming to the Mets in 1998. Piazza admitted in his Hall of Fame speech he didn't see it. Entangled in his own contract controversy, he hadn't noticed Todd Hundley was sidelined. But feelers were put out, offers were made and accepted, Franco sacrificed No. 31 and, lo and behold, it appeared on Piazza's back at Shea Stadium.

Now it is going to be retired at Citi Field. Mike is about to join the world's most exclusive club. The United States Senate has been called that, but they have one hundred members. The National Baseball Hall of Fame, fairly exclusive in its own right, grew in 2016 to 312 denizens, or one more than the total wins compiled by Tom Terrific. The membership of those who'd had their numbers retired by the New York Mets was four . . . and only two because of how they played as Mets. Seaver was always indisputable. Piazza had just taken a while, but there was never a good reason not to do it.

The Mets use the occasion to freshen their numerical presentation, moving the numbers and names they choose to honor from the wall behind what is now known as the M&M's Sweet Seats to a more exalted level above Promenade, affixed to the facade that wraps the left-field foul pole. Thirty-one's predecessors are already up there when Howie Rose starts the ceremonies. He introduces Mike's wife Alicia, their two daughters, Nicoletta and Paulina, and one son Marco, his parents Vince and Veronica, and his brothers Tony, Tommy, and Vince Jr., then three teammates: Leiter, Alfonzo, and Cliff Floyd. A video rolls. The gray skies clear up on CitiVision as the action moves to the sunny pretaped Citi Field parking lot, specifically to the site of the five-sided commemorative marker that advises you that you are standing on the site of Shea Stadium's home plate from 1964 to 2008.

Or, if you are like the man in the video, you are crouching behind it. As Mötley Crüe's "Home Sweet Home" plays, the presence of Piazza comes into full view. Mike touches the plate, just as he had at the crest of the Shea Goodbye ceremonies eight years before, just as he had done regularly between '98 and '05. Having paid the old place homage, he stands in the empty lot where once a ballpark stood and strolls toward its replacement. The Crüe is interspersed with familiar voices making familiar calls. Murph's when he crushed Ramiro Mendoza. Howie's on 9/21/01. Ted Robinson's after Carlton Fisk's record fell.

Soon, in real time, our pedestrian is inside. Mike emerges from the tunnel and into the home dugout, shaking hands with Collins (an acquaintance from when both were stationed in the Dodgers' system), catcher d'Arnaud, all the current Mets. He stops to stand on a logo bearing his likeness and semi-circles the bases, waving all the way around, until he

lands at the podium behind second base. After another, longer video presentation attesting to how Mike had made this night necessary, Howie
calls the roll.

"The number retirement we are about to witness," the post-Murph
Radio Voice of the New York Mets declares, "is a big deal. It is a really, really
big deal. It is, quite simply, the highest honor a team can bestow upon one
of its players. Consider, for a moment, the select few who have earned this
honor in the fifty-four year history of our team." He reads off the numbers
and names. "This is the pantheon of New York baseball elites that Mike
Piazza joins this evening."

Rose asks one and all to direct their attention up above the left-field
corner, where the six discs representing those icons are about to be complemented by a seventh. The soundtrack switches to Aaron Copland's "Fanfare
for the Common Man," which also played to close out the Shea Goodbye
tribute in 2008. A blue canvas with an orange NY is lifted and 31 is revealed.
From right to left, the pantheon is now Robinson, Shea, Kiner; Stengel,
Hodges, Seaver, Piazza. "Congratulations, Mike," Howie adds. "Citi Field
is all yours."

He can add it to his collection, right next to Shea Stadium.

For Mike, the date might as well be October 2, 2005. He says thank you
a couple of times, but the crowd won't stop cheering or chanting, same as it
ever was on the day he played his final Mets game. "You guys are unbeliev-
able," he says. "Wow." All he can do for a spell is wave as he did eleven years
earlier.

When he finally gets some words in edgewise, he assures the fans that
they are on his Cooperstown plaque, even if they are not each listed individually beside him. "No one goes into the Hall of Fame alone," Mike tells his
second ballpark. "Each and every one of you is in there with me." He raises
his index finger as he did in 2013 when he told Mets fans that he counted
them as his true friends. As such gestures go, it's a helluva lot more effective
than Rafael Palmeiro's version.

Mike can do pretty much anything he wants with his crowd. He gets
it, as a sports team owner himself (that of an Italian soccer club), to give a
grudging round of applause to the Wilpons. Fred and Jeff bore the brunt
of customer dissatisfaction during the lean years, but Mike reassures
his friends in the stands who first boo when their names are mentioned.

"Nobody wants to win more than them," Mike says, and for the moment, his endorsement carries weight.

"I think I better get going so we can get this game in tonight," is Mike's way of wrapping up, but the crowd isn't having it. The 2016 Mets are hovering a little above .500 and lately disappointing their followers. Mike, enshrined in a perpetual state of sepia slugging, can do no wrong. As in his final game as a Met, he doesn't want to overstay his curtain call, but he's also learned to take a hint. "No?" he vamps. "You wanna hang out a while?" One more round of *MIKE PI-AZ-ZA!* ensues.

"I wanna say just a little bit of what it means to have my number retired for this great franchise and for you amazing fans," Mike continues. "That means I will always be with you." Again, he takes out the index finger and points up above left field, up at 31. "So every time these guys"—he points toward the Mets dugout—"and you need a little bit of inspiration, just give a little peek up there to Ol' Mikey, and *know* that I'm back home, watching you guys on TV, saying a lot of prayers"—he crosses himself—"prayin' for the Mets."

The catcher then turns secular but grows serious. "I truly love all you guys," Mike testifies, "and I just want you to know, you have given me an honor no man deserves and no player deserves. And I think about all that we went through and all we lived through, from the beginning to the end, and today, it's a new beginning, and I look forward again to coming back many, many years.

"God bless you guys. God bless your families.

"And LET'S . . . GO . . . METS!"

* * *

You couldn't say that all those years in Queens hadn't taught Mike Piazza how to speak the language. And, after a few rough weeks in August, once enough injuries had healed, you couldn't say his prayers went unanswered. Or perhaps enough peeks up at Ol' Mikey did the trick. However it happened, the Mets went on a tear similar to the one Mike's Mets pulled off in 2001. They captured twenty-seven of their final forty games and, on the second-to-last day of the season, clinched one of the National League wild cards. At 87–75, they earned the right to host the Giants, who clinched their berth on the last day, in the last game ever called by Scully. Unfortunately, it also earned them the right to face Madison Bumgarner in an institutionalized one-game playoff that didn't work out quite as well as the one Leiter threw against the Reds. Noah Syndergaard pitched wonderfully for seven innings, but Bumgarner was brilliant for nine, and San Francisco eliminated New York, 3–0. No repeat pennant, still no successful World Series sequel to 1986.

True to his word, Miami's most famous Mets fan was watching. At 1:09 A.M. on October 6, nearly two hours after the final out at Citi Field, @mikepiazza31 tweeted, "A frustrating end to an otherwise exciting stretch run, you Mets fans will always be amazing, your hope is Inspiring! God Bless, #LGM, #mets."

Another Mets flag would not be raised the following April, but Mike Piazza was guaranteed to be forever a part of the fabric in Flushing.

ACKNOWLEDGMENTS

There are few phrases in the Met lexicon more exhilarating than "Piazza on deck as the potential winning run." Thanks to Mike for defining anticipation for us for eight seasons. Thanks, too, for inhabiting our memories for a lifetime. To paraphrase his answer to the one question I had the opportunity to ask him, the games were long, the years were sublime.

How did anybody write a baseball book before the advent of Baseball-Reference? That may be the only baseball question whose answer I can't look up on the most vital website known to fan and author alike.

My fellow Mets fans and I weren't shy about communicating our ire toward the BBWAA three Januarys running, demonstrating to me just how much this book's title character meant to us. We shouldn't have had to have gotten so ticked, which is to say we shouldn't have had to waited four ballots for Mike's call to the Hall, but the passion we expressed on Piazza's behalf, particularly via tweets of discontent, perversely served to inspire this project. Good goin', #MetsTwitter!

As I attempted to describe this book to my occasional spiritual guide Mark Mehler, he clarified my thinking for me. "It's about the Mets fan's relationship to Piazza," Mark suggested, "like the Bible is the story of the relationship between God and the Jewish people. I would call it a love story, but with a surfeit of blood and guts, idol worship and incest. True love never runs smooth." I think he was talking about religion there, but it also sounds quite a bit like the Bobby Valentine years. In that vein, I tip my blue and orange yarmulke to Matthew Callan, a true Talmudic scholar in the realm of the 1999 Mets.

The idea that there was a thread to be spooled from 1993 to 1999 to the Hall of Fame election results of 2016 wasn't an obvious one, but it appealed to Ken Samelson, and I thank my Skyhorse editor for seeing it and patiently encouraging me to pursue it. When it comes to sports books, he is Spartacus.

I have a perfectly wonderful biological sister, but in baseball matters, I swear I'm related by genetics to Jodie Remick. She looked out for my best interests in 2016, seeing to it I'd experience the retirement of No. 31 from just the right angle. Like her, I sort of wondered why we had to replace Todd Hundley . . . and like her, I came around pretty quickly.

A season of baseball writing, on a blog as well as at work on a book, is better because of the steadfast support of friends like Sharon Chapman, Kevin Connell, Rob Emproto, Ryder Chasin, Dan Gold, Andrea Foote, David "Skid" Rowe, Mark Simon, Kevin Chapman, Joe Figliola, Rob Chasin, Jon Springer, Garry Spector, Christopher Halleron, Matthew Silverman, Jeff Reiter, Jim Haines, Jay Goldberg, Ben Rosenfield, Charlie Hangley, Ed Witty, Brian Sokoloff, and the blessedly wonderful readers of *Faith and Fear in Flushing*. I am also grateful to John Coppinger (*Metstradamus*), James Schapiro (*Shea Bridge Report*), and my FAFIF partner Jason Fry for sharing their writing on a going basis with Mets fans like me.

Thanks to Ethan Wilson, director of the Mets media relations department for furnishing just enough access for a writer/fan. Gratitude forever to the late Shannon Forde for taking bloggers seriously and engaging us lovingly in the first place. Kevin Carey of MLB lent a hand tracking down a long forgotten at-bat. Kevin Sornatale represents SNY well. Gary Cohen, Howie Rose, Josh Lewin, and Pete McCarthy are broadcasters and people of the highest order. The bequeathed 1993 archives of Ron Kaplan turned into a masochistic boon. A good soul at Retrosheet revealed the name Herm Wehmeier to me and what he had to do with Curt Schilling in 1999.

Jeff Hysen is the best street team, sounding board, and pal an author ever had. *Mi pana* Carlos Briceno paints a bandwagon like nobody's business. Mr. and Mrs. Stem remain the inverse of Mets fans, but they couldn't be any more appreciated by this Mets fan.

One of the last pieces of news I got to share with my father was that I was writing this book. Charles Prince died during the All-Star break in

2016 and was memorialized on a day the Mets played the Cubs at Wrigley Field. Next thing you know, the Cubs win the World Series. Coincidence? I couldn't say, but my dad was a champ.

Stephanie Prince has listened to me urge on hundreds of ballplayers and read aloud thousands of work-in-progress words. It is her voice, however, that remains the sweetest thing I've ever heard.

SELECT BIBLIOGRAPHY

BOOKS

Angell, Roger, *A Pitcher's Story: Innings with David Cone*. Warner Books, 2001.

Corcoran, Dennis, *Induction Day at Cooperstown: A History of the Baseball Hall of Fame Ceremony*. McFarland & Company, 2011.

Delsohn, Steve, *True Blue: The Dramatic History of the Los Angeles Dodgers, Told by the Men Who Lived It*. William Morrow, 2001.

Green, Dallas and Alan Maimon, *The Mouth That Roared: My Six Outspoken Decades in Baseball*. Triumph Books, 2013.

Klapisch, Bob and John Harper, *The Worst Team Money Could Buy: The Collapse of the New York Mets*. Random House, 1993.

Linn, Ed, *Hitter: The Life and Turmoils of Ted Williams*. Harcourt Brace Jovanovich, 1993.

Martinez, Pedro and Michael Silverman, *Pedro*. Houghton Mifflin Harcourt, 2015.

New York Daily News, *Piazza*. Edited by Victoria Marini. Sports Publishing, 2000.

Piazza, Mike and Lonnie Wheeler, *Long Shot*. Simon & Schuster, 2013.

Rosenbaum, Dave, *If They Don't Win It's a Shame: The Year the Marlins Bought a World Series*. McGregor Publishing, 1998.

Rubin, Adam, *Pedro, Carlos & Carlos! and Omar: The Rebirth of the New York Mets*. The Lyons Press, 2007.

White, Theodore, *America In Search of Itself: The Making of the President 1956–1980*. Warner Books, 1982.

NEWSPAPERS, PERIODICALS, NEWS AGENCIES, & WEBSITES

Advertising Age
Adweek
AmazinAvenue.com
Associated Press
Baltimore Sun
BaseballHall.org
Baseball-Reference.com
BaseballSteroidEra.com
Boston Globe
CBS.com
Chicago Tribune
Cincinnati Enquirer
CNN.com
ESPN.com
ESPN the Magazine
Galesburg Register-Mail
Hartford Courant
Houston Chronicle
Los Angeles Times
MBTN.net
Mets.com
MetsDaddy.com
MLB.com
MTV.com
Mudslide.net
Newsday
New York Daily News
New York Mets Media Guide (1993, 1994, 2001, 2016)
New York Mets Official Yearbook (1994, 1995)
New York Post
New York Times

The New Yorker
Orlando Sentinel
Philadelphia Inquirer
Pocono Record
RealityShack.com
Retrosheet.org
Rolling Stone
The7Line.com
St. Petersburg Times
San Francisco Chronicle
Seattle Post-Intelligencer
Southeast Missourian
Splitsider.com
Spokane Spokesman-Review
The Sporting News
Sports Illustrated
SportsonEarth.com
SportToday.org
Star-Ledger (New Jersey)
Sun-Sentinel (South Florida)
Time
Topeka Capitol-Journal
UltimateMets.com
United Press International
USA Today
The Village Voice
The Wall Street Journal
Washington Post
Washington Times
Wine Spectator